SHOPPING CENTER MANAGEMENT

SHOPPING CENTER MANAGEMENT

International Council of Shopping Centers
New York

ABOUT THE INTERNATIONAL COUNCIL OF SHOPPING CENTERS

The International Council of Shopping Centers (ICSC) is the trade association of the shopping center industry. Serving the shopping center industry since 1957, ICSC is a not-for-profit organization with over 37,000 members in 75 countries worldwide.

ICSC members include shopping center

- owners
- developers
- managers
- marketing specialists
- leasing agents
- retailers
- researchers
- attorneys
- architects
- contractors
- consultants
- investors
- lenders and brokers
- academics
- public officials

ICSC sponsors more than 300 meetings a year and provides a wide array of services and products for shopping center professionals, including publications and research data.

For more information about ICSC, write or call the
International Council of Shopping Centers
1221 Avenue of the Americas
New York, NY 10020-1099
Telephone: 646-728-3800
Fax: 212-589-5555
www.icsc.org

This publication is designed to provide accurate and authoritative information in regard to the subject matter covered. It is sold with the understanding that the publisher is not engaged in rendering legal, accounting, or other profes-sional services. If legal advice or other expert assistance is required, the services of a competent professional person should be sought.

—From a Declaration of Principles jointly adopted by a Committee of the American Bar Association and a Committee of Publishers.

Published by
International Council of Shopping Centers
Publications Department
1221 Avenue of the Americas
New York, NY 10020-1099

Cover Design: H. Roberts Design
ICSC Catalog Number: 173
International Standard Book Number: 1-58268-005-1
Printed in the United States of America

Contents

6. Marketing 123

Marcy Carter-Lovick, SCMD

7. Maintenance 143

Don Paul, CSM, RPA

8. Security 163

Anna C. Northcutt

About This Book

This book covers the following topics that a shopping center manager will want to be knowledgeable about:

- Financial concepts
- The lease and its language
- Tenant mix and leasing strategies
- Administration
- Marketing
- Maintenance
- Security
- Risk management and insurance
- Crisis management
- Redevelopment and renovation
- Legal issues
- Retailing.

Some topics, such as maintenance, are a part of every shopping center manager's responsibilities. Other areas, leasing and marketing, for example, are executed by some managers and not others but are topics most managers will want to know about. An issue such as redevelopment and renovation may not be an immediate area of concern to a shopping center manager but may be some day.

Each chapter has been contributed by a shopping center professional, who explains the principles and practices of each topic—plus some of their own personal insights and tricks of the trade. Practices may vary from center to center. What may be applicable to a neighborhood strip center with off-site management may not be appropriate for a regional mall in an urban area with on-site management. The viewpoints are those of the authors and are not policies or recommendations of the International Council of Shopping Centers (ICSC).

Shopping Center Management contains forms, illustrative examples and common-sense advice. Please keep the following in mind when reading the text:

• Numbers, which are often impacted by the geographical location of a center, the current economy and other factors, are only used to illustrate examples. Where dollar amounts or other figures are used, they are used for illustration only and are not meant to suggest industry standards or guidelines.

• When developing policies and practices, each individual shopping center manager should consult the owner and shopping center counsel, among others.

• Similarly, forms, lease clauses and other documents are samples only and can be adapted for use for the reader's own shopping center. They are not to be construed as being endorsed or recommended by the contributor or ICSC. Readers are again advised to consult legal counsel to devise appropriate documents for their centers.

• All lease remedies and lease rights are not exercisable without legal risk. The right to change the locks or remove persons by force can result in claims for loss of quiet enjoyment and assault. The removal of property can render the landlord liable for its care and preservation. The detention of a purported shoplifter can lead to claims of false arrest. Dissemination of suggested procedures for security, loss prevention, emergency assistance and the like can result in claims of negligence if not followed by the owner or manager authorizing them. Towing an employee's car, while the employee is shopping after the end of his or her workday, can lead to a damage claim. Even the best policies can lead to trouble if improperly instituted. Checking with legal counsel before formulating and implementing policy is always advised.

For guidance on how to get additional information tailored to meet more specific needs, here are additional resources you may want to consult:

• For those who need explanations of terms, see the Glossary at the end of the book.

• The handy index of the book will help you locate information. For example, Common Area Maintenance (CAM) and other terms may be discussed in more than one chapter.

• The *ICSC Keys to Shopping Center Management Series,* published by ICSC, provides coverage of the fundamentals of shopping center management. Core topics and key points and definitions are succinctly covered.

• For those who want more advanced or specific information on each topic, see the list of Resources and Recommended Readings at the end of most chapters.

• The ICSC Albert Sussman Library is available to respond to requests for specific information and additional resources.

Shopping centers are dynamic, changing institutions. ICSC's programs and services, such as its specialty conferences on temporary tenants, law and finance, among others areas, will keep you up-to-date on changes in the industry.

For more information on ICSC, write or call:

International Council of Shopping Centers
1221 Avenue of the Americas
New York, NY 10020-1099
Telephone: 646-728-3800
Fax: 212-589-5555
ICSCNET: www.icsc.org

Acknowledgments

The International Council of Shopping Centers acknowledges the following shopping center professionals who contributed the chapters that appear in this book:

Alan A. Alexander, SCSM, CPM
Senior Vice President
Woodmont Real Estate
    Services, Inc.
Belmont, California

Shannon Alter, CPM
Owner
Retail Management Services
Tustin, California

Marcy Carter-Lovick, SCMD
Principal
Carter Marketing Works
Southlake, Texas

Joseph P. Cilia, SCSM
General Manager
Simon Property Group
Roosevelt Field Mall
Garden City, New York

Charles R. Cope, SCSM, CLS
General Manager
Tysons Corner Center
McLean, Virginia

Colin M. Gromley, Esq.
Attorney-at-Law
Altman, Kritzer & Levick, P.C.
Atlanta, Georgia

Mark London, SCSM, SCMD
Senior Vice President of
    Redevelopment
General Growth Properties
Chicago, Illinois

Robert Nelson
Senior Vice President
Sedgwick James, Inc.
San Francisco, California

Anna C. Northcutt
Owner
Center Security Management
San Juan Capistrano, California

Wayne T. Okubo, SCSM,
 SCMD, CLS
Principal
Okubo Real Estate
Redwood, California

Don Paul, CSM, RPA
Vice President of Business
 Development
SSC Service Solutions
Vairico, Florida

Kate M. Sheehy
Vice President
Lend Lease Real Estate
 Investments, Inc.
Atlanta, Georgia

Kurt Sullivan, SCSM
Vice President, Property
 Management
TrizecHahn Centers
San Diego, California

Kevin M. Walsh, Esq.
Attorney-at-Law
Altman, Kritzer & Levick, P.C.
Atlanta, Georgia

The International Council of Shopping Centers gratefully acknowledges the following individuals and their companies for the time and
expertise they offered in reviewing this publication:

Mark J. Levick, Esq.
President
Altman, Kritzer & Levick, P.C.
Atlanta, Georgia

Oscar R. Rivera, Esq.
Partner
Siegfried, Rivera, Lerner, Delatorre & Sobel, P.A.
Coral Gables, Florida

SHOPPING CENTER MANAGEMENT

1 | Introduction

Mark London, SCSM, SCMD

Shopping centers are more than a type of real estate, or a means of distributing goods, or an entity that contributes local taxes or a major employer. Since their inception, not long after World War II and the Korean War, shopping centers have taken on social and cultural implications—particularly in the United States and Canada—that have given them an iconic niche in the context of everyday life. Shopping centers have greatly evolved and diversified since their inception in America's giant postwar, suburban boom; they have also moved from being perceived by consumers as having a special status in the 1950s and 1960s to a far more commonplace, ubiquitous status in the late twentieth century.

In fact, the past fifty years of proliferation and diversification of shopping centers have created a national consumer population that has come to expect the service, convenience, value, and selection of shopping centers. Although consumers have progressed to the point of expecting the focus and range of options offered by a highly evolved and mature shopping center industry, they rarely consider the functions and processes that underlie centers of all types. While shopping center function is not of great interest to shoppers, generally, the names of the nearest large, enclosed malls are often among the most remembered and "top of mind" names in community after community, reinforcing their iconic nature in our society.

Shopping centers are unique as a real estate format in that they serve a variety of special audiences in addition to consumers, retailers and their owners. Often such audiences include the communities in

1

which shopping centers are located. Community service can take the form of economic or other types of support. From staging high school fund-raising car washes to providing emergency shelter, many shopping centers are an integral part of community life. Shopping centers have become greater than the sum of their components.

This book will attempt to inform you about the key areas and parties involved in shopping centers. Since there is great variety among the types and specific natures of shopping centers, this chapter will introduce many of the core concepts that are basic to most or all. The chapters beyond will focus on specific details related to the key areas of shopping center management.

Retail Real Estate Is a Unique Format

It has often been said that the dynamics of retail real estate are three-dimensional, while those of most other real estate formats are two-dimensional. The reasoning behind the comparison is that most nonretail real estate—office, apartment and warehouse formats, for example—are based upon a simple landlord-tenant relationship. Shopping centers and other retail real estate formats are based upon a more complex dynamic which includes the same two parties *plus* consumers, who must patronize the tenants' stores in order for the process to work—thus creating a three-party process. The complexity results from the additional challenges related to finding the appropriate assortment of tenants (or merchants) who can effectively attract enough consumers to support the business plan, including paying the landlord's rents.

Shopping centers are also unique in the world of real estate because they typically evolve and change—adapting to various challenges and opportunities—more rapidly than most other real estate formats. In fact, shopping centers are inherently designed to facilitate change by virtue of the makeup of the stores or other components within them. The more complex three-part retail dynamic requires that landlord and merchant work together to achieve success with a third party—consumers. The shopping center's on-site staff is typically tailored to meet the needs generated by these three parties and by the type of center.

Key Parties: Fundamental to Shopping Centers

For most of its life cycle thus far, the shopping center business could be summarized as revolving around the interactions of the three parties identified in the preceding section plus one additional party—not unique to shopping centers—lenders.

1. *Shopping center owners* or *landlords* and *operators* (operators—if different from a shopping center's owners—are those parties managing and operating a shopping center from day to day)
2. *Tenants* (or *merchants*) who occupy space in the shopping centers, paying rent for such space
3. *Consumers* (or *shoppers*) who are patrons of the shopping center and its tenants
4. *Lenders*, who provide much of the capital needed by shopping center owners to build, purchase or finance a center

The vast majority of shopping center functions, details and nuances relates directly to the listed key parties. Often, the perspectives of the four parties can differ from each other in regard to the same issue. In many ways, the role of capable shopping center management is to strike a working balance between the interests or perspectives of the key parties, relevant to a specific issue. For example, if a landlord leases space only to merchants from whom he could get the best rents, consumers' interests may not be best served because the stores that they prefer may not be offered. The give and take between the ongoing need to serve consumers, while meeting the needs of a shopping center's owners and merchants, creates the necessity for a dynamic balance. Moreover, if these areas are performing in harmony, the goals for lenders are usually going to be met.

One of the most consistent challenges in shopping center management is to identify, understand and meet the ongoing needs of consumers, merchants and landlords.

This introduction to shopping centers will focus on the various roles of the shopping center in relation to the key parties and situations. The balance of this chapter will provide an overview of shopping centers from the perspective of three of its major roles:

1. As a place of business
2. As an investment
3. As a property

Shopping Centers as a Place of Business

BASIC STRUCTURE AND FORMAT

Among the points to know about a shopping center's basic structure and format are the following:

- Almost all shopping centers consist of a site, comprising the land that it occupies and some type of building(s), which houses tenants or merchants offering goods and/or services.
- The precise amount of land required to support a building will vary according to its natural topography, local zoning, certain tenant-driven parking requirements, the nature of the overall site design and other situational factors.
- The space occupied and leased by tenants is measured in square feet (sf); a shopping center's total leasable space is known as its gross leasable area (GLA).
- Freestanding, usually peripheral buildings, often supported by their own dedicated parking lot, are known as outparcels, or as pads or pad sites.

The purpose of a shopping center's site and paving—roadways and parking areas—is to allow a customer to efficiently access a parking space in relation to visiting one or more stores at the shopping center. Larger sites usually have entry drives that connect the road surrounding a site to its inner parking areas; such drives usually occur intermittently along the site's perimeter. The largest sites, supporting the largest buildings, usually have ring roads circling around the building. A ring road immediately surrounding a building is known as the inner ring road, while one further from the building, usually located between parking areas and an entry drive(s), is the outer ring road. The ultimate design of a site's topography, parking areas, roadways and buildings is primarily a function of:

- Original topography
- Parameters—such as parking and roadway/ring road specifications—as defined by certain key stores

- Parameters as defined by the local zoning authority
- The landlord's goals and resources
- The type of center
- Community and neighborhood resources

TYPES OF SHOPPING CENTERS

The format of the site and major building(s), as well as the retail stores, entertainment facilities or services that it contains, all differentiate the basic types of shopping centers. The most fundamental differentiating feature is the specific nature of the accessibility to the stores—whether they are directly accessible to shoppers from the adjacent parking areas (in an unenclosed shopping center) or if there is an enclosed, nonstore area in which shoppers can travel, protected from the elements (as in an enclosed shopping center).

Shopping centers with enclosed nonstore areas are known as malls. Shoppers usually refer to the enclosed, nonstore areas or the whole building as the mall. The industry term for the nonstore area of any building and any exterior parts of a site is *common area*. The specific nature of the types of stores making up a shopping center's tenant base, or its merchandise mix, generally determines the center's type.

Shopping Center Definitions. The table on page 6 is meant to provide guidelines for understanding major differences among the basic types of shopping centers. Several of the categories shown in the table, such as size, number of anchors and trade area, should be interpreted as "typical" for each center type. They are not meant to encompass the operating characteristics of every center. As a general rule, the main determinants in classifying a center are its merchandise orientation (types of goods/services sold) and its size. It is not always possible to precisely classify every center. A hybrid center may combine elements from two or more basic classifications, or a center's concept may be sufficiently unusual as to preclude it from fitting into one of the eight generalized definitions presented here. There are other types of centers that are not separately defined in this table but nonetheless are a part of the industry.

Type	Concept	Sq. Ft. Inc. Anchors	Acreage	Number	Typical Anchor(s) Type	Anchor Ratio*	Primary Trade Area**
Neighborhood Center	Convenience	30,000–150,000	3–15	1 or more	Supermarket	30–50%	3 miles
Community Center	General merchandise; convenience	100,000–350,000	10–40	2 or more	Discount dept. store; supermarket; drug; home improvement; large specialty/discount apparel	40–60%	3–6 miles
Regional Center	General merchandise fashion (Mall, typically enclosed)	400,000–800,000	40–100	2 or more	Full-line dept. store; jr. dept. store; mass merchant; disc. dept. store; fashion apparel	50–70%	5–15 miles
Superregional Center	Similar to Regional Center but has more variety and assortment	800,000+	60–120	3 or more	Full-line dept. store; jr. dept. store; mass merchant; fashion apparel	50–70%	5–25 miles
Fashion/Specialty Center	Higher-end, fashion-oriented	80,000–250,000	5–25	N/A	Fashion	N/A	5–15 miles
Power Center	Category-dominant anchors; few small tenants	250,000–600,000	25–80	3 or more	Category killer; home improvement; discount dept. store; warehouse club; off-price	75–90%	5–10 miles
Theme/Festival Center	Leisure; tourist-oriented; retail and service	80,000–250,000	5–20	N/A	Restaurants, entertainment	N/A	N/A
Outlet Center	Manufacturers' outlet stores	50,000–400,000	10–50	N/A	Manufacturers' outlet stores	N/A	25–75 miles

* The share of a center's total square footage that is attributable to its anchors
** The area from which 60%–80% of the center's sales originate

In addition to the shopping center definitions shown in the table, the following trends should be noted:

• Neighborhood centers. These centers are located as close as possible to where their customers reside so as to best serve them.
• Community centers. Community centers can be located either near a residential base of customers or within a business district with other freestanding and shopping center retail stores.
• Regional centers. The development of new regional centers continues, but far more slowly than in the 1980s. Category killers or "big boxes" are being included as part of the complex in some cases.
• Superregional centers. Most recent design or formats of superregional centers have incorporated adjacent category-killer merchants in an effort to thwart nearby power center competition.
• Fashion/Specialty centers. These are often located in heavily trafficked tourist areas.
• Power centers. Power centers are often located very close to regional or superregional malls.
• Theme/Festival centers. These centers have evolved into a subset category known as lifestyle centers, featuring entertainment and retail, but without conventional department store anchors.
• Outlet centers. Outlet centers have evolved into two primary formats—the large 1–2 million square foot "Mills," which are very large and service a wide trade area, and the more traditional unenclosed and smaller types. The proximity to conventional enclosed centers is growing smaller.

MERCHANTS (OR TENANTS)

Merchants are usually classified according to the size and nature of their stores, in addition to the size of their parent company or ownership. A group of stores within a company is usually known as a chain, and thus the individual units as chain stores. The largest stores within one shopping center are usually known as anchors. Department stores, often 50,000 to 300,000 sf in size, usually anchor malls and sell various types of general merchandise, such as apparel, cosmetics, luggage and other items; they are divided into separate areas or departments within the store. Anchors in unenclosed centers can range from department stores to other large-format stores, such as grocery, warehouse, office supply, book or electronic goods stores. These stores will usually range from about 25,000 sf to 200,000 sf in size.

One of the underlying principles of shopping centers is the idea that anchors are the main attraction for shoppers. Other, smaller stores that occupy nonanchor space benefit from the shopper traffic created by the anchor(s). Found most often in strip centers, the ever-evolving group of large, specialized anchor stores have become known as big boxes; they can be found in malls, as well, and their merchandise is highly focused around a specific niche or use—such as toys, office supplies or books. The smaller stores in shopping centers are often known as specialty or small shops.

Another key principle is that the attraction of any shopping center to potential consumers is partially based on the center's tenant or merchandise mix— that is, the unique combination of various stores offering specific types of products or services. While apparel was the key merchandising element in the early days of the shopping center business, today other types of goods are increasing in demand while ready-to-wear related offerings have been somewhat reduced. For example, home furnishings and related products are growing in importance in many markets today. The media have reported that home furnishings overtook apparel in regard to consumer purchasing as of 1997.

Merchants and landlords enter into formal agreements, known as leases, governing most key areas of the relationship between the two parties. Merchants rent the space that they occupy. In the case of anchors, they often own the land related to their building and parking (their parcel). In such cases, the landlord and anchor enter into a reciprocal easement agreement (REA). These REAs also govern both parties' rights, obligations and, often, the specific operating details of a center—such as exterior building signage limitations for the whole center or the number of parking spaces required to support the anchor store, specifically, and, usually, the entire center.

The shopping center industry has evolved to a point where most merchants occupying space in malls and the larger unenclosed centers are either part of a national chain or a licensed/franchised operation of a national or regional chain. Local merchants are often referred to as mom-and-pop operations. Many merchants have an affiliation with a company that issues franchises or licenses to operate under its name, and most of the franchisers of major national franchising concepts have a framework of corporate expertise to support them.

Another result of the evolution of shopping centers has been the growth of service-type tenants within most center formats. While there has been little such growth in the outlet sector, convenience-driven uses—such as mailing/packaging services, prepared foods, ticketing services, etc.—have multiplied since the early days of shopping centers. In most instances, the tenants in shopping centers sell goods or services. In certain situations, special tenants—such as libraries, educational programs or hospital outreach programs—may occupy space. However, shopping centers are primarily a means for the distribution of retail goods and services—although the assortments of goods, services and formats in which they are organized are constantly evolving in an effort to maximize consumer interest and merchant sales productivity.

Merchants are usually represented at the mall level (or on site) by either an owner or a manager. The chain store merchants are usually organized in a pyramidal hierarchy, with district or regional managers overseeing a group or region of stores, often organized geographically. In larger chains, there may be one or two levels above the regional position, each overseeing larger groups of stores. The turnover—through both attrition and promotion—of store associates and management is a common, ongoing, everyday reality in shopping centers. Often there is great benefit to the landlord in monitoring store manager turnover, performance and continuity. The landlord's on-site representatives often maintain a relationship with both a chain store's local manager and regional manager; in the case of most chain stores, the local manager has modest authority, usually focused upon employee hiring/evaluation/scheduling and basic store operations.

SHOPPING CENTER ON-SITE STAFF

The nature or purpose of a shopping center is usually the chief determining factor in regard to the profile of its on-site staff. As the reader might anticipate, the larger the shopping center, the more staff and types of roles that it has on-site. Malls and other large centers usually support several on-site functions.

Management. Most enclosed and large unenclosed centers usually have a general manager (GM) on site. The GM oversees the operation of the centers on a day-to-day basis. Larger centers often have an assistant or associate manager in support of the GM. The specific responsibilities of a GM and an assistant can vary greatly according to both the philosophy of the landlord and the center's performance. For example: Some landlords want their GMs to devote significant time to leasing space, usually locally, while others do not engage on-site associates this way.

Operations. Similar to the parameters concerning the variation in the roles of GM, most larger enclosed and many unenclosed centers have an operations department on site. The function of this unit is to clean (housekeeping) and maintain the property. Whether or not the center has a central plant or separate heating, ventilation and air-conditioning (HVAC) units has a major impact on the type and nature of staffing in this area. A central plant produces conditioned air through the operation of a centralized system, which then distributes it to the enclosed common areas and usually the merchants' stores. The anchor stores usually handle this function independently. Most unenclosed centers do not have central plants. In many smaller unenclosed centers, there may only be one operations associate, or one might cover several centers.

Operations must oversee day-to-day housekeeping, emergency repairs, ongoing maintenance—including landscaping—and usually long-term maintenance, as well. Most often, there is an operations manager or director overseeing all areas and reporting to the GM. The balance of the staff required is increasingly more likely to be contracted through a third-party resource rather than be in-house staff, or landlord's employees. Even with such contracted workers, there are often key maintenance associates, and/or assistants, who are direct landlord employees.

Note that while merchants are usually responsible for the maintenance and housekeeping of their own stores, the landlord maintains all common areas, including the roof over most merchants' stores. Anchor or large stores often have individual arrangements specific to their lease or REA. Merchants collectively contribute to a common area maintenance (CAM) fund—usually allocated on a pro rata basis to nonanchor stores. Merchants share the cost of operating the common areas of the center.

Marketing. Marketing is another shopping center landlord function that varies greatly by center type and even within specific classes from landlord to landlord. As with previously discussed areas, in general, the larger the center, the more likely that there will be on-site resources dedicated to marketing. Somewhat like the concept of shared common area costs, most shopping center leases require merchants to contribute to some type of pooled marketing resources—usually known as a marketing fund. While this amount tends to be minimal for anchors, regardless of center format, enclosed mall merchants tend to contribute substantially more to marketing than strip center merchants.

The role of marketing is another facet of shopping centers that has been evolving since the earliest days of the business. In an enclosed mall, the role of marketing can range from community support and public relations to traffic-building promotions to merchant relations and even merchants' associate training, and covering much more in some cases. In the largest centers, there may be one, two or more full-time associates devoted to marketing. Generally, the chief roles of marketing are considered to be:

- Public (and community) relations—local
- Merchant relations and on-site support
- Shopping center sales productivity and market share maximization
- Special income area, such as sponsorships

Security/Public Safety. The role of security in shopping centers, particularly in larger centers, has become increasingly high profile since the bombing of the World Trade Center in New York in the early 1990s. Unlike many of its European counterparts, the United States had enjoyed a relatively worry-free existence prior to the World Trade Center attack. This incident marked a noteworthy change in the attitudes of many shoppers in the United States, who began exhibiting more awareness in regard to overall safety issues.

Similar to the preceding center functions, security efforts vary with the size and complexity of a shopping center. The largest centers typically have a specific director of security—usually reporting to the operations manager or GM—a security staff, one or more vehicles and sophisticated communications equipment. Security's main purpose is to protect the landlord's property and common areas of the shopping center. For the most part, security within each merchant's premises is that merchant's responsibility.

However, as the role and perception of security have evolved, on-site security aims increasingly to deliver a message of personal safety to shopping center consumers—where appropriate. At the same time, each visitor has a responsibility to conduct himself/herself prudently. Security also will help a merchant with special situations from time to time. For example, the mall security may assist a merchant by detaining a shoplifting suspect until the police arrive. As a final thought in this area, it should be noted that the part-time use of off-duty local police is an increasingly common practice, supplementing local security teams in many malls. The addition of local police outreach facilities—

such as part-time offices within a center—is becoming more and more frequent. Finally, security may be in-house or contracted.

Other On-site Functions. The other on-site functions—which may include short- or long-term leasing, accounting/bookkeeping and various types of administrative support—vary by landlord and shopping center type. The preceding descriptions have usually outlined the maximum scenario—in relation to the largest, most complex centers. Most strip centers do not have a full-time, on-site manager. Most centers of this type are overseen regionally, in groups of five to twenty-five, by an individual or a team focusing on key functions, often in a remote office. It is quite common for the strip center's managerial role to be combined with a leasing role. Leasing is the function of renting space to tenants. Leasing is the sales function in shopping center management. It is also increasingly common for landlords to expect their on-site GMs and local teams to lease space in larger formats, as well. For the majority of strip centers, the most frequent on-site landlord representative, if any, is someone overseeing the maintenance and operations areas. The role, often found in large strip centers, is usually somewhat less varied and complex than the operations managers found in malls.

CONSUMERS

Consumers—also known as shoppers or customers—are the ultimate key to making any type of shopping center perform. Making any generalization about consumers enhances the probability that it will be found to be invalid; however, having noted this, the best way to understand the challenges and opportunities related to consumers is to review a short list of the key trends that have affected or continue to affect greatly both their behavior and the shopping center business.

Most reliable trend and demographic resources view two key factors or trends that have had the greatest impact on consumer behavior since World War II. These are *time famine* and the *increase of women in the workforce*. Since World War II, there has been a steady and relentless increase in the number of working women—from below 40 percent before 1950 to upward of 70 percent, by most reconciliations, in the late 1990s. This has had a sort of good news/bad news effect on shopping centers by increasing household incomes with two wage earners in most and decreasing the amount of free or leisure time available to shop. In effect, households today have more money to spend for discretionary purposes, but less time to do so, than prior generations—even taking inflation into account. The impact has been rippling through shopping centers, particularly malls, for many years. The impact can be confirmed in several ways.

- During the past fifteen years, the number of stores visited per shopping trip has decreased. The duration of most trips has also decreased. However, these factors have been offset by increases in the amount of spending per trip. Consumers are spending less time shopping, visiting fewer stores, but spending more in the stores visited. These statistics reference enclosed malls, where the most research has been done.
- The existence of time famine—not enough time to do everything—has been identified as a reality in many households. There has been a tandem increase in the focus on convenience for consumers and time savings throughout the merchant/store and shopping center sectors.

Although shoppers have less free time, they also have already chosen most of their favorite stores. Retailers have capitalized upon this by growing their stores, offering more choices in the same store. If consumers are visiting fewer stores per visit, but spending more money per visit, it is logical that the size of stores has increased. Many chains are using two to five times the space that they did ten to fifteen years ago.

Consumers cross-shop across channels of distribution. A woman may buy her cosmetics at a traditional department store, panty hose at the grocery store and sundries at large discount stores. Time and convenience are issues, as noted. Many landlords are creating hybrid shopping centers with components from more than one type. For example:

- While the big bookstores started outside of malls, many landlords are putting them in malls to satisfy customers, rather than enduring them across the street.
- A new type of unenclosed center, the so-called lifestyle center, has begun to be developed. It includes entertainment components—a movie theater and restaurants—big-box stores and small shops from many sectors. In concept, it offers many of the best components of mall merchandising—with drive-up convenience.

There is an almost infinite variety of consumer issues and factors that will both drive shoppers' behavior and the response to or anticipation of it by shopping centers. These range from the increasing diversity in the ethnic makeup of consumers to the continuous rise of single heads of households. Both merchants and shopping centers must anticipate the key factors in order to best serve consumers. There is an old saying about the retail business: "The only constant is the fact that things will continue to change."

COMMUNITY

It is logical that shopping centers would often serve their communities—defined by the size and nature of the center—in a multitude of ways. Shopping centers must be good neighbors in regard to issues such as lighting, noise, traffic, trash, parking lot runoff (water) and so on. The GM or other landlord representatives often play leadership roles in community organizations ranging from chambers of commerce to schools to various nonprofit groups. Both the landlord's company and those members of its on-site team must be aware of, focused on and supportive of community issues, concerns and initiatives.

There are a variety of ways in which a shopping center can raise its community profile. It is much harder to steer or manage such a profile in a particular direction. This is largely because various groups or community members can have an infinite variety of agendas and issues with which they are concerned. Overall, the larger a center, the more effort that should be made continuously to reach out and maintain a dialogue with its community. At the same time, regardless of size, most centers will benefit by maintaining a posture of ongoing community sensitivity.

Shopping Centers: An Investment Perspective

TYPES OF INVESTORS OR OWNERS

As an asset class, shopping centers have always required capital, generally produced reliable cash flow and incorporated a broad range of risks. For most of its history, the shopping center industry has focused on building. Typically, developers of shopping centers could be classified into several different categories based on their ultimate ownership strategies:

- *Merchant builders:* developed shopping centers in order to sell them, fairly quickly, after creation

- *Long-term holders:* usually held center indefinitely or sold at the point of their perceived peak value

Banks and other financial institutions usually provided loans to developers which funded the initial construction of centers. Once a center was stabilized after its creation, a developer intending to hold the asset usually sought long-term financing from various banking or lending-related sources.

It is critical to understand that shopping centers are valued based upon their cash flow or operating profitability. As with stock market companies, the value of shopping centers is based on a multiple of cash flow. The multiple is determined by a capitalization, or cap, rate. Cap rates are usually driven by overall market factors, the specific type of asset or shopping center and the agreement between two parties—owner and buyer or lender. For example, a shopping center producing $4 million in annual net operating income (NOI) would be worth:

- $50 million @ 8 percent cap rate (12.5 multiple)
- $40 million @ 10 percent cap rate (10 multiple)
- $53.3 million @ 7.5 percent cap rate (13.3 multiple)

For most of its history, the shopping center industry has focused on the creation of value as the ultimate goal for landlords and their operating agents. Value could be created by enhancing the center's NOI and/or theoretically lowering the cap rate, thereby raising the value multiple. Raising value through cap rate change has usually been related to lowering the asset's risk factor in regard to its long-term stability. These theoretical cap rate changes occur only through major actions such as the addition of an anchor or cinemas.

For most of their history, the ownership of most shopping centers has traditionally passed to pension funds and insurance companies. While many banks, lending institutions and some special financial instruments have been owners as well, from the late 1970s until the late 1990s pension funds and insurance companies have owned the majority of the real estate assets, relative to their value. The reasons for their ownership are fundamental. Pension funds are the product of the retirement or pension assets of major companies and organizations, such as teacher or state employee groups. Both pension funds and insurance companies annually generate vast amounts of capital, which must be invested to produce consistent financial returns for the eventual benefit of their owners. Real estate has traditionally functioned as a hedge investment amongst a variety of assets held by investors. This is because most real estate formats can theoretically benefit from periods of inflation—as costs increase, theoretically so will rents.

During most of their history, shopping centers were built by developers, often were managed by the same or specialized organizations and were sold to the institutional investment community—pension funds, insurance companies and the like. This continued right through the mid-1980s, when development peaked and lenders were providing capital with little scrutiny. Most of the real estate industry—including shopping centers—then endured a severe recession, "crunch" or slowdown. From the late 1980s through the early 1990s, few centers were built or sold. Lenders began requiring 20 percent and more in equity capital to finance new projects; just a few years before, loans for new construction were available without equity requirements.

The industry began to recover from its most difficult period in the mid-1990s, subsequent to beginning the current period of public ownership of shopping centers through real estate investment trusts (REITs). (REITs are highly specialized entities that offer its investors special benefits. REITs must distribute 95 percent of earnings to investors annually as dividends, and, as a result, they do not pay the usual corporate taxes.) While this REIT period has brought about several strategic changes in regard to some fundamental aspects of the shopping center business, it has also brought stability and consolidation.

The growth of the public sector ownership of shopping centers since 1993 has added several important nuances to the balanced harmony between the key parties by removing much of the need for lender capital through fund-raising in the public markets. As REITs acquire more and more properties, there are greater numbers of owner entities managing their own shopping centers, reducing the need for those companies specializing in operating properties for owners. Public ownership adds further complexity to those companies operating as REITs, with a few issues trickling down to the shopping center, or on-site, level.

Many institutional owners—often supported by third-party advisory companies with fiduciary responsibilities—have been carrying on their books shopping center assets for which they apparently overpaid during the "go-go" days of the mid-1980s.

The high performance of the current REIT era has encouraged many institutional owners to sell their shopping center assets because asset values have risen to their highest levels of the past decade, as cap rates have fallen. After the very challenging recent era, ownership of REIT stock is preferable to direct asset ownership for most institutional owners. Theoretically, the stock is far more liquid than the actual asset. At any rate, shopping centers—as well as other real estate assets—are being sold and acquired in quantities that are unique in history. The results of the current REIT period will likely be as follows:

• While there always has been and always will be some private shopping center ownership, the majority of assets are being sold to the REITs; this is not only for the reasons mentioned previously but because the REITs need such assets in order to maintain their growth rates, particularly as they become larger and larger.
• While some institutional owners will continue to seek direct ownership, the majority probably will not.

In summary, the recent enormous growth of REITs has altered the shopping center's nature as an investment. The majority of historical investors appears to favor investment through the REITs rather than direct ownership. The secondary effects of these current trends are reducing the long-standing emphasis on value enhancement in favor of cash flow to serve the needs of the public markets. The REIT era has also brought a significant focus on redevelopment of existing centers.

ASSET AND PORTFOLIO MANAGEMENT

As pension funds and other institutional owners absorbed so much of the shopping center real estate—and other formats, as well—the concept of asset management arose within the shopping center industry. Asset management involves the oversight of assets in order to maximize their value in keeping with the owner's objectives. With institutional owners, asset management has acted as an interface between the operator of the center and ownership, attempting to achieve the original performance goals established for the asset or group of assets.

During the past ten years or so, institutional asset managers have generally tried to learn much about most facets of shopping center management and operations. Often, the asset manager must decide whether to proceed with a particular course of action as recommended by the shopping center operator. A challenge can arise when the pending action may be the right thing to do for a center but in conflict with the specific goals of the owner. The operator and asset manager must work it out. Normally, the better the two parties understand each other's goals, the more likely that a prudent action will result.

The asset manager normally takes a long-term view with respect to most decisions regarding a shopping center. Again, the REITs are changing the process. REITs, as public companies, utilize internal asset managers for many of the same purposes as the institutional owners did. REITs are far less likely to sell properties, for reasons relating to their financial structure and tax and earnings issues. Thus, the asset managers play a key role in overseeing all phases of a property's productivity—on both an immediate and a long-term basis.

In summary, the important role of asset and portfolio management was first driven by the investment goals of the institutional owners and is transitioning to the public REITs, who have parallel asset management functions within the framework of their own structure and goals.

The Shopping Center as a Property

Ultimately, the role of shopping center management is to maximize the productivity of a property. The evolving nature of so many of the key parties—consumers, foremost, along with merchants and landlords—can be very energizing and even dizzying at times, but never boring!

Enhancing a shopping center usually involves long-term teamwork, as well as a commitment to a well-thought-out and researched strategic plan and consistent fortitude. Many supporting disciplines contribute to the successful operation of a center—ranging from insurance and risk management to on-site and home office administration to various types of legal and other support, depending upon the issue at hand. These topics will be covered in detail within the following chapters.

It is critical to remember the three-part complexity of shopping centers while at all times maintaining a vigilant eye on the consumers. For most on-site team members, it is often easy, after a while, to lose the perspective of consumers; stepping back and ensuring that the general manager or marketing manager assesses each circumstance from a consumer's perspective is both challenging and ultimately rewarding. In many ways, shopping center management requires the classic jack-of-all-trades approach, since there is constantly so much to know and evaluate. However, it pays to know much about many areas rather than a little about many areas. In today's environment, resources such as the Internet facilitate one's ability to glean valuable information that was not available in such a manner previously. The reader may find valuable consumer trend information in newspapers or buried in sophisticated marketing studies.

In a classic business sense, one can only improve profits in one of three ways—improving income, decreasing costs or achieving both.

In shopping centers, increasing sales usually leads to improved rents, merchants and consumer loyalty. To some degree, it's part art and part science in shopping centers. Sometimes an intuitive hunch, prompted by a valid observation, can lead to success. In other cases, rigid conformation to classic rules such as site traffic parameters is often critical.

While no one book or experience can truly prepare one fully for the challenges and excitement of successfully operating shopping centers, a tremendous effort has been made to incorporate as much as possible of the information that you'll need in the succeeding chapters of this handbook.

Recommended Readings

Altoon, Ronald A., FAIA. *International Shopping Center Architecture: Details, Concepts and Projects*. New York: International Council of Shopping Centers, 1996.

ICSC Keys to Shopping Center Fundamentals Series. New York: International Council of Shopping Centers, 1996.

ICSC Keys to Shopping Center Management Series. New York: International Council of Shopping Centers, 1992.

Shopping Centers Today. Monthly. New York: International Council of Shopping Centers.

Winning Shopping Center Designs 1998. New York: International Council of Shopping Centers, 1998.

This chapter was contributed by Mark London, SCSM, SCMD, Senior Vice President of Redevelopment, General Growth Properties, Chicago, Illinois.

2 | Financial Concepts

Wayne T. Okubo, SCSM, SCMD, CLS

One of the most important reasons you have been employed as a property manager is to facilitate the shopping center owner's goals and objectives. This is the first area you will need to have clarified. You will need to know how long the owner will keep the property, how the owner wants the property maintained, why the owner wants to acquire the property and what the owner wants to achieve by owning the property.

In some instances you will be thrown into fighting fires, racing from problem to problem and trying to solve them to everyone's satisfaction. If this is the mode of operation, you may have problems paying bills, juggling vendors who want to get paid, getting vendors to do work and effectively solving problems, all while trying to please the owners. It is much easier to work proactively, performing preventive maintenance, budgeting and providing a scheduled working environment. These are considerations to keep in mind when you are interviewing a possible employer or client.

Once you have made the commitment to manage a property, you have committed yourself to perform your duties in accordance with the owner's expectations. Therefore, you need to understand the owner's goals from the outset. This will determine how you do your job, and maybe even whether you can or will want to work for a particular landlord.

As a property manager you have a number of constraints that determine how you execute your tasks. You are regulated by both federal and state real estate laws, requiring in most cases that you have a real estate license. Besides having the department of real estate govern your activities, you have a number of trade organizations that enforce their standards and code of ethics.

Real estate laws state that you have a fiduciary responsibility to the owner. In other words, you have a financial responsibility to the owner and must have a contract outlining how you carry out responsibilities. Important aspects of your duties include how much you are authorized to spend, under what circumstances and at what point you are to obtain owner approval before engaging contracts, services or purchasing products.

All of these elements must be considered in your decisions. Remember—ignorance of the law or "I was just following instructions" are no longer viable defenses.

Value Enhancement

IT'S PART OF THE JOB

One of your most important tasks is to enhance the value of the property or find value in the property and capitalize on it. If you understand how value is derived you will be able to enhance the value of the property. Naturally, finding value where there was none is the greatest trick of all. How do you do this? Quite simply, you look for areas where you can generate additional income—from pay phones, temporary tenant programs, increasing the gross leasable area (GLA), and so on. All of these areas increase your net operating income (NOI), which increases your cash flow and also increases the value of the property.

You have to be careful, because sometimes you can get caught up in generating value without understanding the cost. You will need to perform a cost-benefit analysis to determine if an improvement is worth implementing.

HOW DO YOU MEASURE IT?

The most common measurement of value enhancement is the payback period, which entails measuring how long it would take to have the initial investment returned. You would simply divide the increase in the annual cash flow into the initial investment, which will provide the number of years that it would take to pay off the investment. In most cases owners of properties would consider the investment worthwhile if the payback occurred within two years.

Investment/Annual Increased Cash Flow = Payback Period in Years

The most common method of measuring returns is the return on investment (ROI). In this case you would divide the increased cash flow by the initial investment. This measurement is usually over the period of a year.

Annual Increased Cash Flow/Investment = Return on Investment

The next step is to factor the time value of money (TVM) into your return. There are two methods of measuring returns over time. The first and most used method is the internal rate of return (IRR). Most financial calculators have this function, which entails the input of the initial investment and then each year's cash flow, positive or negative. There are two drawbacks to the IRR. In some instances, when you have a number of negative cash flows you will actually have more than one IRR; that is why you must guess what the IRR is in the formula. The other drawback is that the IRR reinvests the cash flow at the same rate of return. In most cases, when the reinvestment rate is quite high, the IRR will be unrealistic and you would, therefore, achieve less than the depicted results.

In order to overcome the pitfalls of IRR, another TVM calculation was created—the financial management rate of return (FMRR). In this case you have two rates, one for negative cash flow (where you have to borrow money to finance this shortfall) and the reinvestment rate of the positive cash flow based on where you place this money (passbook, certificates of deposit, individual retirement accounts, stocks, bonds, etc.). This calculation requires you to discount negative cash flows into the prior year based on the finance rate and move positive cash flows into the future based on the reinvestment rate. This is the most accurate method of determining TVM, but unfortunately this calculation is too complicated to be installed into a financial calculator at this time. Naturally, when you are programming this type of calculation into a spreadsheet, you will have to incorporate a number of "if-then" contingent formulas that would take into consideration positive or negative cash flows, which would bring the amount forward or backward.

DOES SIZE MATTER?

In the case of returns, size does matter. In addition to size, the time frame of the return is also important. There is considerable risk as the bulk of the return occurs further in the future. It is hard enough to forecast a budget into the next year, let alone a pro forma that goes several years into the future. In performing your TVM calculation, if the cash flow over five years, say, were the same under two scenarios, but in one you have a more immediate return, the TVM will reflect this with a higher return (naturally reinvesting the cash flow). Therefore, the risk associated with the returns of TVM determines if it takes too long to enjoy the returns, which dilutes the effect with the risk and must be taken into consideration. In most cases a lower but immediate return is given priority over a higher return obtained over a prolonged period.

The Credit Check

The first step at value enhancement is to lease out the center's space. Who do you approach for a lease? Is the prospective tenant within the tenant mix? Does the tenant have credit? Is it a national tenant? Will the lender approve the tenant? Does its use violate any existing exclusives?

The true intent of credit checks is to determine if the risk of entering into a lease with a prospective tenant is worthwhile and to decrease possible exposure to bankruptcy. It is worth noting that if a tenant has gone into bankruptcy to reorganize its business recently, like so many of our department stores and national tenants, it could re-enter bankruptcy to liquidate its business. Therefore, the fact that a tenant has gone into bankruptcy recently is no protection from the tenant's further financial difficulties.

The financial stability of the tenant provides an insight into the nature of the prospective tenant's business and its ability to be flexible to the changing needs of consumers. Remember: you are embarking on a long-term relationship between owner and tenant, a financial marriage that will determine if the property can perform according to the owner's expectations.

WHO IS THE TENANT?

In some cases, you will be desperate to find a tenant. Even then, you need to perform a credit check. In most cases you will be able to determine how much credit the potential tenant has, the nature of its payment history, any public occurrences (bankruptcy, liens, public filings, governmental taxes, etc.), terms of payment, the number of inquiries for credit, delinquencies and, most important, evictions. Sometimes credit bureaus are only able to check credit for a tenant in a restricted area. You will need the tenant's name, trade name (doing business as, or "dba"), address and affiliated companies, among other facts. If it is a public corporation, there is much more information available than is the case with a private company or a mom-and-pop business.

SOURCES AND LEGALITIES

There are a number of credit bureaus that you may choose from. Most of the large databases of tenants are quite reliable, but in the past several were plagued with inaccurate information. It is important to determine if the information reported is accurate. A rule of thumb is to only use reputable credit bureaus, but even those have had problems with errors.

There are disclosure laws that dictate how you utilize credit reports. In the past, credit bureaus made a number of mistakes, reporting erroneous credit ratings for companies. Occasionally, when accurate information could not be obtained from the company under investigation, the credit bureau left erroneous information in its place. When a credit report was performed for this company the erroneous report was generated, forcing the company to straighten out the records and provide the information that was previously unobtainable.

Legislation has been enacted to prevent this from happening, essentially by permitting the credit report to be challenged. In some cases, if a potential tenant was turned down based on the credit report, the tenant would receive a copy of the report and have the ability to challenge the reporting credit bureau.

Ask the credit bureau to provide you with the reporting requirements in your area.

IMPACT

The financial impact of having or not having a tenant is apparent. What is not apparent is to what extent the tenant will impact the value of the shopping center. In most cases, appraisers and lenders are looking for national credit tenants. These are tenants who are in good standing, having better than average credit, who operate a chain nationwide. Appraisers and lenders will not discount the value of these rents, thereby preserving the value of the center. In other cases, lenders will discount the rents being paid by a mom-and-pop tenant, which will decrease the net operating income and the value of the shopping center. (See "Income Capitalization," p. 33.)

Rent

MINIMUM RENT

Typically, minimum rent—the basic rent paid per square foot—is the rent that is focused on, the root of a center's value. This rental rate is relative to the other rents and the free rent concessions that are given. Most owners and institutions look at this as only a part of the entire center's financial picture. The scheduled rents may at times be misleading, due to delinquencies. That is why you have estoppel certificates in which tenant and landlord reaffirm that the lease is intact and the rents have been paid.

PERCENTAGE RENTS

Percentage rent, a percentage of the tenant's total annual sales (above a predetermined level) that is paid in addition to minimum rent, has been an area of controversy in leases, for two reasons. First, many tenants don't know how the percentage rent works. Second and foremost, those who *do* understand how percentage rent is applied may not reach the sales level required to pay percentage rent.

In most cases, purchasers/underwriters do not consider percentage rent as value enhancement because you are unable to rely on it on a consistent basis. Therefore, shopping centers that are generating a high degree of percentage rents may want to negotiate in their leases the ability to convert 75 percent of the percentage rents into minimum rents. They will then have an automatic mechanism in place that converts percentage rents into an increase in minimum rents, which will not be discounted in valuation.

Centers may also want to have a kick-out clause in the tenant's lease, stating that if the tenant does not reach a certain level of sales and percentage rent, the center has the option of terminating the lease. In that scenario, the tenant may pay an increased minimum rent reflecting the unachieved sales.

TRIPLE NETS

Triple net refers to common area maintenance, property taxes and insurance, which are your recoverable expenses. If any of these items are included in the rent, then it would be considered less than a triple net lease. A gross lease would include all of the triple net expenses. A single net lease or modified gross lease would include both property taxes and insurance in the lease rent. A double net lease would usually include the property taxes in the lease rent. Notwithstanding inclusion in the rent, there may be escalation clauses for recovering some of the increases in these costs.

Typically, the triple nets in a strip center are based on gross leasable area (GLA), which would utilize all of the space in the shopping center as the denominator and the tenant's space as the numerator in the formula used in determining the tenant's pro rata share. In most centers, the triple net costs first deduct the department stores' contributions, then prorate the expenses in several categories (enclosed mall, parking area, food court, etc.). When prorating the expenses in the center, use the occupancy at the start of the quarter. This is usually tricky, because a number of tenants negotiate restrictions on the square footage or categories used. Other tenants negotiate a cap on the increases in these expenses, especially with the sale of the center, which dramatically increases the property taxes. These conditions to the lease are known as slippage. Slippage is the amount the landlord has to pay for additional costs, such as the triple net charges and/or tenant repairs, because of favorable leases that have provided relief to tenants under certain conditions. In other words, with a lease that has a cap of $0.32 per square foot per month for common area maintenance (CAM) costs and actual costs of $0.45 per square foot, the landlord will have to come up with the $0.13 per square foot. After a while this starts to add up, especially if large tenants have negotiated these conditions into their leases. The impact of slippage erodes net operating income (NOI), which reduces the value of the property. It is always important to remember the impact of slippage when agreeing to concessions.

AMORTIZED IMPROVEMENTS

The norm is to amortize improvements over the initial term of the lease. What about during the option period? The option period is the extension of the lease that is a unilateral right of the tenant. This gives the tenant control over the occupancy of the space, where the extension may not be exercised. Therefore, it is uncertain whether centers will be able to collect any amortized improvements during this period. More important, is it financially sound advice to collect the amount over the initial period, rather than speculating the recovery over an extended period? In early terminations, the unamortized portion of the improvements and leasing commissions are usually included as part of the termination fee. In many cases, centers can use 10 percent as their financing cost to amortize the improvements. Naturally, this figure will go up during periods of inflation.

MARKETING FUND (MERCHANTS' ASSOCIATION FUND)

Contributions to this fund are based on the square footage of the tenancy. As the square footage increases, the amount decreases. In other words, for 1,000 square feet the tenant might be charged $0.50 per square foot and for the next 1,500 feet the rate might decline to $0.45 per square foot. Department stores typically negotiate to pay no or token amounts while remaining voting members of the merchants' association.

Typically, the owner will contribute 25 percent of the collected fund up to a predetermined maximum.

ADVERTISING FUND

This is a fund that is funded by each tenant for a structured advertising campaign set forth by the center's marketing director. This would include tabloids, inserts and seasonal campaigns. In some instances, instead of following the four seasons, it may more advantageous for your tenants to advertise during their selling seasons, spreading the advertising throughout the year. Because the advertising is purchased in bulk, the rate is usually much better than the tenant would be able to obtain.

Once again, the owner may contribute 25 percent of the collected fund, with a cap.

EFFECTIVE RENT

This is the rent that is obtained on behalf of your landlord, including both minimum and percentage rents. This is tricky, because you must deduct all of the concessions that you or the leasing broker have provided as an incentive to attract the tenant to the space. The impact of free rent (CAM only), commission premiums, extended construction/fixturization periods (all rents), tenant improvements, ceilings on CAM, floors on the numerator used to calculate CAM and other concessions can be quite dramatic.

Minimum Rent over the Lease Term − (Concessions, Free Rent, TIs, Caps on CAM, etc.) ÷ Term = Effective Rent

You finally divide this amount by the square footage to determine the effective rent per square foot.

Effective Rent ÷ Square Feet = Effective Rent per Square Foot

Financial Statements

PURPOSE

What is the purpose of a financial statement? The financial statement is primarily used for determining the financial position of the project at the end of an accounting period. It will illustrate the relationship of income versus expenses, assets versus liabilities and the return on the equity. In other words, the financial statement tells you if the project is making the desired return on a real-time basis. Unfortunately, an analysis of the financial statement is needed to determine the exact nature of the investment and the profitability that is recognized at that point in time.

Relate Income and Expenses. There are a number of ways of looking at income and expenses. The most common is the expense-to-income ratio specifying the efficiency of the project and the actual profit margin. The margin is derived by subtracting the operating expenses from the income, arriving at the net operating income. The net operating income is then divided by the income to provide the proper margin percentage. The debt service and capital expenses are subtracted from the net operating income to obtain the net cash flow. The net cash flow determines the bottom line for the real estate project.

Means of Analysis for Investors and Management. The financial statement is the starting point to determine the financial fitness of a project. Unfortunately, too many investors look only at the financial statement and not at the other aspects that make a project successful. This is because the financial statement is the one quantifiable element of a project. The other aspects of determining the feasibility of the project are at times very subjective.

PREPARATION OF FINANCIAL STATEMENTS—DIFFERENCE IN TIMING

The actual preparation of the financial statements for the projects that you are involved in may vary according to the investor requirements. The following are two of the principal ways entries may be treated.

Cash-basis Accounting. Cash-basis accounting recognizes income and expenses when the cash is received and/or disbursed. In other words, the accounting is done on the basis of "money in and money out." This basic method of accounting is utilized by a majority of property management companies.

Accrual Accounting. Accrual accounting recognizes revenue when earned and expenses when incurred. These transactions are recorded at the end of each accounting period even though the cash has not yet been received or paid. This provides a more precise picture of the financial situation at the end of the accounting period. In this statement the income that may be anticipated from a tenant is added as a receivable and indicates that this income still needs to be collected. On the expense side, you will include the adjustment of expenses that are either recurring (e.g., utilities, janitorial, security, etc.) or expended through purchase orders, which are payables that need to be invoiced and paid.

COMMON ELEMENTS OF THE FINANCIAL STATEMENT

Balance Sheet. The balance sheet is the statement showing the project's financial position at the end of an accounting period. The statement includes:

- assets (cash, accounts receivable)
- liabilities (loans, accounts payable). These may be short term (anything under a year) or long term
- equity (venture capital, stocks)

It shows the net effect of the operating statement, and is also where prepaid rents and security deposits are reflected.

The relationships of assets, liabilities and equity are important in computing certain financial ratios that determine where the company is in relation to industry standards. The most common *solvency ratios* are as follows:

Quick Ratio = (Cash + Accounts Receivable)/current liabilities
This shows liquid assets that are available to cover current debt.

Current Ratio = Current Assets/Current Liabilities
This measures the margin of safety to cover a reduction in current assets.

Liabilities to Net Worth = Liabilities/Net Worth
Compares debt to venture capital, high debt levels indicating high risk.

The most common *efficiency ratios* are as follows:

Inventory Turnover = Sales/Inventory
This shows the rate at which merchandise is moved, indicating stock levels.

Assets to Sales = Assets/Sales
This indicates the level of investment that is needed to generate the sales.

Sales to Working Capital = Sales/(Current Assets – Current Liabilities)
This measures the efficiency of using short-term assets and liabilities to generate sales.

The most common *profitability ratios* are as follows:

Profit Margin = Net Profit after Taxes/Sales
Profit earned on a per dollar of sales, measuring efficiency.

Return on Assets = Net Profit after Taxes/Assets
A key indicator of profitability.

Return on Net Worth = Net Profit after Taxes/Net Worth
Analyzes whether the return on venture capital is suitable.

Income and Expense Statement. The income and expense statement is also referred to as a profit and loss statement. This statement shows the net operating income and the net cash flow income for the specified accounting period. Most owners are interested in the "bottom line," which in most cases is the cash flow, or what the owners can put in their pockets.

Transaction by Detail. The transaction by detail statement provides detailed income and expenses for each account code or category. This statement is especially useful when there is sufficient detail, allowing one to understand what was included in each income and expense category. Each account code or category must be well defined, providing the necessary description of what items are included in each. Every month the transaction by detail chronologically lists income and expense items as they are entered. As each item is entered, a description field is provided, allowing you to annotate what the item is for, such as a late charge or emergency plumbing repair.

Rent Roll. The rent roll is very important in that it shows the payment or the lack of payment by each tenant. This statement includes an aging report that shows the charges that have accumulated for the tenant, and whether the tenant's payment is current. In many instances, if you just look at the rental variance you may not notice any delinquency in the payments, because the tenant paid rent in that particular month. In reality, the tenant may be far behind in rent, information which is depicted in this report.

Most accounting packages allow for the flagging of rent increases and percentage rent reports.

Cash Receipts Journal. The cash receipts journal is a statement that accounts only for transactions involving the receipt of cash. The statement will identify the receipt of cash and the application to the specific categories (rent, percentage rent, CAM, taxes, insurance, marketing fund, media fund, reimbursements, etc.). In addition, the cash receipts journal lists the income from pay phones, vending machines and other revenue sources.

Cash Disbursements Journal. The cash disbursements journal is a statement that accounts only for the transactions that involve the disbursement of cash. The statement is categorized by the vendor and the checks that have been disbursed, regardless of the application of the expense (e.g., the handyman gets a check for plumbing, electrical and masonry repairs).

Check Register. The check register is a detailed list of the checks that have been processed. The statement primarily lists the checks in numerical order, which should reflect the chronological order in which the checks were processed. There is a provision for manual and computerized checks, which may cause confusion when a check is cut on a manual basis. If the manual checks are improperly entered into the system, an overdraft situation may seem to exist because the debits from the manual checks were not reflected.

General Ledger. The general ledger is a record of the project's accounts. The general ledger contains the accounts that make up the project's financial statement. Separate accounts exist for individual assets, liabilities, equity (stockholders, individual or corporate), revenue and expenses. A trial balance of the general ledger accounts is prepared at the end of the accounting period to assure the correct reflection of debits and credits.

Bank Reconciliation. Very rarely does an ending balance in a bank statement agree with the cash account of the books. This is natural, since there are disbursements made that are not reflected against the account. In addition, there are bank charges, interest and bank errors, any of which will throw off the balance of any account. Therefore, a bank reconciliation is needed to adjust the book balance. Journal entries are then made to update the records and arrive at an ending balance in the cash account that agrees with the ending balance of the bank statement.

Valuation Methods

INCOME CAPITALIZATION

The "income approach" to appraising is multilayered and complex. This approach is the most common method of evaluating shopping centers. There are many intricacies in this process and many ways for the value to be rationalized. Essentially, the income approach processes the net operating income to indicate its capitalized value (the amount of the investment that produces it).

Net operating income is the income that is derived from the property by subtracting the operating expenses. The operating expenses include all of your monthly expenses, but exclude any debt service, capitalized expenses, leasing commissions, reserves, depreciation or tax implications. The elements that make up the operating expenses are those that are necessary for running the shopping center, including management fees, even though an owner may not charge a fee.

Other valuation methods relying on gross rent (gross rent multipliers) do not calculate a return for the real estate project, but rather an estimation of what may be expected from the project based on income only. The gamble is your ability to manage normal or minimal expenses to obtain the return that you desire.

The expense items below the net operating income (NOI) lines are all arbitrary items. The items considered below NOI are debt service, capitalized expenses, commissions, tenant improvements, reserves, depreciation, income tax, etc. Debt service is usually the largest one. Capitalized expenses may be incurred, or perhaps nothing is put back into the property. You may lease the property yourself, so you may not have to pay out any commissions. It is up to you how much reserves, if any, you set aside. Depreciation is based on how your accountant interprets the legality of cost segregation and its application. Tax implications deal with how the ownership entity is structured. Examples are C corporations (double taxation); S corporations (individual taxation); the limited liability company (LLC), which affords the protection of a C corporation without the strict reporting requirements; general partnerships; limited partnerships; the limited liability partnership (LLP), which provides the flexibility of a partnership with the limited liability of a corporation; and a myriad of ownership forms that are variations of previous forms, such as a syndication or a joint venture. These are all items that differ from owner to owner.

Calculation. The easiest way to remember the income capitalization approach is to remember "IRV." IRV is the formula that provides the necessary components to perform this function.

$$V = I / R$$

V = Value
I = Income (net operating income)
R = Rate (capitalization rate or return)

This is the simplified basis for determining value. There are three methods of determining the "rate," or cap rate (capitalization rate): direct comparison, band of investment and summation.

Direct Comparison Method—The direct comparison method of obtaining a cap rate involves the "market approach" to determine the cap rates that were used in like project transactions. This would involve the identification of comparable project transactions that have taken place in similar communities. The cap rate is then assessed according to the NOI per square foot of the project. The cap rate is adjusted with the possible additional income of that project, whether there is additional land that may be sold or additional square footage that may be built onto the project.

There are many institutional sources for cap rates that provide confirmation of the actual cap rate that is derived. These sources are based on institutional investors that have been surveyed and who have provided the basic criteria for their investors. Furthermore, the market cap rates that are obtained through recent transactions in the area are qualified by appraisers.

Band of Investment Method—The band of investment method, or the "debt-constant equity-dividend method," is the approach that a majority of appraisers utilize. It employs the percentage of the project that is based on a loan that is multiplied by its mortgage constant. The remaining equity percentage of the project is then multiplied by the desired yield rate. Both of these are added together to obtain the cap rate. Additional loans or equity partners may be added to the formula.

Summation Method—The summation method, or the built-up rate, of determining a cap rate involves adding together several different types of elements. The basis of this rate is started by assessing the safe rate (the passbook rate at a bank or savings and loan) and then adding or subtracting elements that affect this rate. Below is an example of how the cap rate is thereby established.

Safe Rate	4.0%
Investment Risk	2.5%
Entrepreneurial Fee	1.0%
Non-Liquidity Burden	2.0%
Recapture Rate	2.0%
Cap Rate	11.5%

Discount Rate/Discount Factor—Now that you understand how to apply income capitalization and how the capitalization rate is determined, you will need to apply a discount rate to your calculations. Income capitalization reflects a static point in time, based on a single year. In evaluating property in appraisals you perform income capitalization to determine value in addition to taking into consideration cash flows over a period of years, which reflects the ups and downs of tenancy. When you evaluate a property over time you smooth out the ups and downs of cash flow and have it discounted to present value. Typically, in determining value you would evaluate the cash flow over a ten-year period.

The discount rate or discount factor is the percentage that is used to reduce an amount based on the risk, and percentage, that an owner feels is required in order to hold on to the investment over a period of years. The most common use of the discount rate is in determining the present value of cash flows.

One of the problems in evaluating investments is that time and the actual size of the cash flows generated by alternatives make them difficult to compare. You may have two differing cash flows (as seen below) that total the same amount, but have a different value once the element of time is introduced.

Year	Property A	Property B
1	$ 50.00	$60.00
2	30.00	10.00
3	25.00	70.00
4	45.00	20.00
5	50.00	40.00
Total	$200.00	$200.00

The technique of discounting allows future cash flows to be expressed in terms of their present value. To determine the present value of an income stream of cash flows, a discount rate must be chosen to find the discount factors for future years. The discount factor, when multiplied by the appropriate future cash flow, gives the present value of that cash flow. You would naturally discount both the cash flow and the value that you have depicted based on the cap rate to present value. This is a much more complex calculation than just capping out a value, because you have to take TVM into consideration. Assuming a discount rate of 8.5 percent, the present value of the above cash flows can be calculated. These factors are based on the financial calculation solving for the present value, using the discount rate of 8.5% and a future value of $1.

Year	Discount Factor	Property A	Discounted Property A	Property B	Discounted Property B
1	.922	$ 50.00	$ 46.10	$ 60.00	$ 55.32
2	.849	30.00	25.47	10.00	8.49
3	.783	25.00	19.58	70.00	54.81
4	.722	45.00	32.49	20.00	14.44
5	.665	50.00	33.25	40.00	26.60
Total		$200.00	$156.89	$200.00	$159.66

It becomes apparent that the cash flow in Property B is incrementally higher than that of Property A, only due to the impact of time on the cash flows. In other words, if you have cash flows that are higher in earlier years even though the total dollar amounts are the same for A and B, the present value, by discounting the cash flows, shows an advantage and higher value for the cash flow of B.

Combining these discounted cash flows with the residual value or the terminal value (tenth year value based on the eleventh year NOI) determined from the income capitalization determines the present value of the property.

This makes it a little more complicated—and accurate—than just capping out the NOI of a particular year and saying that is the value of the shopping center. A developer subtracted the cost of building the project from the newly determined value to determine the profit margin, ignoring the time it would take to obtain the entitlements, building permits, lease-up period and so on, not to mention the additional expenses associated with this lapse of time (interest carry, property taxes, insurance, security, additional unanticipated expenses, etc.).

REPLACEMENT VALUE (COST APPROACH)

This method is used for the valuation of shopping centers for two key reasons. First and foremost is to create the replacement value of a project for insurance purposes. The second is more subjective, in that it provides the inherent value that may be attributed to the restoration of a historic project or the employment of differing construction techniques for a modern-day monument for the investor.

Cost of Replacing Damaged Property. The replacement value goes into detail as to the construction of the real estate project. It does not delve into what you may have paid for the construction of the project, but rather the cost today of having a contractor complete the project. The cost of the land is based on the comparable values that are found in the market. There are logistics of rebuilding the center, where time delays, cost overruns, change orders, layout changes, anchor tenant changes and other factors may not be accurately depicted today (just the cost). In other words, this method does take into consideration the fact that you have gold-plated faucets, that you have converted a historic factory into a retail complex, built an extremely modern shopping center with retractable roof, and so on.

Insurance Purposes. The value that is derived from this and from subsequent appraisals will determine the amount that should be insured. The project then should be insured for this amount so that, should there be a disaster that is covered by the insurance company's policy, you will be able to obtain a full settlement to rebuild the shopping center. There are a number of items that will be deducted from the settlement amount of an insurance claim, including deductibles, coinsurance and the depreciation of the investment.

COMPARABLE VALUES (MARKET APPROACH)

This is probably the easiest and the most performed valuation approach for the residential brokerage community. This is a very important part of determining the market rate for undeveloped commercial property and the determination of a cap rate used in like property. In the realm of shopping centers, especially large ones, you may have to go to other similar communities outside of the state that you are in, so that you will be able to find comparable projects. There are companies that track the closing of these types of transactions and make these figures available for determining comparability of most properties. This provides the information that you need to analyze the efficiency of the property and determine if there are any correlations to the cap rate used to determine the purchase compared with the NOI per square foot. Many appraisers extrapolate the varying cap rates and NOI per square foot to arrive at a cap rate that is applicable to the subject property. In any event, the market approach is instrumental in ascertaining the cap rate used for the direct capitalization method of determining the value of a project, as well as providing the land value for the replacement value approach for the project.

Budgets

INCOME

Try to forecast your income for all of the income categories, minimum rent, percentage rent, CAM recoveries, tenant improvement (TI) recoveries/loans, promotion/marketing funds, miscellaneous income (pay phones/vending machines) and other revenue-producing operations at your centers.

Rents. Look at each of your leases. Hopefully, you have lease summaries in the front that will provide the rent increases at a glance. Reflect the change in rent in your income schedule.

Your percentage rents should be based on an incremental increase or decrease in sales, based on your past experience with the tenants' sales and competition, not only in the shopping center, but also in shopping centers around you.

Recoveries. In many cases your recoveries are based on the start of the quarter occupancy of the shopping center after you have deducted the department stores' contributions. You will have to make assumptions regarding the occupancy of the shopping center, based on your leasing projections. Be conservative; if a space has never been rented and you have no prospects for occupancy, you will have a tough time supporting the inclusion of income for this space in the next year.

In some cases you will have minimum denominators that have been negotiated into the lease agreement, so again check the lease to confirm these amounts.

Check your leases regarding applicable recoveries. In the case of department stores they exclude certain categories, since they pay directly for these expenses. Even if this is the case you may still assess a portion of these costs, such as for trash removal, since there is common area trash for the customers in the shopping center.

There are cases where tenants have negotiated caps on increases in common area charges, property taxes and/or insurance. There is a dramatic increase in this cost when a property is sold, which cannot be passed on to these tenants. This is called slippage and the owner will have to pay for this expense.

Tenants usually do not pay a management fee on property taxes or insurance.

Further, percentage rents may offset tenant improvement recoveries. In this case, in lieu of obtaining a tenant improvement recovery there may be a threshold amount of percentage rent that would be credited before the tenant improvement recovery kicks in.

EXPENSES

Expenses often outpace income during a flat economy. This becomes scary for the owners, especially if they purchase a high-maintenance shopping center. This type of shopping center has costs that continue to rise, regardless of the increase in rents. Therefore, you must always project your costs based on the possible increases that are expected in the next year.

Contracts. This should be an easy exercise. You may want to review your contracts with your existing vendors and negotiate next year's rates or put them out to bid. Either way, you will be able to pinpoint this amount quite readily.

Labor. This is a very important part of your operations. Labor rates—either union or nonunion—need to be projected. Look at an affordability index to determine if your personnel can actually survive on the wages they are earning. This is important, because if they cannot survive they may augment their wages by other means.

Labor rates are also tied into contracts, such as elevator and escalator contracts that are tied into cost of living allowances (COLA). This will automatically impact these contracts and need to be considered in projecting your budget.

Materials. There is an index that determines the increase in cost of materials. In most cases you will be able to negotiate with your vendors not to exceed an amount based on a certain volume of sales. If you do not achieve the sales level expected you will be charged at a slightly higher rate.

Once again, a portion of your contracts will be impacted by a percentage of these rates, such as your elevator/escalator contracts.

Utilities. You will need to contact your utility companies to see if they are projecting an increase in their rates. Utility companies cannot arbitrarily raise your rates. They must apply to the public utility commission (PUC) to justify and receive an increase in their rates. This is a long process, so the utility companies know their plans regarding rates long in advance.

In the case of getting PUC approvals you may want to get a group together who will lobby for rates to remain at current levels instead of increasing.

Property Taxes. In most counties the property taxes are scheduled according to different bond measures that are applied to your tax rate. This probably has a greater impact than the increase in reassessing the property's value. You may be within a state that has a cap on increases, such as California, where Proposition 13 holds increases to 2 percent a year, unless the shopping center is sold, where it is automatically reassessed according to the new purchase price (base year).

There are property tax appeals that you can embark on either by yourself or with a property tax appeal company. You may negotiate their fees anywhere from 50 percent to 25 percent of the savings or a fixed fee.

Insurance. In most cases you will be able to have input from your insurance agent regarding the increases in your insurance, depending on the experience rating (number of claims) of the shopping center and how the market will receive your product. The market is the underwriters available to insure the risk; the product is the property type—

the shopping center. Always try to shop the market by working with independent brokers that cover different companies. From year to year there are new insurance companies that become bullish on a certain product type, and it may be yours.

Pro Formas

Pro formas are multiyear budgets that use assumptions to provide a picture of how a center will perform. This will take into consideration the lease-up, re-lease of space, projected changes in the economy and the impact of costs to the bottom line. In this case you will use the most "what ifs" in crystal-balling the future.

FUTURE INCOME PROJECTION

How does one project the future income of an existing project? This is a little easier if there is a track record to follow in determining the assumptions to project the income for a property. What if there is no information available for a new development? What do you do? Talk to the governmental bodies that are "in the know," such as the chamber of commerce, the franchise tax board and public officials, to enlist their expertise in obtaining a base to start your pro forma. Next, start creating differing scenarios based on different assumptions. If you subject the project to a number of assumptions that you have taken into consideration, this will allow you to understand the project forward and backward.

Income is based largely on bodies. This means you need to know how many people live and work in the area where you are thinking of developing a shopping center. Next you need to know how much disposable income each of these people has and if they are going to spend it in your shopping center. If the population base is unstable the resulting sales will be erratic, which will impact your rental rates. Sales provide the rental rates. If the rent is too high then the tenant will no longer be able to be in business and will leave. The result may be that the project will fail.

TIME VALUE OF MONEY

In the most universal sense the time value of money must take into consideration the cycles of any type of investment. The most cost-effective time in the cycle to purchase the investment is the start of the upward spiral. Market conditions flow in a sine-wave curve for each type of investment. The duration of this curve varies in length of time, anywhere from twelve to eighteen years. Typically, the real estate cycle follows the business cycle. As the market takes off, a frenzy is created, which stimulates the number of investors who buy at the top of the market. Who profits by this buying frenzy? The local investors who develop these projects.

The problem for developers and investors is the lack of ability to use computers to quickly analyze projects. Instead, real estate developers and investors use a single sheet of future-stabilized cash flows that are capitalized to obtain a value of the completed project. The single sheet pro forma does not address the questions of when the project will happen and over what time period. The project is created without taking into consideration the need to get zoning changed, entitlement established, the project leased and the return provided. The time span can dissolve the profit margin of a project. The cost of money (interest, preferred return, etc.) can also make many projects negative, if the "interest carry" eats all of the profits, even if the project is performing according to its one-sheet pro forma.

Rationale: The Impact of Interest Payments on Value of Money Over Time. As stated earlier the cost of money (carrying costs) impacts the project. Once the project is started the carrying costs start, and if the timing of the project does not meet the needs of the consumer the project's profit margin will be eaten up. The interest payments—or in some cases, a "preferred return," the guaranteed return for the initial investment in the project—will hinder the profitability of the project, especially if the project is marginal or if it takes a great deal of time before these amounts are reduced. Regardless, the interest in a project has to be given serious consideration because the project may fail, due to the lapse of time and the accrual of interest.

Amortization. Amortization is the gradual reduction of a principal amount over a specified period of time. The payments include the specified interest and a residual principal that incrementally increases over time.

In addition, with adjustable rate mortgages (ARMs) you will be able to forecast the rise and fall of the interest rates over a period of years. This should coincide with the rise and fall of the consumer price index (CPI). Although the CPI may remain flat for a period of time, you still should try to forecast a smooth increase and decrease in the CPI that coincides with the real estate cycle.

ASSUMPTIONS

Projected Lease Renewal Rates. As with everything that is dependent on time there is a cycle to work with in projecting lease renewal rates. Assume, for example, that the development will start off great and will start to increase in rental rate, but with increasing competition from new shopping centers, the rates will start to decrease. As the lease rates decrease, the market will stop building, since the developments will no longer be able to support the project with an increased basis in land and construction cost, decreasing the margin and return on investment. The lease rates will then start to rise again, since the available space will be absorbed due to lack of construction. The cycle then begins once again, but this time involves the redevelopment of shopping centers in this now mature area. This cycle is dependent on the continued growth of a community. If consumers leave the area, or if the cycle stops for another economic reason, there will be a sharp change in the rates.

Projected Tenant Sales. Tenant sales are always very difficult to predict. This will take research, and again, you will have to contact the local chamber of commerce and the department of taxation to determine the retail sales for the city and county. This, coupled with the total inventory of retail space, will help you determine the starting point for the sales. The sales of a new center will start with a bang and will slowly decrease over a six-month period. Sales comparison will increase over the next three years at about the double digit mark, if you have a captive customer base for that period. The sales will then taper off and plateau.

New Leasing Activity. There are a number of methods of determining the absorption rate—the net square footage leased annually, adjusted for new and demolished buildings—that you will be leasing at a certain shopping center. Unfortunately, this is determined by the market that surrounds you, even though you may have a superior product. The old adage is "buy an inexpensive house in an expensive area," which will make your property appreciate because of your neighbors'. This holds true to a certain extent with leasing a shopping center in an area that has a great deal of vacancy. This will allow the bargain hunters to go where the bargains are located, but also may push down lease rates and increase concessions.

One thing to remember: If your shopping center is 100 percent occupied most of the time, you are probably leasing your center at too low a lease rent. It is a tough act to balance the lease rent with supply and demand.

Projected Expenses.

Operating Expenses—Most of your expense projections should be tied to the rise and fall of the CPI. This will allow the expenses to keep pace with the economy. You may want to just multiply your expenses by the CPI, which is the easiest to complete. In some states the property taxes have caps on the annual assessments or assess only on a cyclical basis. Either way you must introduce these additional items into your calculations. If you fail to introduce this element your pro forma will actually perform better than real life and disappoint the owners. Try to be conservative in your projections of expenses. In other words, consider all aspects. Otherwise, something will surely pop up that you didn't consider.

Renovation—If you are proposing a renovation of a real estate project, always remember that time will affect the cost assumptions used by contractors. There are many factors that drive the cost up or down, such as if the contractor was busy, if the contractor needed your job to get other jobs or if the contractor's estimator was wrong in adding up the numbers. Either way, these situations change as time passes. You can almost always count on job costs to go up. In rare instances, where the economic climate is devastated, your job costs may go down. Therefore, always add a contingency buffer for inflation, cost overruns and other fluctuations.

Replacement of Major Capital Items—A reserve may be created in most real estate projects for the big repair and maintenance items whose costs may be passed through to the tenant. A similar reserve needs to be created to replace major capital items. This reserve should reflect the need over years to renovate the facade of the real estate project, if necessary.

Cost of Leasing Space.
The cost of leasing space is dependent on the market, and if you are not in the appropriate range you are out of the "ball game" for leasing commissions, tenant improvements, rent concessions, caps, exclusive rights and so on. Advertising and marketing are based on the rates that are available for the area. Remember, if you give something up in the manner of concessions, monetary or otherwise, you are impacting the project.

Depreciation. The additional items that need to be considered are how property and its improvements are depreciated. The current depreciation basis is derived from a 33.5-year term for permanent improvements. There are many ways of looking at the tenant improvements, as they may be depreciated with the building or with the life of the lease.

There are tax ramifications that also need to be considered. This is left to the accountants, who will advise you of tax credits and loopholes that may be utilized. The project may have been built with tax exemptions for redevelopment areas or tax credits for historical areas.

Property Tax Appeals. A major issue today is property tax appeals that will reduce the basis of the taxes for the project, especially if the project is not up to its full money-making capacity or the property was purchased at a higher-than-normal value. Any of these conditions warrant the investigation of a tax appeal. If won, the tax appeal will reduce your taxes on an interim basis, but most times the assessment must be appealed on a year-by-year basis. In economic lulls, the county tax assessor's office will be swamped with appeals, making them scrutinize your appeal more carefully. Every dollar that they give back in a tax refund is a dollar less for your community. Retain a qualified specialist (whose fees can be negotiated) to represent you on a contingency basis.

You may also appeal your property taxes when you have a tremendous amount of deferred maintenance. This is a bit harder to prove to the county assessor's office, but still a viable property tax reduction technique.

Vulnerability of Assumptions. If conservative, assumptions may make you a hero; if too aggressive, they may make you a failure. It is the balance between these two extremes that must be met in order to retain your credibility. It is very hard to project past the first several years, since there are a number of external forces that impact the economic feasibility of your real estate project. Therefore, it is paramount that you research your area to see if there are any developments that will impact your project.

Projections Based on Past Trends. The real estate market is based on cycles. In many areas, the cycles run in twelve-year or eighteen-year cycles, or somewhere in between. Historical market trends provide a basis for today's market trends, allowing a calculated guess about the future based on past patterns and economic conditions. This permits the investor and developer to time a project's success with the real estate outlook in that area. Understanding the cycles and the triggers that investors use to make decisions allows you to better poise a project for success.

Longer Time Frame than Pro Forma. The time frame outside of a pro forma has always been the single drawback of forecasting. There are so many factors that need to be considered that it would be impossible to create an accurate pro forma. Who will file bankruptcy this year? Will there be a market for mid-market regional malls? How long will the power centers be successful? The questions go on and on; all you do know is that retailing is always in a state of transition.

Declining Accuracy as Time Increases. The accuracy of forecasting is based on the information that was obtained on the day that the projection was completed. Who could have projected the fall of the Eastern bloc countries, which literally stopped the economy of the former Soviet Union? The fall of communism and the ramifications for the defense industry in the United States has had a tremendous effect in military base closures. The base closures have stalled the economy in the surrounding communities.

These kinds of developments could not be imagined during the assembly of a pro forma, but they have had great impact in shopping centers. They demonstrate that the industry is not isolated from the whims of the world. Does this mean that you need to be a world scholar to present a pro forma with the assumptions that are needed? No, this just means that you cannot assume that world economics will not impact your business. Quite the contrary; you must be sensitive to what is going on in the world and how it affects us.

Players

INSTITUTIONS

There is a proliferation of institutions that are investing in shopping centers. These institutions, in the form of life insurance companies, pension funds, multinational corporations, among others, have begun their move on the shopping center market by way of real estate investment trusts (REITs). Prior to the change in legislation that allowed institutions to participate in REITs, they had to either underwrite loans or directly invest in a project. Unfortunately, with a portfolio of mostly stocks and bonds, the money managers were investing a majority of time into managing the real estate investment.

This all changed with REITs, since this allowed the institutions to invest in the way that they invested in stocks. They would review the shopping center management company to understand its track record and its philosophy of running these centers. This makes the transaction more liquid; if they do not like how the portfolio of shopping centers is being managed, they simply sell the stock in minutes. In prior years, if the institutions invested in shopping centers and did not like the results, they would have to sell the property over a period of time to eliminate it from their portfolio.

There are still institutions that invest in real estate projects directly, but this is becoming less common.

REAL ESTATE INVESTMENT TRUST (REITS)

Real estate investment trusts (REITs) are companies that manage a real estate portfolio for shareholders. The advantage is in its ability to qualify for special tax treatment, by having a minimum of 100 shareholders and distributing at least 95 percent of its income. REITs that qualify and distribute their income typically avoid taxes and act as a conduit for the shareholders' real estate investments. Unlike corporations (except subchapter S corporations), the income is taxed only once and at the shareholders' level. A trust is not permitted to be a personal holding company, nor can it be used to hold property mainly for sale to customers.

Economics. REITs have allowed Wall Street and the general public to get into the real estate game, but with costs. REITs were first introduced in the 1970s, but quickly disappeared, due to the high rate of inflation and the reinvestment of the REIT dollars into certificates of deposit and tax-exempt IRAs. The money industry is continuously in a state of flux. As inflation and interest rates change, so do the returns and the respective investments into differing vehicles. Wall Street is currently sweeping up the stocks, with unprecedented growth. The bull market has driven the price of most stocks to astronomical points, which puts incredible pressure on REITs to acquire undervalued projects, redevelop well-situated projects or develop new projects. As money is thrown at the REITs, they must place it in some type of real estate.

Financial Models. A number of REITs are using a multitude of computerized models to analyze the purchase of real estate projects. For the most part, the REITs have been industry-specific and have kept to an area of expertise. This has allowed for a number of REITs to form, filling specific niche requirements. These requirements are dictated by a project type (anchored strip center, regional enclosed mall, power center, etc.) with a secondary concern for the amount of property in the portfolio for each geographic area. This is a matter of having enough of a base in a geographical area to allow the control of the investments through the generation of fees that would be able to sustain a management staff.

FOREIGN INVESTMENT

In the 1970s and 1980s the Japanese were investing a great deal in the United States, Australia and Europe. Most of these transactions were based on investing in trophy properties rather than the financial feasibility of the investment. The feasibility was most naturally overlooked with the devaluation of the dollar, which made real estate a bargain, at 40 percent off. Furthermore, the prime rate in Japan at the time hovered around 4 percent.

The industrialization of Asia has brought additional entities to real estate. This next generation of real estate investors is investing in the United States for many reasons, but it boils down to economics. If there is a deal that is secured by real estate and the returns are great, the deal will be done.

Many foreign investors are using the income capitalization method of determining value based on today's income stream. The upside potential of the project will only make the project more desirable. In today's market, there are numerous real estate projects available at less than the cost of building the project (sometimes 50 percent of the cost of the project). If the foreign investor purchases a real estate project at an 11 percent cap rate on today's income of 70 percent occupied, the possibility of upside is very great. If the market turns in an area or if the investor works on tenanting the project, the return becomes an exponential boom.

The key to working with a foreign investor (or any investor) is to develop a strategic alliance with that investor. This means that you will work to make the investor money and not to be fee-driven. The profitability of a safe investment is the paramount concern of the foreign investor. No one invests money to lose money.

Long-term Prospects

WHEN TO SELL

The old adage says to "buy low, sell high," but no one has a crystal ball to predict when this will happen. There are ways to determine the point of the cycle that you are entering and when you will reach a peak. In different regions there are economic cycles that vary anywhere from twelve years to eighteen years. There are indicators that tip you off when a cycle may be approaching; for instance, Arizona has historically had a peak in the economy before California had its peak.

Many projects have lacked the provision of the exit strategy. Why? The exit strategy provides the relinquishing of the project. This is contrary to the development or investment of the project. If the project is so good, why sell the project? The answer is that the most productive part of the cycle has passed and investors are ready to place the profit into another project that will start on its upward spiral. The exit strategy is critical in that it usually illustrates that the project is thin in margin and must be completed in its entirety to obtain a profit. An exit strategy needs to be created for each stage of the development and the investment in order to determine the best point to dispose of the project. The majority of foreign investors look at exit strategies before purchasing the property. The foreign investor wants to understand the risk of owning and possibly selling the property.

One of the main keys to investing in real estate today is to determine the exit strategies that are available for the project. If these alternatives, even in a worst-case scenario, illustrate the feasibility of the project, the project may be purchased. Many investors today are demanding projects that they are able to dispose of at a moment's notice, without any loss of the investment, but rather a discount of the return. The easiest answer to the question of "when to sell" often is: at the peak of the market.

HOW TO MAXIMIZE VALUE

One way to maximize the value of a shopping center is to use foresight in the development of the project, allowing it the flexibility to change as the market changes. This permits a strip center to be converted to an enclosed mall or an enclosed mall into a mixed-use development. If certain principles of design are used in the development, the shopping center will be able to be converted into a number of differing uses that will cater to the changing needs of the community. This means that the tenanted spaces need to be flexible, so that a number of tenants and differing configurations may be utilized.

The direct way to maximize the value of the shopping center is through the minimization of expenses. You must accomplish this task without exposing the investor to liability claims or undue deferred maintenance that will reduce the value of the investment. Look at all of the expenses; even though they are passed through to the tenants, these expenses represent an occupancy cost that could be translated into rental income.

Marketing is another key aspect of maximizing a shopping center's value. Marketing positions the center in the community. This is the most inexpensive method of rallying the tenants around the "cause" of generating sales. The more sales that are experienced, the more rent that may be afforded. If the tenants have tremendous sales, they are, within reason, willing to pay for the ability to continue to generate these sales.

Resources

The American Council of Life Insurance publishes the *Investment Bulletin* that summarizes the underwriting transactions of life insurance companies. Peter F. Korpacz publishes the *Korpacz Real Estate Investor Survey,* which is used by appraisers, in addition to a number of in-house surveys. These are just a few of the sources that are available providing summaries of cap rates for particular project types in different geographical areas.

The Dollars and Cents of Shopping Centers, published by the Urban Land Institute, and reports published by the International Council of Shopping Centers (ICSC) and the Institute of Real Estate Management (IREM) can provide you with information needed to make accurate income projections.

Recommended Readings

Alexander, Alan A., CSM. *Preparing a Budget for a Small Shopping Center.* New York: International Council of Shopping Centers, 1988.

Alexander, Alan A., CSM. *Shopping Center Lease Administration: A Manager's Guide to Improving Financial Record Keeping.* New York:

International Council of Shopping Centers, 1986.

Alexander, Alan A., CSM. *Shopping Center Rent Administration: A Manager's Guide to Avoiding Cash-Flow Problems*. New York: International Council of Shopping Centers, 1990.

The SCORE: ICSC's Handbook on Shopping Center Operations, Revenues and Expenses. New York: International Council of Shopping Centers, 1997.

This chapter was contributed by Wayne T. Okubo, SCSM, SCMD, CLS, Principal, Okubo Real Estate, Redwood City, California.

3 | The Lease and Its Language

Kurt Sullivan, SCSM

Whether you are new to the shopping center industry, a particular company or a specific center, achieving an understanding of the basic template upon which this business is conducted is critical to your success as a shopping center management professional. And that basic template is *the lease*.

It should be noted at the onset of this chapter that the term "lease," while having a specific definition in the dictionary, should be regarded in a broad sense when used in reference to shopping center management technique. While it is true that shopping center managers deal in large part with leases as the governing document in their relationships with the various users and clients at their properties, the lease is not the only such document that a good manager must understand and be able to use in the course of a day's work. Others, such as reciprocal easement agreements (REAs), separate agreements, specialty licensing agreements and temporary occupancy agreements, all bear on the way in which shopping center professionals must approach their work, deal with respective constituencies and determine courses of action as they go about the business of managing their properties.

First take a look at definitions that apply to the above terms.

- *Lease:* the signed agreement between a landlord and tenant that establishes the duties, rights and responsibilities of each with respect to the use and possession of real property
- *Reciprocal easement agreement (REA):* the signed agreement between common landowner parties in a project that establishes the relationships, rights and duties that apply to those parties

- *Separate agreement:* the signed agreement supplementing a base document, such as an REA, in which specific responsibilities and rights between two parties to that base document are called out
- *Specialty licensing agreement:* the signed agreement between a licensor and licensee in which rights, duties and standards are outlined for application in short-term activities such as cart, kiosk and retail merchandising unit operations
- *Temporary occupancy agreement:* the signed agreement between a short-term occupant licensee in an in-line space, similar to the specialty licensing agreement

Common among the above definitions is the term *signed agreement.* This is an item of key importance to the shopping center professional since, to be valid and enforceable, a fully signed and executed document must exist. The wise manager makes it a practice to work with only formalized documents and ensures that each is executed by an authorized representative for the respective entity. It is true that verbal agreements have been found by the courts in some cases to be enforceable. However, this typically does not work to the benefit of any of the parties to such an agreement since litigation or, at a minimum, significant disagreement, is usually the precursor to such action, which might have been avoided if a written document were used rather than reliance on oral agreements. So, to enhance your safety and security when dealing with the various aspects of leasing some portion of your property, starting out with a policy of formalizing all such agreements onto fully executed documents will always serve the interests of the shopping center owner and manager.

A Notable and Significant Difference

In dealing with the specialty store aspect of a shopping center, the typical agreements that come into play are the lease, the specialty licensing agreement and the temporary occupancy agreement. Whereas the lease grants an irrevocable right to use and possess real property for a specific period of time and under certain defined criteria, both the license and temporary occupancy agreements grant permission to use either real property or personal property (e.g., a cart or kiosk), with such permission being revocable at the discretion of the licensor. Therefore, the lease carries with it more permanent, longer-term qualities that are not present in a license.

It could be asked why one would consent to a lease and its inherent long-term and irrevocable nature when a license agreement would yield more flexibility for the owner of the property. The answer lies in the needs of the respective parties. Take a look at two situations in which someone wishes to utilize the same portion of a property and how a lease would be more appropriate in one versus the other.

The first example is that of a fast-food operator who plans to engage in a franchise pizza operation. Prior to coming to the landlord with the intention of finding space for this business, the operator has sought and obtained a franchise agreement enabling him or her to operate as an authorized franchisee and must adhere to a specific set of criteria for the construction, operation and ongoing maintenance of the franchise. The operator will need to construct the necessary cooking, preparation and serving areas, and there will be a significant cost associated with this improvement work. Additionally, you as the shopping center representative want to ensure that a certain level of quality is achieved in the build-out of this store. In such a case, the significant financial investment to be made by the operator calls for a suitable guaranteed term of use to be achieved so that the construction costs can be appropriately spread and amortized over that period of time. While the shopping center owner may desire to commit to a shorter period of time, providing flexibility in order to regain the space should the operator not perform well, it is unlikely that a merchant who is faced with significant up-front costs will consent to such an uncertain time frame for its occupancy. Therefore, a lease, with the long-term and date-certain nature of the agreement, is the appropriate document form to use.

Looking at another situation for the same space, an independent operator wishes to sell licensed apparel in conjunction with a current trend that has evolved in which such apparel is in demand. The nature of the operator of this business is one who obtains products from various suppliers on a periodic basis determined by the amount of business it does in a given period of time. The build-out of the space does not involve high-priced equipment but rather can be accomplished through the creative use of display fixtures and a limited amount of cosmetic and structural improvements. The operator may well desire to secure the location for an extended period of time so as to ensure its ability to fend off competitors and continue operation. However, the relatively low investment in fixtures and improvements to the space results in no need to spread the cost over a long amortization period. In addition, the trendy nature of the product being sold may not guarantee its long-term endurance, further reinforcing the argument for short-term flexibility on the part of the center. In such a situation, the shopping center owner may do well to maintain its flexibility and consent only to a license agreement in which control of the space could be regained should business conditions change and the operator is neither successfully generating sales nor presenting an appropriate standard of operation within the property.

Whether to *lease* or to *license* can many times be determined based on the level of financial commitment required of each party to effect a suitable arrangement for the conduct of business. Through discussion, review of information and detailed understanding of an operator's business development and operation, a shopping center manager can be in a position to make the determination that works for everyone involved.

Another prime concern in the decision to implement a lease or a license is that of the owner's financing needs for the property. In order to secure long-term financing, it is typically a requirement of a lender that a certain percentage of the center's area or income be produced under permanent leases as opposed to the less permanent license agreements. Lenders want to have assurance of the cash-flow stream upon which the financing is granted, so that they have a justifiable basis for assuming that the income will be produced over the term of the financing contract. It is also not uncommon to have provisions in the financing agreement that call for the lender to be advised or even give its approval prior to terminating leases. This facet of managing the center's occupancy needs to be considered by the manager.

Understanding and Using the Lease

Depending on the center or company in which you work, you may encounter a wide variety of lease forms. These can vary in length from a few pages to fifty or more pages of articles and provisions. In some cases where a short lease form is used, you may be able to develop not only an understanding of the entire lease but, through repeated use, you may even find yourself being able to quote large sections from memory. This contrasts to situations in which you will deal with a lengthy document with more numerous and more detailed sections. In either case, your job is to know the lease and be able to apply it to all situations that may arise at your property.

To develop your own understanding of the lease in use at your property, make the commitment to read it. It may not be the most exciting reading you will do, but it is a necessary exercise for you, as well as those on your staff who may not have primary responsibility in administering it. Reading through the entire document when you have a long form in use can seem quite tedious. Here's a way to make the process much easier and far more productive than starting on page 1 and reading it through to the end in just a single sitting. Since most leases don't contain more than thirty articles (that's the lease term for sections of a lease), view lease familiarization as a one-month process and break up the task by reading one article each day. Even if you transfer within the same company to a different center, and know that the same lease is in use, you should still take the opportunity to do your one-a-day lease article reading exercise. Now, a few things happen when you do this.

First, even though you may be rereading familiar material, you become more proficient at knowing the document without having to actually refer directly to it. Second, you will realize as you read that there are nuances and facets that you did not fully appreciate and absorb (mainly because you have not had to use a particular section recently), and the reread turns on the light for you. And third, it's a confidence builder as you reinforce to yourself just how much you actually do know about that lease in going over the subjects one more time.

While the thirty-day process will ensure that the lease will get reviewed within a maximum of one month, you will probably be finished in far less time. That's because the articles are, in many cases, fairly short and you will find yourself just wanting to continue reading. So, instead of doing one each day, you will probably find yourself going through three or four articles and moving the task along in a quick manner. But there is a time when adhering to the one article per day routine is beneficial—when an especially detailed or technical article is being read. In this case it is more important to just do the one article, so as to make certain that you really understand it, than it is to do several in an effort to reduce the review time.

A good rule to follow when reviewing a lease is to never allow a single word to pass by your eyes unless you know what it means. Sometimes this applies to groups of words or even multiple sentences, so it is important to make it your policy that you will not retire an article until you can confidently explain all of its contents in your own words. You can test yourself on this by creating a "What if . . ." scenario in your mind and then using the lease language to sort and work through it. If you hit a roadblock on some term or phrase, it's time to get some help. It may only require a quick consulting of your dictionary or company literature. But in some cases you may need to talk with your attorney to have the issue properly explained. Whatever it takes, be sure to put in the effort so that, at the end of your thirty-day review, you have it down cold.

Key Components of the Lease

While a lease document may be lengthy and consist of many sections and parts, the process of understanding the contents of a lease can be simplified if you think in terms of its containing provisions that address certain key areas of the landlord-tenant relationship. While not totally inclusive, since each property has its own nuances and particular features which may require separate and special lease language, below is a listing of key elements that are typically contained in a lease. By grouping your thoughts into specific areas such as these, you may find it easier to catalog for yourself the kinds of provisions you need to consider and how they relate to the overall picture as you review a lease document.

1. Definitions and Basic Provisions
   - Defined lease terms
   - Physical specifics of the center and leased space
   - Duration of the agreement
2. Economic Provisions
   - Rental costs and calculations
   - Pass-through costs and calculations
   - Additional rents (taxes, marketing, insurance, etc.)
   - Indemnity and insurance requirements
   - Deposits, penalties, interest costs
3. Uses and Control
   - Tenant space
   - Common areas
4. Tenant Obligations
   - Operation of the store
   - Repairs and maintenance
   - Construction

5. Landlord Obligations
   - Operation of the center
   - Duties respecting tenant
   - Initial facility construction and tenant space turnover
6. Major Situations
   - Reconstruction in event of major destruction
   - Condemnation
   - Landlord sale of the center
7. Legal Process
   - Consents
   - Defaults
   - Notices
   - Assignment and subletting

As mentioned earlier, the above listing is not all-inclusive for every property, but it does represent the key components of the relationship between the parties which need to be addressed and delineated so that everyone has a clear understanding of who must do what and the processes to be followed throughout the tenancy.

As you review a lease form, it may be helpful for you to organize your thoughts in terms of determining where a given provision fits within the above matrix. This will be helpful to you as you later administer the lease with respect to specific tenant situations. For example, prior to a meeting with a tenant on the subject of nonpayment of rent, you would want to know that the sections on Definitions, Economic Provisions and Legal Process will be the most likely sources for your information on this particular subject. It would be less useful for you to prepare for such a meeting by reading through sections that concern center operating rules or reconstruction in the event of major destruction, given that your focus is on the economic area—that is, the tenant's obligation to pay rent. Likewise, if you are about to take up the issue of a tenant's desire to remodel its store, you would be most interested in the areas of Tenant Obligations and Legal Process.

Another reason to think in organized terms when approaching the lease is so that you can develop the ability to quickly assess a situation, determine all of the areas of the lease which may bear on the issue and be ready to apply them to the issue. While saving the manager's time in the above examples is a benefit derived from a thorough and organized knowledge of the lease, it is essential that your understanding of the lease and its contents allows you to know where all references are in the lease that may pertain to a given issue. For example, it is clear that the issue of what a tenant is allowed to do in the common area will be covered in provisions pertaining to use. But it may be quite helpful, and even essential for you, if you also know that the economic group of lease provisions contains language under indemnity and responsibility which holds the tenant fully liable for its actions in the common area arising from its operation of its store.

Remember—think in terms of organizing your review of the lease so that, as you consider a particular issue, you will be able to quickly assess the kinds of lease provisions that address the subject, as well as those that can also bear on the issue in an indirect manner. You will find that understanding the lease and what is inside its pages will be a far more manageable task, making the lease a tool that you will be able to utilize quickly and efficiently.

Lease Summaries

Having copies of the lease on file in your center office is extremely helpful to not only the manager but the entire management staff in handling the various issues that arise in tenant relations at a center. Many companies go so far as to have original leases on site in the management office; others will have copies of the lease (keeping the original on file with an attorney or in the owner's offices), while some may simply have summary information of the major lease provisions filed at the center location. Having the actual lease is of major benefit because you will have the ability to research an issue fully and not be limited to a summary of key facts or points. However, having such summaries can also be of value for you and the administrative personnel who also administer portions of the lease.

The term *lease abstract* is often used to describe a summary of lease information. Even if you have an original lease on file in your office, it is quite helpful to prepare one or more abstracts that detail specific information which is used regularly. For example, while most tenants are required to pay rent on the first day of the month, some leases may call for a different date. You can prepare an abstract listing the rent due date for each tenant and then have this information available for your bookkeeper, accountant or even yourself as a quick reference each month. This will enable you to get a handle on your rental receipts in relation to lease obligations without having to research all of the individual leases. This abstract could be enhanced with information on the amount of late charges which would apply for late payment as well as the date on which each tenant would be subject to such a charge. Or you could prepare an abstract showing the insurance requirements that apply to each tenant, listing amounts of coverage, special coverages which the lease may require or any other data on this area of the tenant's obligations.

In addition to specific abstract sheets that are focused on a particular area of the tenant's responsibility, a general abstract is also helpful. This would contain an overview of each tenant and consist of the key information that one might like to have on a single sheet of paper to provide you with a quick reference source for all tenants. Here is a list of some of the information you may find helpful in a general abstract:

- Tenant trade name
- Tenant address for notices
- Space identification and size
- Brief use clause summary
- Percentage rent and breakpoint
- Rental due date
- Unusual lease provisions
- Rent start date
- Lease expiration date
- Rental escalation dates
- Tenant legal name and legal entity
- Phone and fax numbers
- Dimensions of the space
- Minimum rent amount
- Common area maintenance (CAM), tax, utility, marketing fees
- Late fee amount and application date
- Security deposit amount
- Possession date
- Option dates
- Insurance requirements

The above information can be quite useful when organized in a concise manner; often, it will prevent you from missing something that would otherwise go unnoticed if you had to pull a lease and read through it fully to find the information.

Another value of preparing an abstract, in addition to the ongoing reference tool you will then have at your disposal, is the abstract process itself. By doing a thorough review of each new lease and noting the standard and nonstandard information contained in it, you will have a process by which your leases receive a full review so that critical data can be noted for future use. This would not be so important if all leases were written on a standard form with no modifications. But, unfortunately, this is typically not the case. Today's merchant is quite sophisticated and will often have an outside attorney review the lease, if not someone who works in a dedicated lease documentation department within the merchant's organization. This review will invariably result in modifications and changes to your standard language which will have an impact on you and the tenant over the course of the lease term. You need a way to find any such changes; a process for keeping them handy for the appropriate people; and a tool to track respective responsibilities under these unique lease provisions. The abstract process will accomplish this for you.

As you review a lease it is important to know what is and what is not standard language. In some cases, each lease is an original document prepared using a word processing program. In such a situation, there may be no indication as to changes that have been made against the standard form. In contrast to this, your company may use a standard form that is preprinted, on which any changes are clearly indicated by lining out a section where a deletion or a change is needed, and then including asterisked additions at the bottom of the page to show the new or additional language. The latter method makes picking out the exceptions a relatively easy task; you can often page through it quickly, both in your abstract review and later throughout the lease term, to see the significant changes from the standard language.

However, with computer technology becoming more a part of the business, shopping center managers are seeing many original documents produced that have all terms merged into the draft without the need for typewritten additions. In such cases, there is a way that you can facilitate the process of finding changes and exceptions. This involves having a *red-line* version of the lease produced in addition to the original document. The red-line is exactly the same as the original document except that it is not executed as a formal copy of the lease, and any changes to standard language are clearly shown with deletions being crossed out and additional wording being underlined. If you are fortunate enough to have your leases produced by someone with a word processing program that will handle this automatically, that makes it even easier because you will be furnished with this marked-up version of the lease. But if you do not, it is strongly suggested that you do an initial lease review and, using a copy of the actual, original lease, make your own red-line version by highlighting any nonstandard language. It is a time-consuming process to do this red-lining yourself, but you will find the resulting tool to be of great use over the duration of the lease as you need to refer back for information.

Being a "Lease Savvy" Manager

Knowing your lease form and the contents of each article contained within it is a solid first step to your being able to deal with the important area of lease management and administration. But beyond this starting point of lease understanding, you need to develop a method of doing business that makes full use of the lease and also ensures that the lease document remains effective throughout the lease term. This involves the way that you handle lease-related affairs and amounts to your own style of management in this regard. A few tips in this area may be of help to you as you handle lease issues.

CONFIDENTIALITY

The lease is a legal agreement within the context of a real estate–related relationship between two parties. As such, many states have very specific laws that guard the confidential nature of the lease, and you must be aware of and abide by them. It is not uncommon for someone to inquire about a certain tenant's lease. A manager could be asked by another tenant about something in a store's lease, or perhaps even an employee of a store may inquire about provisions contained in that store's lease. It is very important for you, as the custodian of this confidential material, not to divulge anything contained in the lease, even in an informal or casual manner.

TIMELINESS

In many leases one will find the phrase "time is of the essence." This is quite typical in real estate matters and it is an important issue in the shopping center business. The lease will contain obligations and requirements on the part of each party to that lease. There are usually timelines and deadlines associated with various issues in the lease, and the "time is of the essence" provision calls for the parties to act in accordance with those time frames. Thus, when you receive any official notification (usually delivered by certified or registered mail), it is imperative that you immediately review the matter, determine from the lease language if there is any action required on your part, make sure that you take that action and (very important, here) make sure that you record your action for the file. In cases of dispute, which is where the lease document is typically scrutinized extensively, inaction by one party on an item that called for swift, or at least timely, handling will invariably turn the situation against that party. So be sure to be a highly responsive manager when it comes to lease-related matters.

QUOTING THE LEASE

It is important for a manager to know the lease and be able to apply it to certain situations. In doing so you should recognize that, unless one of you has obtained your law degree, neither you nor your tenant is an attorney. You may find the language of some leases to be overwhelming in both structure and terminology. Thus, simply quoting the lease, either verbally or in writing, is typically not the best way to start the process of dealing with a lease-related issue. You should develop the ability to review a provision of the lease and then discuss it in conversational terms. Likewise, when writing to a tenant to explain its duties under the lease, a similar manner of presentation will serve the purpose. By approaching issues in a business manner rather than in a legal manner, you will often be able to achieve resolution more readily. Conversely, the use of legal phraseology, either verbal or written, can escalate a simple issue which is in need of discussion to one of legal proportions. This is something to avoid if you are able to do so.

However, sometimes it becomes necessary to actually quote the lease exactly as it is written. Formal demand letters, "last resort" letters, legal notices and other official correspondence will require that you indicate the applicable lease provision verbatim so that there is no misunderstanding as to the actions required. And, if you are in a discussion dealing with a situation which has degenerated from a normal exchange of business ideas to a confrontational or antagonistic issue, you would do well to literally have the lease and read from it the provision in question. Whenever you are faced with these kinds of scenarios, precision and accuracy are critical to your case. Double-check what you are about to write or say because you can be sure that your counterpart in the matter will be doing just that.

INTERPRETING AN ISSUE

You cannot begin reading a lease document without shortly thereafter becoming aware of the large amount of punctuation and more elaborate sentence structure contained in it than is ordinarily found in casual reading. Some sentences in a lease can extend for ten lines or more and have a series of colons, commas, parentheses and other punctuation that makes the reading an intricate process. In approaching this kind of document structure, you need to dissect sentences into separate segments, being highly aware of the punctuation, so that each part can be understood. For example, look at the following lease provision:

Tenant shall pay its share of common area costs, without setoff or deduction, based on the total sums expended by Landlord for the operation, maintenance and repair of said common area (as the same has been previously defined), and such sums shall include the addition of a 15% charge to compensate Landlord for its accounting and record keeping with respect to said common area operations.

If we break down the above sentence, we find the following provisions being stated:

1. Tenant pays for the cost of common area maintenance.
2. Payment must be made, irrespective of any dispute by Tenant.
3. All money expended by Landlord will be part of what is billed to Tenant.
4. Earlier in the lease, common area was defined specifically.
5. A 15 percent markup by Landlord is considered part of the billable expenses.

By thinking in segments rather than trying to digest an entire sentence or phrase, you will not only find that you understand what is being called out but you will also be much better at explaining it to your tenants and other staff members. As you read through the various sections of the lease, if you come across an area where the language appears to be complex and lengthy, try writing down the elements of each statement in the manner shown above. When you do so, you should find that it becomes easier to understand. By doing this a few times in writing, you will eventually develop the ability to mentally break apart such sections and achieve the same kind of understanding.

The Reciprocal Easement Agreement (REA)

As discussed earlier, while not fitting perfectly into the definition of a lease, there are other agreements by which a relationship between two or more entities can be effected for use in the shopping center context. Among these is the *reciprocal easement agreement* (REA). Whereas the lease is used to establish the relationship when an owner gives to another party the right to use a portion of that property, the REA is used to formalize the relationship between two or more parties who own their respective pieces of property but nonetheless need to establish a legal framework to establish the relationship between each and outline how each party will perform and interrelate with the other parties. The REA may define operational aspects of the relationship, such as the rights and responsibilities with respect to maintenance and repair of the different pieces, or parcels, of land which make up a given project. It may also define the initial development of the project and include the various construction and design requirements, site and building improvements and all other facets of the multiparty relationship within a single project.

A typical situation in which an REA is used would be in a shopping center project containing a mall area of specialty shops owned by one party and one or more anchor store buildings owned by different entities. The anchor stores need not be connected to the specialty mall building, although this often occurs in large, regional shopping centers. Even a pad site (the parcel of land on which an anchor store's building stands) that is freestanding, but still part of the overall project, could be an owner party in an REA.

One contrast between the function of a lease arrangement and that of an REA of particular note to the shopping center manager is the issue of approvals. Typically, the landlord in a lease has reserved many rights to itself which result in the landlord being able to do a variety of things to the property without obtaining permission of the lessee. Such items may include alteration of the mall building, changes in parking patterns or numbers of spaces, construction of additional store area and so on. However, since you are dealing with actual owner entities in the REA relationship, often there will be very precise and rigorous requirements stated in the REA pertaining to the need to obtain approvals of all parties prior to any one party making changes to its parcel or anything built upon it. So, before you decide to make a change to the property, be sure to read and know the approval provisions contained in your REA.

THE OPERATOR

Another item covered in the REA is typically the designation of an operator for the project. The operator will be the entity responsible for the day-to-day operation and management of the overall project. This operator may be one of the parties to the REA, such as the mall developer or a subsidiary, or it may be a third-party manager retained by the parties to independently manage the project. You, as the center manager, will most likely work for the operator, so you will want to know exactly what requirements are placed upon you in this document. Items such as operating rules and regulations, storefront construction criteria, parking ratios, common area costs and prorations and other essentials to the project will be discussed and detailed. Your obligation as manager is to adhere to all of these provisions and to make certain that the various parties adhere to their responsibilities and obligations under the REA.

NOTICES AND APPROVALS
A typical situation you may encounter is that of one party advising you as the operator of a change that it intends to make on its parcel. This change may be something simple, such as the addition of another exterior or an illuminated sign, or perhaps a repainting of the building. Or it may be something as significant as that party's intent to change its use or add to its building with an expansion. While you will want to review such a request thoroughly as manager of the project and determine if you wish to approve this plan subject to the operating rules and procedures you are charged with upholding, you should be aware that the REA could require approval from the other parties to the REA. One way to handle such a situation properly and consistently with both your role and duties under the REA would be as follows:

1. Review the request and determine if it is something that makes sense to you in terms of the day-to-day operation of the center. If so, then you may be in a position to give approval from the perspective of the property manager.

2. Next, check the REA and determine if the request is something that needs to be brought to the attention of the other parties.

3. If so, you will either find a provision that the other parties be advised or you may find that approval must be given by the parties. In such a case, you as manager could convey the issue to the other parties, or you may find it easiest to communicate to the requesting party that it is responsible to make the necessary notifications and obtain appropriate approvals prior to commencing the work. In this case, be sure to require that the party provide to you proof of the other parties' approvals before commencing such work. Most REAs provide for each party securing its own approvals from the others, so, unless you actually want to insert yourself in the process, it should not come as a sur-

prise to a party if you advise it of your approval as manager, but that it also must obtain its own approvals from other parties.

With respect to any contacts made to the parties, you may find *addresses for notices* clearly defined in the REA. Make certain that any correspondence you send on any REA-related matter is sent in strict accordance with such addresses and any procedures calling for certified mail. Should some dispute arise over an REA issue, your ability to defend your position may hinge directly on being able to prove that the right persons were afforded the appropriate information in the correct time frame. Often this will come into play with the concept of *deemed approved*. (Deemed approved means that, absent a specific denial, approval is deemed to have been given upon expiration of a stated period of time.) This concept is found in many REAs in the section pertaining to requests for approvals. It typically would be written in a manner indicating that a party requires that certain things be submitted to it for approval. However, in order to prompt the parties to respond in a timely manner, there may be language that states essentially the following:

> The request for approval shall be sent via certified mail, postage prepaid, to the Address for Notices specified in this REA, along with all supporting information to enable the party to make an informed decision on said request. The receiving party shall have thirty (30) days from receipt of said request to indicate either its approval or disapproval of the request. In the event no such indication is received by the sending party within thirty (30) days, the request shall be deemed to have been approved by the receiving party.

Under the kind of provision stated above, the deemed approved provision makes sure that the parties are not held up by each other simply because one party failed to respond to the issue. You as manager should also look for such language in the REA which has a bearing on items sent to you, since it could also be provided for in the document that you, too, must respond or your approval will be deemed to have been given.

Separate Agreements

In addition to the provisions in the REA, there may be other agreements between some, but not all, of the parties. This would typically be the case in matters where one party wishes to negotiate something that, while pertaining to its obligations at the project, does not have an impact on all other parties. For example, if one party wished to reserve some area of the parking lot for its exclusive use, this would certainly affect all parties as to their ability to use the project's parking; therefore, this kind of issue would be found in the REA itself. However, perhaps one party has negotiated that its common area contribution to offset enclosed mall specialty store CAM is to be a flat, specified amount. Enclosed mall specialty store CAM is the cost of maintenance and operation of interior common areas which is borne by stores which front on those interior common areas. This would affect the developer of the specialty store portion of the mall but probably not be an issue for the other parties. Thus, it would most likely be mentioned in a separate agreement between only the developer and that party.

As manager of the property, you should make sure that you are totally familiar with the base REA document and any separate agreements that may exist. There is nothing more embarrassing than finding out after the fact that you had an obligation or even an opportunity (the right to take some action) in an issue that has since passed and can no longer be addressed. Knowing your REA and any support documents will ensure that this does not happen to you. To effectively keep track of REA provisions, you can use the same "read an article a day" approach recommended for lease study, and also employ an abstract of the REA that contains all of the day-to-day matters discussed within it. This handy and quick reference tool will prove to be invaluable to you as issues come across your desk requiring you to make certain that appropriate actions are taken.

Conclusion

This chapter opened by identifying the lease (along with other occupancy and use documents) as the basic template of the shopping center business. Nearly everything you do as a manager flows from the fact that a relationship with users of your property is in effect and that you have certain rights, obligations and responsibilities as a result of those documents. In order to carry out any of the other aspects of your work as a shopping center manager, you need to ensure that you are properly equipped to deal with the initial platform of leases and agreements that forms your property's foundation. Reading and understanding those documents will equip you in the proper manner. And even though your business is multifaceted and complex, you can view the lease as both your starting point and a checkpoint in dealing with almost any issue related to your property. By doing so you will ensure that you abide by your obligations and temper your decisions with consideration of all of the provisions contained in these agreements.

Glossary

The glossary that follows is a listing of key definitions compiled from this outline, with several terms not defined in the outline added for your information. The terms are defined within the context of this shopping center management topic.

Addendum   Lease change or addition usually inserted at the end of the original lease form.

Assignee   New tenant that assumes the rights and responsibilities of the original tenant.

Assignment   Transfer by the tenant of all tenant's obligations and rights to a new entity.

Commencement date   Day on which tenant's lease term begins, not to be confused with occupancy date.

Common area maintenance (CAM) charges   Charges shared among tenants for landlord's maintenance and operation of common areas.

Exhibits   Attachments, usually to the end of an original lease, specifying site location, legal description and tenant's construction specifications.

Indemnification   Protection against suit or expenses.

Kick-out clause   Option that allows a landlord or tenant to terminate the lease before the end of the term.

Letter of intent   Generally a nonbinding document submitted prior to a formal lease. It serves to delineate the intentions between the landlord and the tenant. Basic issues, including minimum rent, percentage rent, pass-through expenses and other major points of negotiation, are outlined.

Minimum rent   Rent that is not based on tenant's sales.

Pass-through expenses   Tenant's portion of expense composed of common area maintenance, taxes and insurance and any other expenses determined by landlord to be paid by tenant.

Percentage rent   Rent based upon a percentage of tenant's sales, usually paid in addition to a minimum or base rent.

Radius restriction   Specific trade radius in which tenant may not operate another business, usually of the same type or name.

Relocation clause   Gives landlord the ability to move the tenant to another location within the shopping center premises.

Termination   Interruption of the lease before the term expires.

Trade name   Name under which tenant operates a business.

Trade fixture   Item specific to a tenant's business, usually not attached to the walls or floor; usually removed at lease expiration.

Use clause   Outline of the exact type of merchandise to be sold or business to be conducted in the premises.

Recommended Readings

Alexander, Alan M., CSM. *Shopping Center Lease Administration: A Manager's Guide to Improving Financial Record Keeping*. New York: International Council of Shopping Centers, 1986.

Crafting Lease Clauses: Meeting Shopping Center Landlord and Tenant Objectives. New York: International Council of Shopping Centers, 1994.

ICSC Keys to Shopping Center Leasing Series. New York: International Council of Shopping Centers, 1995.

The ICSC Temporary Tenant Handbook. New York: International Council of Shopping Centers, 1994.

Key Shopping Center Legal Issues: Understanding Current Laws Impacting Leasing and Management. New York: International Council of Shopping Centers, 1995.

Keys, John R., Esq. *The Antitrust Aspects of Restrictive Covenants in Shopping Center Leases*. New York: International Council of Shopping Centers, 1994.

Leasing Small Shopping Centers. New York: International Council of Shopping Centers, 1997.

Messinger, Stephen, and Barnett Ruttenberg. *Understanding Major Lease Clauses.* New York: International Council of Shopping Centers, 1991.

Shedlin, Andrew, Esq., and Roy Green, Esq. *Lease Negotiations.* Audiocassettes. New York: International Council of Shopping Centers, 1988.

Shopping Center Study Lease. New York: International Council of Shopping Centers, 1994.

Wolf, Irving, CSM/CMD, ed. *Essential Factors in Shopping Center Leasing.* New York: International Council of Shopping Centers, 1992.

This chapter was contributed by Kurt Sullivan, SCSM, Vice President of Management Resources, TrizecHahn Development Corporation, San Diego, California.

4 | Tenant Mix and Leasing Strategies

Charles R. Cope, SCSM, CLS

The leasing of space in a shopping center is one of the most critical elements to a center's success. Leases determine the income and productivity of a center. Successful leasing requires knowing who the players are, analyzing the center's trade area, prospecting for tenants, determining rents and negotiating the lease deal. Just as the success of a center involves profitable leasing, the success of center management is often based on effective, profitable leasing. When a project is fully leased or exceeds the leasing goals, management succeeds. When there are too many vacancies or the economic side falls short, management falls short of the goal.

Experience on a leasing team is often the best way to learn all the elements that go into making a leasing deal possible, whether negotiating, merchandising or motivating staff out in the field. The goal of this chapter is to connect what you learn from reading directly to your leasing experiences and to enhance your success in leasing efforts.

Long before the lease is signed, the business of leasing begins. Leasing is a process that begins with understanding the tenant mix of a center and then utilizing several leasing strategies with the goal of merchandising a center with a unique mix of tenants who define the center, attract shoppers from the center's primary trade area and register profit for the tenants and the center. This chapter examines some of the factors that contribute to an effective tenant mix and profitable leasing strategies.

Tenant Mix

Tenant mix is the combination of store types and price levels of retail and service businesses in a shopping center. Whether a center has ten stores or two hundred, an effective mix strengthens the center by creating a synergy calculated to appeal to a range of center customers, increase traffic at the center and—through placement and price —encourage customers to make multiple purchases or cross-shop at different types of retailers. A center mix typically includes different percentages of the following types of retailers:

- Specialty shops
- High-end stores
- Women's ready-to-wear
- Menswear
- Shoe stores
- Specialty restaurants
- Fast food
- Gifts
- Accessories
- Cards and stationery
- Jewelry
- Music, records, videos
- Entertainment
- Services

EVALUATE THE TENANT MIX

While it is essential for shopping center managers to understand the different classes, categories and classifications of retailers, it is also necessary to acknowledge that what applies today may not necessarily apply tomorrow. Therefore, at times it may be necessary to break out of the mold and explore other tenant mix possibilities for a center. There is no exact formula for a right or wrong tenant mix. In a small center, a grocery store, a dry cleaner, a Chinese restaurant and a hobby shop may represent four key tenant categories that bring success. In a mall, fashion, services, entertainment and food, intermingled with department stores, are analyzed and balanced to create the right strategic mix. Are the price points aligned with a center's demographics? What is the competition doing?

MARKET ANALYSIS

A *market analysis* examines trends in the trade area and identifies the characteristics that will offer a center an advantage over its competition, attract more customers to the center and extend the length of the customer visit in the center.

CENTER ANALYSIS

A *center analysis* can be accomplished through a simple, more direct evaluation called a *penetration study.* A penetration study examines the gross leasable area (GLA) of each merchandising category and the total volume of each category as a percentage. A productivity higher than the norm suggests the addition of another store to that group. While this evaluation is not foolproof, it does offer an indication of where to improve a center's merchandising. Two very different examples follow. The jewelry category is an example for malls. In instances where this category may comprise 3 percent of the GLA and produce 6 percent of the sales, the result indicates a workable mix. However, in an instance where women's wear occupies 32 percent of the GLA and registers 22 percent of sales, this may suggest replacing an expiring women's wear store with another category use. In other words, the category is not carrying its weight with the center's customer base.

Other analysis and marketing tools that provide invaluable direction for merchandising include focus groups consisting of customers who regularly shop at the center or telephone surveys of those who do not regularly visit the center. Another excellent source of merchandising knowledge is the existing merchants in a center. They are anxious to share their ideas and perceived customer needs with management. The best way to obtain this information is through casual conversation during a mall walk with the center's merchants. Finally, monitor the busiest, most heavily staffed and completely merchandised departments in the center's anchor stores. For example, if they have a very successful line of apparel as a department, explore with that apparel company the possibility of an in-line store.

OWNERSHIP EXPECTATIONS

Many shopping center professionals say that the single most important factor in tenant mix is ownership expectations. An understanding of the owner's goals and objectives will enable the shopping center manager to make more informed decisions in all aspects of management, especially leasing. This is accomplished by:

- Meeting with ownership on a scheduled basis
- Ascertaining the economic value of the lease

Meet at least annually with ownership to learn and acknowledge their expectations for tenant mix and leasing. Incorporate this step into the process of preparing the annual shopping center business plan.

Ascertain the economic value of the leases and how key provisions are negotiated. When the value of a center is determined, a capitalization rate is applied to the income derived from the leases. Expiring leases—where a prospective buyer can realize a positive impact on income through re-leasing—impact the value of the center. Understand the significance of various clauses in the lease, including the relocation clause, percentage rents, breakpoints, and landlord kick-outs or termination clauses. Know the economic issues that contribute to the overall value of your shopping center.

Leasing Strategies

The process of leasing, including building a tenant mix, prospecting, developing strategies and negotiating, represents the work of a team of people, not just one person. This team often includes the:

- Shopping center manager
- Marketing manager
- Accounting staff
- Document coordinator
- Leasing attorney
- Tenant coordinator
- Leasing team member

Since the jobs of each of these people or departments are connected, the following section describes the responsibilities of each team member in light of some of the leasing strategies and negotiating tools frequently utilized.

TEAM MEMBERS AND LEASING STRATEGIES

Various companies will take differing views regarding a manager's involvement, but it is critical for the process that the *shopping center manager* become an integral part of the leasing team. Likewise, it is critical that the manager become familiar with all aspects of leasing and contribute to the team's efforts, becoming as valuable to the team as possible.

The center's *marketing manager* is usually included in various aspects of the process, taking on different tasks. They are pivotal to the shopper survey and focus group process. Marketing frequently maintains good contact with the merchants and is in an excellent position to engage them in a discussion of new retailing ideas under consideration at the center. At present, many retailers are looking hard at required participation in marketing and media funds. Involve the marketing manager early in the negotiations to demonstrate to current and prospective retailers the effectiveness of the center's overall marketing plan. Inclusion of the marketing manager on the leasing team brings new concepts and ideas to the team's efforts. It is also a natural extension of marketing managers' functions to visit other centers, collecting directories and highlighting the stores that they perceive as convincing additions to their center's mix. Finally, marketing professionals maintain strong networking ties with one another and share information about new concepts in practice at centers around the country.

The *accounting staff* is a very important part of the team, setting up a center's budget, pro forma and other financial goals. While the manager establishes the objectives for the financial goals, the accounting staff assists by reviewing with the manager critical provisions of the lease and other documents, including lease termination dates, renewal options, rent bumps and other key provisions. Once the financial objectives are established, the accounting team also assists the manager in matching the economics of a proposed deal with the established objectives. For example, the net present value (NPV) for the to-be-leased space is matched so that the manager can see the total value of the deal and make better, more informed economic decisions. (Exhibit 4 is a sample form for a "Net Present Value Analysis of Proposed Lease.")

The accounting staff also assists in one increasingly critical aspect of prospecting and lease development—evaluating the financial strengths of proposed tenants. The manager collects an annual report, the previous year's financial statement, federal tax returns and credit references from the proposed tenant. If the proposed tenant has other existing store locations, the manager contacts the landlord at another location. That person often proves to be the best reference, offering more information than whether the proposed tenant pays its rent on time. The accounting staff takes all information supplied by the manager and document coordinator and completes a form that categorizes financial areas, states an approval of the deal and describes any reservations concerning the deal.

If staffing permits, designate a *document coordinator*. This can be the shopping center manager, leasing team person, assistant manager or support staff. This team member tracks all documentation from initial contact letters through executed leases, commencement date verification, amendments and finally, if required, termination documents. Working with both tenant and landlord attorneys, the document coordinator closes the gap in the length of time required to execute a lease. In many organizations, documents often delay the delivery of space, construction, openings and ultimately the rent commencement. The rationale for a document coordinator is compelling. For example, say a center completes ten deals a year. If each store is opened just one month earlier, a significant contribution is made to the center's bottom line. Weekly meetings with agendas written by the document coordinator keep staff accountable for meeting established schedules for a center's leasing timetable goals. The document coordinator may also be assigned to handle other contracts, such as roofing and housekeeping, as well as any contracted security services.

The *leasing attorney* is the person who clearly understands the manager's shopping center business goals and objectives. Similar temperaments between the leasing attorney and center manager are helpful, since they work together on pivotal leasing issues. The job of the leasing attorney is to advise the center manager on many issues. The leasing team then makes the best possible decision for the center in light of that advice. However, the attorney must also protect the center from bad legal decisions and guide the leasing team around legal pitfalls. As with the document coordinator, it is also important for the leasing attorney to deliver a prompt turnaround on all documents. Keep track of the time it takes from turnover to execution and discuss ways to shorten that time.

Another key member of the leasing team is the *tenant coordinator*. This team member is especially important for new projects, or when the center enters a re-leasing or expansion phase. This team member can be an operations director or another staff person who focuses on tenant criteria. The tenant coordinator assists in negotiating the construction exhibit of the lease, reviewing and making suggestions, granting approval of the plans and helping the tenant obtain permits. The tenant coordinator assists in enforcing construction rules and regulations that are established and reviewing the construction for conformance to the approved set of drawings. Upon completion, the coordinator produces a checklist for all to review and correct, as well as billing for construction chargebacks, which may include the following:

- Plan review
- Sprinkler shutdown
- Floor materials
- Temporary electricity
- Construction trash
- Other items

Depending on the property management, a center may also have on-site leasing assistance or leasing through the home office, hire a broker to assist or initiate the leasing work internally by staff. For those centers with a leasing person, make sure the leasing person is aware of all of the team members and their respective tasks. The primary objective of the *leasing team member* is to seek out and assess interest of potential new merchants on behalf of the center.

PROSPECTING STRATEGIES

The leasing team member should be thoroughly acquainted with the budget/pro forma and the merchandise mix plan. The leasing team member should utilize a combination of established contacts and cold-calls in those areas with merchandising similar to the center's plan. Shopping center managers, leasing team members and marketing managers should keep detailed files on all of their key leasing prospects. These prospects are the potential tenants to address when the center is planning to remerchandise vacancies, expirations or the recapturing of space. On an ongoing basis, the leasing person maintains good relationships with colleagues in the industry to remain current with new trends and information on what is going on in other companies. For example, the leasing person should know when a retailing company opens a new division and ascertain if that new concept represents a potential new retailer for the center. Likewise, remaining current will highlight information concerning the financial health of retailers presently occupying space within the leasing person's center.

The following steps assist in building credibility when prospecting:

- Get to know the owners of the stores the center is seeking.
- Develop a list of prospective tenant stores ranging from best to worst.
- Obtain referrals from merchants about their competitors.

- Ask questions about the prospects' businesses to build a familiarity with issues they are facing, and what works or does not work.

After prospecting and cold-calling, the leasing team member assembles all necessary background information collected on prospects and presents to the leasing team those prospects who meet the center's criteria.

Negotiating Tools and Strategies

It is often acknowledged that a good negotiator needs to know both sides' positions and goals as well as they do. Always operate under the assumption that the center's negotiating opponents have educated themselves about shopping center issues. It is imperative in negotiations to know your business inside and out as well as have a strong familiarity with your opponent's businesses. Take advantage of opportunities to read industry magazines and articles that indicate trends that retailers are following.

NEGOTIATING WITH EXISTING TENANTS

In some cases an existing merchant is performing so well that its sales are good, it pays rent on time and it diligently follows your center's rules and regulations. It services its customers well and is well staffed and stocked with desirable merchandise. When its lease expires, in such instances, center management will probably want to renew the tenant in its present location or perhaps offer it a more advantageous location that better suits its needs. To determine the renewal proposal, look to see what similar spaces have been renting for, then compare effective rent (a combination of minimum rent and percentage rent) to see if it holds market. In most instances, a center should be able to achieve at least 80 percent of the effective rent if the merchants are paying percentage rent. In many cases it is better to accept slightly below market rents from an existing merchant, acknowledging that the center will incur downtime, potential leasing fees, higher attorney fees, possible construction allowances and other costs with a replacement merchant.

Other key renewal factors include the extent of required remodeling and whether a center can use a new or existing lease or use an amendment to adjust term, rents and any other key factors in the lease document. Do the common area maintenance (CAM) and insurance sections need updating? How about the environmental clause? Seek advice from the leasing attorney and review the existing documents in order to make an informed decision.

NEGOTIATING WITH NEW MERCHANTS

Perhaps the most significant factor in lease negotiations is the perceived strength of the shopping center and the retailer. If a center is fortunate enough to be considered a "dominant" shopping center, it will gain certain advantages: for example, using its own lease form, achieving top market rents, keeping pro rata CAM charges and real estate taxes and maintaining its full marketing plan, as well as having much to say in store design and other critical areas. Should the retailer be in a stronger perceived position, your center may need to use the retailer's form, pay tenant allowances, settle for gross rents and have other terms dictated to it.

Throughout the negotiating process these and many more issues will be decided. This brings the discussion back to the "team" for help in negotiating the lease. It is best to have the center's insurance broker assist with the complicated provisions that seem insignificant now, but are significant to any property that has been involved in a casualty, fire, flood or building failure. Be particularly careful with loss limits and rights to terminate or suspend rents in the event of a casualty.

Seek specialized advice on all construction issues. For example, electric loads are to be calculated to determine if there is enough power to serve the requested needs of the tenant. If power is lacking, costly improvements to the infrastructure will certainly have an impact on the calculated returns.

It is imperative when negotiating the lease to state clearly as much as possible. Who removes existing abandoned heating, ventilation and air-conditioning (HVAC) equipment on the roof? If the landlord is to handle demolition, does the new tenant want the center to leave anything behind? Are utilities to be brought to a location designated by the tenant or just near to the demised premises? When can certain types of disruptive work take place and when is such work prohibited? It is far easier to negotiate these issues up front rather than in the heat of the moment, when the lease or construction is under pressure.

Some basic forms can serve as automatic reminders for some of these issues from the beginning. An effective way to start with local and some regional merchants is the lease application (see Exhibit 1). This form provides the leasing team member with an excellent review of the prospective business. The form states the type of business, how it operates, who is involved in ownership, and lists several business references, credit references and preliminary financial data. Much can be learned about a potential merchant just by how the questions are answered.

The center does not need all this information for national companies, but even with the nationals you should ask for comparative center sales, recent financial statements or an annual report. After the manager or leasing team member has met with and scrutinized the prospective tenant and discussed the basic terms of the lease, document these discussions with a lease term sheet (see Exhibit 2). This form allows both parties to have in writing the key points needed to structure a lease document. While most of these issues are economic, it is helpful to expand the term sheet to include key provisions of the deal that were important to each party in choosing to go forward.

The next form to advance to is the lease approval form (see Exhibit 3). This document serves multiple uses. First, it is used to document approvals through the center's real estate committee and for preparation of the lease itself. Second, it can be used to approve and issue a new lease, or to amend or renew an existing lease. This is an internal document that flows through accounting, management and corporate as necessary, with each signing all approvals as necessary. Once complete, the lease approval form is then used to prepare the lease document. If any major terms are adjusted during negotiations, a box on the upper right-hand corner is checked and the lease approval form can be recirculated to gain written approval of those changes. It is a good idea to attach a copy of the first form circulated and highlight any changes needing approvals.

ALTERNATIVE STRATEGIES

The leasing of carts, retail merchandising units (RMUs) and vacant storefronts has become a major emphasis in enclosed centers. In the early stages of this trend, it was handled by the marketing staff. It has now grown into a specialized field with full-time, highly competent leasing experts who often generate in excess of $1 million in rents and extra charges for their properties. There are several very good companies that specialize in this type of leasing. They provide the equipment, the plan, the management and the merchants. These experts will address a financial income-sharing agreement with a center.

A common practice is to "incubate" retailers from carts to regular in-line stores; however, most operators of carts are better suited to a smaller, less intense type of operation. They can respond quickly to trends. There will be trade-offs. These operations are often manage-ment-intensive; for instance, making sure they open in time to display their goods in a professional manner. Often there are concerns about return policies. The center can assist in this matter by establishing re-turn policies in the license agreement. Another excellent area to ne-gotiate is a "quick" termination, effective either immediately or in one to three days. This will ensure compliance with many of leasing's crit-ical issues.

Some centers also require these merchants to provide a substantial security deposit. Should a default occur, it is often difficult to track them down and collect past-due rents. When merchandising, keep in mind the center's regular, in-line, full-time merchants. Try not to place competitive merchandise in the center, especially in front of a store carrying the same goods.

Planned or unplanned vacancies will occur. Barricades look impos-ing and can make a vacancy appear obvious. Some good solutions in-clude the use of temporary merchants such as Christmas shops, Halloween shops, flower and cart merchants and temporary displays. These temporary solutions are effective in filling any vacant storefront. In the case of temporary merchants, remember to keep termination options short so that space can be turned over quickly to a permanent merchant. Alternatively, most existing stores are glad to use their staff to merchandise these vacant storefront windows for additional mall exposure. In these cases, set high standards for appearance and regu-larly change the displays to avoid a stale look.

Conclusion

Leasing is one of the most important aspects in the overall success of a shopping center, determining income and productivity for a center. Leasing programs must be carefully planned and organized. Study the tenant mix, the physical plant, the market and the competition. Keep detailed records of all leases and consider creative alternative uses for spaces which standard tenants may not lease. Employ prospecting techniques that will result in the best mix for the center. Negotiate so that the tenant and the leasing team are both satisfied with the lease.

Leasing creates value and uniqueness and allows the manager and leasing team members to experiment with new concepts. Leasing al-lows the manager to respond to customer needs, and it is one factor which sets a manager apart from other managers. As a shopping center manager, learn from your experiences, learn to utilize successful ideas from other properties or professionals and learn to be fair in all leasing negotiations.

Recommended Readings

Alexander, Alan A., SCSM, and Richard F. Muhlebach, SCSM. *Operating Small Shopping Centers*. New York: International Council of Shopping Centers, 1997.

ICSC Keys to Shopping Center Leasing Series. New York: International Council of Shopping Centers, 1995.

The ICSC Temporary Tenant Handbook. New York: International Council of Shopping Centers, 1994.

Leasing Small Shopping Centers. New York: International Council of Shopping Centers, 1997.

Shopping Center Study Lease. New York: International Council of Shopping Centers, 1994.

Wolf, Irving, CSM/CMD, ed. *Essential Factors in Shopping Center Leasing*. New York: International Council of Shopping Centers, 1992.

This chapter was contributed by Charles R. Cope, SCSM, CLS, General Manager, Tysons Corner Center, McLean, Virginia.

Exhibit 1:

Sample Lease Application

I. GENERAL

Legal Business Name: _____

Doing Business As:_____

Present (Most Recent) Location of Business:_____

_____

Reason for This Move:_____

Phone: (___)_____

How Long at Current Location:_____

( ) Own ( ) Lease_____

Mailing Address:_____

Landlord or Mortgage Holder:_____

Address:_____

Name of Contact:_____Phone: (___)_____

(If more than one location, please attach additional list of Landlord references.)

II. FORM OF BUSINESS

Unincorporated (Complete Part III (A) and attach Certificate of Assumed Name)

( ) Proprietorship ( ) General Partnership ( ) Limited Partnership

( ) Joint Venture, Association ( ) Other_____

Incorporated (Complete Part III (B) or III (C)

( ) Corporation

( ) Other: _____

Federal Employer I.D. Number (or Social Security # if an Individual):

_____Date Business Started:___/___/___

Type of Business: ( ) Oil & Gas ( ) Real Estate ( ) Manufacturing

( ) Insurance ( ) Finance ( ) Construction ( ) Communication

( ) Legal/Accounting ( ) Other:_____

( ) Retail (Attach Merchandising Plan including Estimated Value of Inventory and Fixtures.)

Note: This is a sample only and is not to be construed as being endorsed or recommended by the author or the International Council of Shopping Centers. Readers are advised to consult legal counsel to devise appropriate documents for their centers.

Hazardous Materials to be Stored in the Space: Yes/No   Attach List or MSDS (Material Safety Date Sheet).

Insurance:
Carrier:_____Agent:_____
Address:_____
City/State:_____Zip:_____
Phone: (___)_____Provide valid certificate for current occupancy or quotation for this occupancy.

III. <u>OWNERSHIP</u>

(A) Complete this section if entity is an unincorporated Partnership, Joint Venture, Association or Proprietorship. Please identify General Partners and/or Principals as appropriate.

Principal(s)/Partner(s) Name:_____Title:_____
Home Address:_____
City/State:_____Zip:_____
Home Phone: (___)_____Social Security Number:_____
Personal Banking Information:
Bank:_____Bank Officer: _____
Address:_____
City/State:_____Zip:_____Phone: (___)_____

Principal(s)/Partner(s) Name:_____Title:_____
Home Address:_____
City/State:_____Zip:_____
Home Phone: (___)_____Social Security Number:_____
Personal Banking Information:
Bank:_____Bank Officer: _____
Address:_____
City/State:_____Zip:_____Phone: (___)_____

Principal(s)/Partner(s) Name:_____Title:_____
Home Address:_____
City/State:_____Zip:_____
Home Phone: (___)_____Social Security Number:_____
Personal Banking Information:

Bank:_____Bank Officer: _____
Address:_____
City/State:_____Zip:_____Phone: (___)_____

(B) Complete this section if entity is not a publicly traded corporation. Please list the Principal(s) and Officer(s) as well as the ownership interest.

Name:_____Title: _____
Address:_____
City/State:_____Zip:_____Phone: (___)_____
Percentage Owned:_____Social Security Number:_____

Name:_____Title: _____
Address:_____
City/State:_____Zip: _____Phone: (___)_____
Percentage Owned:_____Social Security Number:_____

Name:_____Title:_____
Address:_____
City/State:_____Zip:_____ Phone: (___)_____
Percentage Owned:_____Social Security Number: _____

(C) Complete this section if entity is a publicly traded corporation. List all third-party ratings assigned to this entity (i.e., D&B, Moody, S&P).

_____

Provide most recent annual report.
Provide most recent SEC filing.

(D) For (B) and (C) above complete the following:
State of Incorporation:_____Charter Number: _____
State(s) Where Qualified to Do Business:_____
Registered Agent for Service:_____

IV. BUSINESS CREDIT REFERENCES

Supplier:_____Account Number:_____
Goods/Services Purchased:_____Monthly Value:_____

Address:_____

City/State:_____Zip:_____Phone: (___)_____

Supplier:_____Account Number:_____

Goods/Services Purchased:_____Monthly Value:_____

Address:_____

City/State:_____Zip:_____Phone: (___)_____

Supplier:_____Account Number:_____

Goods/Services Purchased:_____Monthly Value:_____

Address:_____

City/State:_____Zip:_____Phone: (___)_____

V. BUSINESS BANKING INFORMATION

Bank: _____

Address: _____

City/State:_____Zip: _____Phone: (___)_____

Bank Officer:_____

Type of Account(s):_____Account Number: _____

Date Account Opened: _____

Bank: _____

Address: _____

City/State:_____Zip:_____Phone: (___)_____

Bank Officer:_____

Type of Account(s):_____Account Number: _____

Date Account Opened: _____

VI. FINANCIAL INFORMATION

A. During the last 10 years, has the entity making this application or any subsidiary, predecessor, officer or principal (provide full details if the answer is "yes" to any of the following):

Filed bankruptcy? Yes/No_____

Been named as a defendant in any legal proceedings? Yes/No_____

Had a judgment or lien filed against it? Yes/No_____

    Have they been satisfied? Yes/No_____

B. Upon completion of this application and prior to its return, please review carefully. In addition, please provide copies of the latest fiscal year and year-to-date financial statements (balance sheet, income statement and statement of cash flows) that you have available for the prospective Tenant under consideration. If unaudited, the financial statements should be certified as true and correct by the Owner or an authorized Partner, Principal or Officer of the business. Your cooperation will expedite the processing of your application.

DECLARATION

Under penalty of perjury, I, the undersigned, declare that this credit application is true and correct to the best of my knowledge, and I am authorized to submit this application. I recognize that _____ will rely on the information provided herein in determining the credit status of this application and that any substantial discrepancies which may come to _____'s attention before or after execution of a lease may result in _____ finding the lease to be in default and may exercise any of the remedies prescribed in the lease.

Further, I authorize any person or entity to release or furnish information to _____as may be requested in connection with their review and evaluation of this application. I UNDERSTAND THAT ADDITIONAL INFORMATION MAY BE REQUIRED WHICH COULD INCLUDE, BUT IS NOT LIMITED TO, BALANCE SHEETS AND INCOME STATEMENTS, PRO FORMAS, TAX RETURNS AND BUSINESS PLANS. I further agree that all financial statements, tax returns, reports and other materials furnished or obtained in connection herewith shall become the property of _____ _____.

Entity:_____

Print Name:_____

Title:_____

By: (Signed)_____

Date:_____

ID: Driver's License #_____

               (State)   (Number)

Exhibit 2:

Sample Lease Term

SUMMARY OF TERMS AND CONDITIONS

LEGAL NAME: _____

BUSINESS NAME: _____

LEGAL ADDRESS: _____

TELEPHONE:_____FACSIMILE:_____

PROPOSED USE:_____

SPACE:_____SQUARE FEET:_____FRONT:_____

                        MINIMUM RENT:

                        LEASE TERM:

                        LEASE COMMENCEMENT RENT:

                        LEASE TERMINATION:

PERCENTAGE RENT:

PRO RATA CHARGES: Tenant shall be responsible for its pro rata share of COMMON AREA MAINTENANCE, REAL ESTATE TAXES and INSURANCE COSTS. Based upon current billing, these are estimated for calendar year ____ to be as follows:

                        Common Area Maintenance:_____

                        Real Estate Taxes:_____

                        Insurance: _____

OTHER CHARGES: Tenant shall also be responsible for the following Other Charges which based upon current billing are estimated for calendar year ____ to be as follows:

                        HVAC Energy:_____

                        Electric: _____

Note: This is a sample only and is not to be construed as being endorsed or recommended by the author or the International Council of Shopping Centers. Readers are advised to consult legal counsel to devise appropriate documents for their centers.

Water:_____

Marketing Fund:_____

Special Assessment: _____

ONE-TIME CHARGES: Tenant shall be responsible for its pro rata share of the following one-time charges:

Sprinkler:_____

HVAC Equipment:_____

Initial Marketing Charge:_____

Landlord's Standard Floor Finish:_____

Temporary Barricade Enclosure:_____

Coming Soon Logo:_____

Plan Review Fees:_____

PRE-OPENING CHARGES: Includes LOD package, temporary signage, temporary electric, water, asbestos abatement inspection report, etc.

Typical Retail Tenants:_____

Food Tenants: _____

SECURITY DEPOSIT: To Be Determined

GUARANTOR: To Be Determined

DESIGN CRITERIA: It should be understood that Landlord will implement a comprehensive control of store design in order to achieve a unified quality tone throughout the project.

NOT BINDING: The business terms and conditions as outlined above are being submitted solely for review. Neither party will be legally bound by these terms and conditions until a mutually acceptable lease has been fully executed by both parties. Once executed, the terms and conditions of the lease between Landlord and Tenant shall supersede the terms and conditions of this Summary.

AVAILABILITY OF SPACE: This proposal is conditioned upon the availability of the above referenced space, and approval by the Real Estate Committee.

FINANCIAL: Tenant lease application, corporate or personal finance statement (whichever is applicable), balance sheet, income statement, tax returns and business plan must be returned with signed Summary of Terms and Conditions before a lease will be drafted.

OTHER: *(INSERT RADIUS, RELOCATION, OTHER NEGOTIATED TERMS TO BE INSERTED IN DRAFT OF LEASE)*

THIS PROPOSAL WILL BE WITHDRAWN IF NOT ACTED UPON BY:

PREPARED BY:_____DATE:_____

ACCEPTED BY:_____DATE:_____

Exhibit 3:

Sample Lease Approval Form

Property:		Date:	
Submitted by:			
☐ New Lease ☐ Renewal ☐ Amendment			
Tenant			
Legal Name:		DBA:	
Contact Name:		State of Incorporation:	
Address:			
Telephone Number:			
Guarantor:		State of Incorporation:	
☐ Full Guarantee ☐ Guarantee Limited to:			
Tenant Notice Address:			
Lease Provisions			
Space No:			

Renewal/Relocation Existing Deal:	Space No.:	Sq. Ft.:	Min. Rent:	Effective Rent:

Use:		

Term	Years:	Months:	Opening Date:	Expiration Date:

Minimum Annual Rent
   Budget:

Years:	Dollars/Sq.Ft.	Dollars/Yr.	% Rent	☐ Natural ☐ Unnatural Breakpoint

Department Store Increase:				
Security Deposit:				
Tenant Allowance Budget:				
Cash to Tenant:	$	/sq.ft.	$	
Abated Rent:	$	/sq.ft.	$	
Abated Extra Charges:	$	/sq.ft.	$	
Recapture:	$	/sq.ft.	$	
Landlord's Work:	$	/sq.ft.	$	
Brokerage Commission:	$	/sq.ft.	$	% ☐ INHOUSE ☐ Outside
Broker				
Total Cost:	$	/sq.ft.	$	

Ancillary Charges

CAM	☐ Full pro-rata $	sq.ft.	☐ Other	
Taxes	☐ Full pro-rata $	sq.ft.	☐ Other	
Utilities	HVAC $	sq.ft.	Electric $	/sq. ft.
Marketing Fund	$ /sq. ft.	Media Fund $	/sq. ft.	
Escalations	Initial Marketing Charge $		Special Assessments:	

Construction Chargebacks:	

Special Lease Provisions:	

Note: This is a sample only and is not to be construed as being endorsed or recommended by the author or the International Council of Shopping Centers. Readers are advised to consult legal counsel to devise appropriate documents for their centers.

Approvals:

Property Manager	Date
Leasing Representative	Date
Asset Manager	Date
Director of Leasing	Date
Director of Shopping Centers	Date
President (If Needed)	Date

Lease Reconciliation Approval

Asset Manager/Final Approval   Date

Attachments	
☐	Credit Analysis
☐	NPV
☐	Press Release

Exhibit 4:

Sample Net Present Value (NPV) Analysis of Proposed Lease

PROPERTY:	DISCOUNT RATE:	10%
TENANT:	MONTHLY OR ANNUAL:	Annually

	LEASING	THIS	APPRAISAL
SUMMARY OF DEALPOINTS:	GUIDELINE	PROPOSAL	ASSUMPTIONS

TENANCY SIZE IN SQ. FT.
LEASE TERM IN YEARS
LEASE COMMENCEMENT DATE
BASE RENTAL IN $/SQ. FT./YEAR: Year 1
                         Year 2
                         Year 3
                         Year 4
                         Year 5
FREE RENTAL IN MONTHS
RECOVERABLE EXPENSES IN $/SQ. FT./YEAR 1
RECOVERABLE EXPENSE INFLATOR
EXPENSE STOP IN $/SQ. FT./YEAR
TENANT CAPITAL ALLOWANCE IN $/SQ. FT.
LEASE COMMISSION IN $/SQ. FT.

DOLLAR AND PERCENT VARIANCE

NPV OF RENTAL INCOME

NPV OF CASH FLOW

CASH FLOW ANALYSIS PER LEASING GUIDELINE: CASH FLOW ANALYSIS PER THIS PROPOSAL:

PERIOD	BASE RENTAL	FREE RENT	EXPENSE RECOVERY	CAPITAL	CASH FLOW	PERIOD	BASE RENTAL	FREE RENT	EXPENSE RECOVERY	CAPITAL	CASH FLOW
0						0					
1						1					
2						2					
3						3					
4						4					
5						5					
6						6					
7						7					
8						8					
9						9					
10						10					
11						11					
12						12					
13						13					
14						14					
15						15					

Comments   Comments:

Note: This is a sample only and is not to be construed as being endorsed or recommended by the author or the International Council of Shopping Centers. Readers are advised to consult legal counsel to devise appropriate documents for their centers.

5 | Administration

Kate M. Sheehy

Administration for shopping centers consists of keeping records and managing income. Administration comprises four aspects: planning, implementing, monitoring and reporting.

The Four Aspects of Administration

Planning refers to the process of budgeting revenue, expense, income and capital for a future period. Implicit in the planning process is understanding the goals and objectives of ownership. Any plan for a property should be directed at achieving those objectives.

Implementing the plan for administration involves both the invoicing of rents and add-on rent charges ("add-ons") and the collection of those revenues from tenants. *Add-ons* are the additional charges to the rent, which may include service charges for maintenance of common areas, merchants' association fees, contribution to the marketing fund, utilities, trash, sprinklers, insurance and taxes.

Monitoring is the periodic measurement of performance indicators such as occupancy, sales and rents. This measurement provides feedback on whether performance is synchronous with the plan—both short and long term. Monitoring is usually an internal function used to inform the management of the firm and the management at a property.

Reporting—or for this discussion, financial reporting—is the last component of administration. Reporting is a process that is directed both internally and externally. While financial statements communicate the results of the business operation to management, financial statements are also shared with clients, lenders and often the broader marketplace.

Planning and monitoring will be affected by the method used for financial reporting, that is, accrual basis or cash basis. In *accrual basis accounting*, revenues and expenses are identified with specific periods of time, such as a month or year, and are recorded as incurred without regard to the date of receipt or the payment of cash. In contrast to the accrual method, *cash basis accounting* records revenue and expense when received without regard to the period in which they apply.

Leases Are the Foundation

The revenues of a shopping center flow from the terms of the leases with the shopping center's tenants. That is why proper management of the leases is at the core of shopping center administration. Successful administration secures the landlord's rights under the leases.

Shopping center leases may be net or gross. A *gross lease* is one in which the tenant pays one amount, namely rent, and the landlord is obligated to pay all taxes, insurance and maintenance associated with the operation of the shopping center. A *net lease* obligates the tenant to pay not only rent but also a share of taxes, insurance, maintenance and other operating costs of the shopping center. A *triple net lease* requires the tenant to pay 100 percent of the taxes, insurance and maintenance costs associated with the center.

The first step in managing leases is to prepare abstracts. An *abstract* is a summary, or a shortened version, outlining the main points of a document. A shopping center lease abstract may summarize any number of lease clauses, but usually contains:

- The tenant's legal name and address
- The tenant's dba (name *doing business as*)
- The permitted use of the premises by the tenant
- The location or space number
- The area or square footage used by the tenant and/or subject to rent
- The term of the lease, rent commencement date, expiration date and option periods

- The fixed minimum rent and the terms of any scheduled or contingent increases
- The breakpoint sales and the breakpoint percentage, as well as any future increases
- The terms, or formulas, for add-ons

The abstract might also contain the initial budgeted rates for add-ons. When rents or add-ons can be affected by occupancy in the center, the abstract will also include any such co-tenancy provisions.

The abstracts of a shopping center's leases are summarized in a *rent roll*. On a single schedule, the rent roll lists all of the spaces in a shopping center, whether occupied or not. Then information about the tenants occupying the center is summarized on the rent roll. Rent rolls generally include:

- The tenant's dba
- Location and area (size)
- Commencement and expiration dates
- Fixed minimum rent
- The breakpoint percentage and breakpoint sales

Different organizations use different forms of abstracts and rent rolls. In designing either, it's important to decide what information is needed to manage the business and what information ownership is interested in having immediately available.

Planning

THE BUDGETING PROCESS

A *budget* is a financial plan serving as an estimate of and a control over future operations. Different organizations require different forms of budgets. The most traditional form is a one-year operational budget that projects revenue (or vacancy) for each space in the center on a monthly basis and expenses by line item, also on a monthly basis. Typically, even if revenue and expense are budgeted for only one year, major (or capital) expenditures are budgeted over a longer period of time, perhaps three to five years. This allows ownership to plan for cash needs and to manage the long-term maintenance of the property.

In cases where ownership appraises the value of a property on a regular and recurring basis, the time line for the budget may be extended
to three or five years. In that event, the budgeted revenues, expense
and capital may serve as the basis for appraisal assumptions.

Long-range budgeting can be performed with the same criteria as a
one-year plan, namely on a space-by-space and line item basis. However, for properties that have been managed or owned by the same
firm for some time, budgeting may be performed using some "global"
assumptions based upon historical data. Such assumptions might include rates of vacancy, renewal retention, sales growth and expense
growth.

OCCUPANCY

A shopping center budget begins with the current rent roll and then
projects the occupancy or vacancy for each space over the period of
time considered by the budget. Completion of the budget requires a
plan for renewal or nonrenewal of every lease expiring during the
course of the period the budget considers.

To complete this plan, a *lease expiration report* must be prepared. This
report lists all the leases expiring each year in an ascending order from
current year to the expiration year of the lease with the latest expiration date. The area of the leases expiring in each year is subtotaled and
a percentage is calculated of (either or both) total leasable and total occupied area.

The occupancy budget is completed by projecting:

- Each lease that is expected to remain in occupancy during the
  budget period
- Each renewal and the replacement tenant for any nonrenew-
  ing leases
- Unscheduled vacancies and the replacement for such unscheduled vacancies
- Tenants expected to fill currently vacant space

Budgeting occupancy is essential whenever the lease(s) of a center
contain a *co-tenancy provision*. A co-tenancy clause stipulates that a reduced rent or no rent is paid until an agreed-upon percentage of the
center is occupied or may allow a tenant to terminate the lease if a certain percentage of occupancy is not maintained. The lease language
will dictate whether such an occupancy threshold is at a point in time
or based on an average occupancy rate over the course of the budgeted

year. Thus, any occupancy budget should not only calculate occupancy by month and at year-end, but also on average over the budget year.

RENTS

The most critical element of any shopping center's revenues is the rental stream from the tenants. In many centers, a close correlation exists between rent and net operating income (NOI; the income remaining after deducting operating expenses from gross income). Rent is the basis of a center's valuation.

Fixed minimum rent, also called base rent, is the amount of basic rent paid by the tenant, usually stated as an amount per square foot charged on an annual basis. Over the life of the lease, fixed minimum rent may be adjusted either on dates established in the lease or on the occasion of events described in the lease.

Rents that are structured so that they increase at specific times during the life of the lease are called *step-up rents.* Such rents may increase by fixed amounts established in the lease. For example, the rent in a ten-year lease might start at $10 per square foot (psf) and increase to $11 psf at the beginning of the fourth lease year and increase again to $12 psf at the beginning of the seventh lease year.

Step-up rents may also be variable, pegged to increases in indices such as the consumer price index (CPI). As an example, a $10 psf rent could be scheduled to increase at the beginning of the fourth lease year by the change in CPI as of the end of the third lease year compared to the CPI as of the end of the first full lease year. If CPI changed by 5 percent over that period, the new rent would be $10.50 psf.

Rents may also increase contingent upon certain events happening. For instance, rents for all tenants that opened their stores before the addition of a fourth department store may increase upon the opening of that fourth department store.

Occasionally, an initial period of free rent is granted to a tenant. In such a case, the initial occupancy date and the rent commencement date will be different. Generally accepted accounting principles (GAAP) require that average annual rent be recognized by "straight-lining" rent over the life of the lease. This results in an equal amount of rent being recognized in each year of the lease. For financial reporting, an entry will be made equal to the difference between lease rents and straight-lined rent. The same principle applies for leases with step-up rents.

To illustrate, assume that a tenant in 1,000 sf pays $10 psf for each of five years but receives free rent for the first three months of the lease. The tenant will pay $50,000 over the life of the lease less $2,500 in free rent, or an average of $9,500 per year. That average is the straight-lined rent for this lease. In the first year, the tenant's lease rent will be $7,500, and there will be an accounting entry (credit) for $2,000. In the second through the fifth years, the tenant's lease rent is $10,000; the accounting entries for those years will be a debit of $500. This is explained in the table below:

	Year 1	Year 2	Year 3	Year 4	Year 5
Lease rent:	$7,500	$10,000	$10,000	$10,000	$10,000
Entry:	2,000	(500)	(500)	(500)	(500)
Straight-lined rent:	$9,500	$9,500	$9,500	$9,500	$9,500

Sometimes a tenant will lease an additional space in the shopping center for storage. Storage areas will generally be unusable as retail space. Storage rent is usually budgeted separately from other rent.

SALES AND PERCENTAGE RENTS

The rents a shopping center can command are predicated on the sales volumes and sales productivity of its tenants. *Sales volumes* are the dollars of sales produced in a store; *sales productivity* is a measure of the sales produced per square foot of store area. The greater the sales, the higher the rents. Thus, sales affect rents in future periods. And it follows that sales budgeting will impact the budgeting of rents.

Percentage rent is a direct function of sales activity. A tenant's sales during a lease year are multiplied by the percentage rent rate stipulated in the lease. Percentage rent may be calculated in addition to fixed minimum rent, in lieu of fixed minimum rent or in lieu of fixed minimum rent and add-ons. In order to operate profitably, a tenant will be willing to pay some percentage of its sales to occupy its space.

Many leases provide that, in addition to fixed minimum rent, the tenant will pay a percentage *(breakpoint percentage)* of its sales over an amount of sales stated in the lease. This amount is called the *breakpoint sales*. Percentage rent of this type is also called *overage rent.*

For instance, a tenant will pay $1,000 in percentage rent if it has sales of $220,000 with breakpoint sales of $200,000 and a breakpoint percentage of 5 percent. If the tenant's fixed minimum rent in this case is $10,000, then the breakpoint is said to be a *natural breakpoint.* A natural breakpoint occurs where the fixed minimum rent is achieved when the breakpoint percentage is multiplied by the breakpoint sales.

In this example, $200,000 × 5% = $10,000. Some leases will contain breakpoints other than a natural breakpoint. A tenant might pay 5 percent of sales over $200,000 even though fixed minimum rent is only $8,000.

Percentage rents paid in lieu of fixed minimum rent or in lieu of fixed minimum rent and add-ons are not subject to a breakpoint. They are calculated by multiplying the lease-stipulated percentage rate by the tenant's sales for the lease year. Such leases may include graduated, or multiple, percentage rates and sales levels. This occurs when the lease provides for one percentage to be applied to sales in a range of sales volume, and then another percentage on another range and so on. As an example, a tenant might pay 6 percent on the first $300,000 plus 5 percent on sales greater than $300,000 up to $500,000, and 4 percent on sales greater than $500,000.

Leases sometimes grant a tenant the right to deduct all or a portion of some expense or investment from all or a portion of percentage rent. This right is called *offset* or *recapture*. For instance, a tenant has a right to recapture 50 percent of its annual real estate tax charge against any percentage (overage) rent. If the tenant's tax charge is $2,000 and there is no overage rent, the tenant pays $2,000. If overage rent is calculated at $500, the tenant pays $2,000 in tax and no overage since the amount of overage does not fully offset 50 percent of the tax charge. If, however, the overage rent is calculated at $2,000, the tenant will pay $2,000 in tax and $1,000 in overage, thus receiving the full benefit of its 50 percent offset.

Budgeting sales and percentage rent can be a time-consuming exercise. As in any budgeting decision, the administrative cost incurred when budgeting on a tenant-by-tenant and month-by-month basis should be compared to the potential benefit. If percentage rent is small or immaterial compared to the revenues of the center, the budget might be prepared with simple growth assumptions. If the budget will be used as the basis for appraisal assumptions, detailed budgeting may be the most prudent choice.

COMMON AREA MAINTENANCE (CAM)

In a net lease, the tenant pays some share of the costs incurred to maintain the *common areas*, which are those portions of the shopping center that have been designated and improved for common use by or for the benefit of more than one occupant of the shopping center. Common areas generally comprise parking lots, walkways, entrances, truck courts and service corridors. The lease enumerates the types of expenditures for maintenance that can be included in common area maintenance (CAM) expenses. Typical expenses may include those for lighting, heating and cooling, repairs, cleaning, security, landscaping and insuring the common areas. In addition to the expenses listed, many shopping center leases provide for the addition of the administrative cost equal to some percentage of the enumerated expenses.

Generally speaking, the amount of CAM assessed to a tenant in each year is estimated in advance using the property's budget for expense and occupancy. Following the end of the year, when actual expense and occupancy are known, the landlord reconciles the estimate and the actual. If the reconciliation indicates that the tenant has paid too much, the tenant's account is credited. If the tenant paid too little, a bill is sent for the reconciled amount. This reconciliation process is also referred to as "true-up" and "settlement."

A tenant's pro rata share is usually determined by multiplying the costs to maintain the common area by a fraction. The tenant's store area is the numerator of the fraction. The denominator may be the gross leasable area of the center, the occupied area of the center or some other measurement determined by the lease. The lease also determines the inclusion or exclusion of the area for department stores or other anchor tenants in this denominator.

Other methods to bill back a share of common area expense include flat rates, rates capped at certain levels, rates in which increases over the life of the lease are subject to limits and percentage rates similar to the calculations for percentage rent.

In some leases for enclosed regional shopping centers, the tenant may be required to pay a share of only exterior common area expense. Care must be taken to clearly define exterior expense and to categorize that expense in separate accounts.

Sometimes a lease will not include insurance in the common area cost definition but will have a discrete clause covering the bill-back of that expense to the tenants. Insurance expense is market driven and can be affected by factors not entirely in the landlord's control. Therefore, a landlord may choose to separate insurance from common area expenses to prevent the recovery of insurance expense from being capped or otherwise limited.

Trash collection, disposal methods and pricing for those services are also subject to strong market forces. Therefore, some leases will provide that the cost of collecting trash for the whole center is in the common area maintenance expense. Other leases will separate the charge for collecting the tenant's trash from its store and the charge for collecting trash from the common area.

Shopping centers with food courts frequently have leases that obligate the tenants in the food court to pay a separate charge for the costs to maintain the common seating area for the food court. This charge may be pro rata or may be assessed as a percentage of sales. Typically, the food court expenses will include any costs incurred above and beyond those that would have been incurred if there were no food court. Cleaning food court tables, repairing food court chairs, removing "wet" trash from the food court and washing food court trays are examples of such costs.

REAL ESTATE TAXES

In a net lease, the tenant pays some share of the real estate taxes for the property. Some leases also obligate the tenant to pay its share of any expense incurred to appeal a real estate tax assessment.

Many lease forms include real estate taxes for the property as part of the common area add-on charge. Other leases provide that taxes be split between those levied on the common areas and those levied on other land and improvements of the shopping center. Regional shopping center leases often treat real estate taxes as a separate add-on charge and do not include any portion of this expense in CAM. There may or may not be an administrative cost equal to some percentage of the enumerated expenses.

When all or a portion of the real estate taxes are billed to tenants as a separate add-on charge, the amount assessed to a tenant in each year is estimated in advance using the property's budget for expense and occupancy. When actual expense and occupancy are known and, generally, when taxes are paid, the landlord reconciles the estimate and the actual. If the reconciliation indicates that the tenant has paid too much, the tenant's account is credited. If the tenant paid too little, a bill is sent for the reconciled amount. This reconciliation process is also referred to as "true-up" and "settlement."

A tenant's pro rata share is usually determined by multiplying the tax expense by a fraction. The tenant's store area is the numerator of the fraction. The denominator may be the gross leasable area of the center, the occupied area of the center or some other measurement determined by the lease. The lease also determines the inclusion or exclusion of the area for department stores or other anchor tenants in this denominator.

Other methods to bill back a share of real estate taxes include flat rates, rates capped at certain levels, rates in which increases over the life of the lease are subject to limits, and percentage rates similar to the calculations for percentage rent.

UTILITIES

Utilities provided to a tenant's store include electricity, heating, ventilation and air-conditioning (HVAC), water and sewer and natural gas. Utilities are made available to the tenant either directly by the utility provider or by the landlord. If the landlord provides the utilities, the tenant's store may be submetered. The landlord reads the submeters to arrive at the tenant's utility consumption and, generally, calculates the tenant's add-on charge by multiplying the consumption times a rate as provided in the lease.

Some lease forms, however, require that the tenant pays some pro rata share of the utility expense similar to the way CAM and real estate tax are calculated. Other lease forms will require that a minimum charge or a fixed charge be assessed each month. This is relatively common with water/sewer expense.

Although generally grouped with utilities, HVAC is more appropriately called a service since it is not usually delivered by a utility company. HVAC can be provided to the tenant space by either rooftop units or a central plant. HVAC charges may be calculated on a pro rata basis, as a flat rate or with an escalation factor. In some shopping centers with central plants, HVAC might be calculated using a formula for demand and consumption described in a lease exhibit and possibly supported by an engineering study.

Utilities are treated as a "consumable" in many lease forms. This means that the amount charged to the tenant relates directly to the amount of utility consumed in the tenant's space. Thus, a restaurant or hair salon will pay more for water than most other tenants because it consumes more.

For budgeting purposes, where utilities are considered "consumable," many landlords calculate utility revenue by multiplying a historic recovery ratio times the budgeted expense. A *recovery ratio* is a fraction, stated as a percentage, in which the numerator is revenue and the denominator is expense. If the utility bills for all of the water meters serving tenant space are the expense (and there's no water consumption in vacant spaces), and the tenants pay the same water rate billed to the center, revenue and expense would be equal, or recovery would be 100 percent.

One cautionary note: many states have enacted or are enacting legislation that prevents landlords from earning a "profit" through the resale of utilities. This does not, however, preclude the landlord from recovering the reasonable cost of managing and administering utilities.

TEMPORARY LICENSES

Many shopping centers are enhancing merchandise mix through the addition of temporary retail uses. These retailers generally sign a license agreement with the landlord for the temporary right to use a space. Most landlords, therefore, segregate the revenues from this source into an account or accounts separate from tenant rents.

Because of the temporary nature of these licensees, revenue is often budgeted by applying a growth rate to historic revenue. The exception to that practice is when these "temps" use in-line space. Then planning will require space-by-space information (provided by the leasing assumptions) in order to avoid budgeting revenue from two different sources in the same space. To illustrate the problem, consider a center where the prior year-end occupancy was 80 percent and the landlord filled some of that space with a Christmas store for the holiday. If the same space is budgeted to be leased in the current year and unavailable for temporary use, it's likely that a decrease in temporary revenue will have to be budgeted.

MISCELLANEOUS REVENUES

Revenue from sources such as telephones, lockers, vending machines and directories are often included in the miscellaneous category. This line in the budget may also include interest earned from cash management or late charges billed to tenants. Yet another source of miscellaneous revenue might be the fees paid by tenants to have shopping center employees or contractors perform service work in the tenant space. Nonrecurring revenue, such as payments from tenants to terminate their leases before the contract expiration date, might also be categorized as miscellaneous. Since the total revenue in this category is usually immaterial when compared to revenues from tenants, budgeting can be as simple as using last year's actual revenue plus or minus any one-time revenues such as lease termination fees.

MARKETING FUNDS AND MERCHANTS' ASSOCIATIONS

Marketing is an add-on charge whereby the tenants provide the primary funds for the overall marketing of the shopping center. At some properties, this function is managed through a *merchants' association*, which is a nonprofit independent organization of tenants that works to advertise and promote the shopping center. Other properties use a *marketing fund,* where the monies collected are controlled by the landlord and administered by the shopping center's marketing director or manager.

Common to both forms is the obligation to spend the marketing funds exclusively on marketing activities. These might include but are not limited to special events, advertising, market research, sales promotions and community relations. Marketing expenses, therefore, are usually budgeted at a level equal to budgeted revenue. The shopping center leases or the bylaws of the merchants' association may also obligate the landlord to make some matching contribution to the marketing funds equal to a fraction of the tenants' contributions.

Tenant marketing contributions are generally subject to some escalation either by CPI or by the change in media costs for the marketplace. Because the marketing add-on is not a pro rata share, there is no annual reconciliation or true-up.

EXPENSE MANAGEMENT

Many landlords practice zero-based budgeting to control and manage expenses. *Zero-based budgeting* is a method of developing a current budget without basing it on any previous years' budgets; the starting point for each budget item is zero. This form of budgeting helps to eliminate errors arising from applying growth rates to previous years' budgets or even actual expenses that may contain nonrecurring, one-time items. This method requires an objective evaluation of the expenditures necessary to operate the shopping center.

An annual bid process generally accompanies zero-based budgeting for the shopping center's contracted services. This bid process allows the landlord to define the scope of service for the upcoming year and ensure the best combination of service and price available in the market. Utilities bear special consideration in the budget process, particularly as deregulation becomes more widespread and competing sources become available.

When a landlord has several properties, expense management may include a comparison of expenses among the properties. Most often, this is done on the basis of expense per square foot of either building or leasable area. As an example: If a landlord has twelve properties and the average cost of janitorial service per square foot of building area is $1.00, and one center has a rate of $1.25 psf, that might warrant additional evaluation. However, climate and market conditions must be taken into account in any comparison of centers in different geographic areas. The cost of janitorial service, for instance, might be affected by the local sales tax or by union rates. The finishes used in the shopping center can also affect cleaning costs.

Real estate tax expense should be managed on an ongoing basis. The landlord needs to evaluate the assessment against any changes in value experienced by the center and against the valuation of similar properties in the market. On occasion, the landlord may need to appeal the valuation and assessment. Many landlords use specialized consultants to do so because the consultants are knowledgeable about local tax legislation and familiar with the workings of the local assessor's office. Tenants also often have lease rights permitting their participation in the appeal process.

MAJOR EXPENDITURES

The most significant step in planning major expenditures is verifying ownership's objectives and constraints. Any major expenditure should be subjected to some financial analysis and compared to ownership's benchmarks or hurdles. One simple measurement is the *payback period,* or the length of time it takes for the income produced by an expenditure to pay back the expenditure. For instance, a tenant allowance equal to the first year's rent on a ten-year lease has a payback period of one year.

Some landlords may require that the rate of return on any expenditure exceed the rate at which they can borrow money. An internal rate of return, or IRR, can be calculated to make this determination. An *internal rate of return* is the rate at which the present value of the cash inflows and outflows is equal. If a tenant allowance for a seven-year lease has an IRR of 14 percent, and the landlord can borrow money at 12 percent, this expenditure might be approved.

Consideration of risk, however, also enters into decisions to approve major expenditures. Even though a tenant allowance and lease rental stream produce a favorable IRR result, a landlord might still turn down the proposed expenditure if the tenant's credit history is poor or if the venture appeared too risky.

Risk for some major expenditures can be mitigated if they can be passed through to tenants in CAM charges over one or more years. The ability to recover expenditures through tenant billings is entirely driven by the language of the individual tenant leases. Any such decision to pass through an expenditure should be supported by a thorough review of the leases.

Implementing

SALES COLLECTION

Most shopping center leases require that tenants report their sales to the landlord on a periodic basis. It may be monthly, quarterly or annually. Often, the lease will require payment of percentage rent at the same time the sales report is due. Additionally, leases require that the tenant certify the accuracy of the sales at the end of the lease year, with a report signed by a designated officer.

Because of the importance of sales to the revenues of the center, the landlord must enforce timely and accurate sales reporting from the tenants. This may include periodic audits of the tenants' sales. The landlord's rights and responsibilities in conducting those audits are spelled out in the lease document.

BILLING

Billing the amounts due under a lease falls into three categories: monthly charges, annual reconciliations of add-ons and percentage rents. Although the process of notifying a tenant as to the amount due pursuant to a lease clause is called billing, an invoice may never be generated or sent. Many leases begin with a summary of terms that sets out the charges due to the landlord each month. Some landlords send a letter to the tenant whenever the amount of a charge changes, such as a step-up in fixed minimum rent or adjustments in CAM estimates. Other landlords provide the tenant with a book of twelve monthly coupons for the upcoming year on January 1. And still others do, indeed, send the tenant an invoice each month.

For annual reconciliations of charges such as CAM and real estate taxes, on the other hand, most landlords will send the tenant an invoice and a copy of the calculation to expedite processing of the payment on the tenant's side. For that reason and to comply with the language in some leases, the landlord may provide additional support with the annual reconciliation, such as a copy of the paid real estate tax bill from the taxing authority.

Some leases permit the tenant to audit the expenses and the calculation for its annual CAM amount or the amount of other add-ons. The rights of the tenant and the landlord about the timing and conduct of audits are spelled out in the lease document. Rather than manage tenant audits, some landlords prefer to have a public accounting firm certify the accuracy of the expenses and provide that information to the tenant.

In the case of percentage rent, the tenant can calculate the amount due when submitting its sales report. Many tenants will remit payment simultaneously. If the tenant does not remit payment, the landlord will usually provide a letter or invoice with an accompanying calculation.

The lease may require that the tenant make payment or submit sales by a certain time, but the lease may also require the landlord to process such things as annual reconciliations of CAM in a timely manner. It is incumbent upon the landlord to know those dates.

COLLECTION OF ACCOUNTS RECEIVABLE

As important as it is to prepare tenants' billings and invoices accurately, it is probably more essential to collect the tenants' rent and add-ons promptly. Whether a landlord uses the accrual or the cash method of accounting, the quality of the income stream can be adversely affected if the collection history at a shopping center is poor.

On a cash basis, any failure to collect rent(s) means that revenues are not recognized and may adversely affect the landlord's ability to distribute dividends or to pay lenders. On an accrual basis, the failure to collect rent(s) promptly may be recognized in an account called *bad debt allowance* or *credit loss*. This allowance is for uncollectible or uncollected billing balances and reduces both the current year income and the assets on the balance sheet. In an appraisal, the historical proportion of accounts receivable to total revenue may adversely affect the valuation.

If a tenant fails to pay rent(s) in the billed amount and at the time set forth in the lease, the tenant is in default. A *default* is a failure to comply with the terms of the lease. The lease will spell out the remedies available to the landlord if the tenant fails to cure the default. In addition to the specific lease language, local law will also govern the landlord's ability to collect rent(s). Many leases provide for the landlord to charge a late fee, or interest, on any unpaid balances.

For optimal performance, any collection policy should be written, consistently applied and measured. The collection policy should conform to the language of the majority of leases in the center but must recognize exceptions arising from unique leases. The first component of successful collection is recognizing when accounts are due. Typically, the monthly payment of fixed minimum rent and add-ons is due on the first day of each month. Other billings, such as percentage rent or reconciliations of common area maintenance or real estate taxes, will have specific payment terms.

Many landlords use a dunning letter to notify a tenant of a failure to pay before the cure period in the lease is expired. Usually, the letter is sent after phone calls fail. Once the cure period lapses, a notice of default should be sent to the tenant in accordance with the notice provisions of the lease. If the tenant fails to respond to the notice and cure the default, the landlord has several options. These include suit for performance and suit for possession. In a *suit for performance*, the landlord takes the tenant to court to compel payment; in a *suit for possession*, the landlord seeks to evict the tenant and regain the space. The steps to accomplish collection or repossession are specific to the lease and to the jurisdiction; they are also very time sensitive. Therefore, care must be taken to follow correct procedure.

Because lawsuits are both expensive and detrimental to the landlord-tenant relationship, some leases provide for arbitration to resolve conflicts. For collecting small arrearages, especially from tenants no longer in occupancy, some landlords use collection agencies. The agency receives a percentage of the collected amount as a fee, but this cost may be less than the cost of the landlord's time.

Monitoring

OCCUPANCY

Most landlords prepare a report at the end of each month that describes the status of occupancy or leasing for each space in the shopping center and summarizes that information, as follows:

	Area (SF)	% of GLA
Leased and occupied:		
Leased not yet occupied:		
Out for signature:		
In negotiation:		
Vacant:		
Total:		100.00

This reporting not only identifies the current occupancy of the center but also provides a ballpark estimate of future occupancy when the first two or three categories are added together. While the monthly occupancy/leasing status report provides useful information, its value as an analytical tool will be greater if the current year statistics are compared to the budget, the prior year or both.

SALES

Few things tell as much about the performance of a shopping center as the sales of its tenants. That is why many organizations devote considerable time to sales reports. Since percentage rent is derived from sales, the most basic of sales reports will capture information about tenants' sales volumes. This information is generally presented for the current month, year-to-date, this month in the last year and year-to-date last year. Comparison to prior years helps to establish trends, and many landlords also prepare five-year sales volume reports for that reason.

Understanding the shopping center's sales is critical to successful leasing and merchandising. Maximizing sales with the right merchandise mix is the first step to optimizing rent and value. Because of its relationship to rental rates, sales psf is a key performance indicator. Sales psf may be quoted on an annual, annualized or rolling twelve-month basis. The sales of the tenants are usually sorted by merchandise category and often subtotaled by comparable and noncomparable stores. One definition of a comparable store is a store occupying the same space for two full years.

Another key performance indicator is the calculation of occupancy costs as a percentage of sales. *Occupancy cost* is the sum of a tenant's fixed rent, percentage rent and add-ons. This measurement can be calculated for the center, for a merchandise category, for a wing or level of the center or for individual tenants. Comparing occupancy cost to sales can indicate whether a particular store is "healthy" or whether the landlord is realizing market rents. Preparing an occupancy cost schedule for each tenant in the shopping center is an excellent aide to the budgeting process for leasing and merchandising.

LEASING RESULTS

Many landlords rely on the occupancy/leasing status report as sufficient information on leasing results. Others, however, monitor leasing productivity as a leading indicator for occupancy and net operating income. For instance, if a property budget calls for 20,000 sf to open on November 1 and lease(s) for that space are executed by August 1, those store openings may have a good chance to occur on time as far as budgeting is concerned. On the other hand, if there were no leases even out for signature on August 1, the likelihood of making budget could be diminished.

Landlords who monitor leasing results separately from occupancy usually track the execution of new and renewal leases. If the property is leased by a broker, brokerage fees may be paid upon execution and/or opening. So such monitoring is essential for processing payment of the broker's commissions. Similarly, a property manager might want to monitor the productivity of internal leasing agents.

Few organizations budget the timing of lease executions; rather, they budget the opening of the stores. If a landlord wants to monitor the timing of lease executions against a benchmark, a historical average of the number of days between lease execution and store opening would have to be calculated. To arrive at a budget for lease execution, the property budget for store openings would be stepped back in time by that historical average. To illustrate: For the last two years, the time elapsed between execution and opening for Property Manager X has been 120 days. A tenant is budgeted to open on November 1. Using the 120-day average, the lease for that tenant is budgeted to be signed on July 1.

Monitoring renewals is similar to monitoring lease executions for new deals. Lead time, however, tends to be a little longer because renewals often have a lower priority than new leases for business people and attorneys on both sides of the transaction. The failure to execute renewals in a timely fashion, however, can have a negative impact on the cash flow of the shopping center. Most renewals include some increase in fixed minimum rent or change in add-ons. Tenants will not usually pay those increases until the renewal lease is executed. Given that the revenue budget is probably based upon renewals being in place on time, an unfavorable timing variance will result if renewals are late.

Because the budgeted leasing assumption includes both leases expiring during the year and tenants expected to renew, the landlord might be more proactive by sending reminders to the broker or internal leasing agent 150 to 180 days in advance of the original expiration date. This reminder program can continue until the renewal is executed.

RECOVERIES

Recoveries are the relationship between revenue and expense for common area maintenance, real estate taxes, utilities and other add-ons where the tenant is paying a share of the shopping center's expenses. If all of a shopping center's leases were "pure" triple net leases, recovery of expense would be 100 percent—or greater if the leases permitted an administrative fee. However, since most shopping centers have a diverse and varied population of leases, recoveries are fairly complex and need to be managed.

On the one hand, management means accurate and timely calculation of tenants' billings and annual reconciliations. On the other, management also means creating a feedback loop to brokers, leasing agents and attorneys to inform the people controlling the beginning of the lease process about the financial ramifications of variations from standard lease language.

Standard lease language in most landlords' leases is written to secure optimum recovery of expense for the landlord. Changes to that language generally reduce the landlord's recovery and create an unfavorable impact on the bottom line. The benefit of having a particular store as part of the shopping center's merchandise mix might far outweigh the cost of a concession on add-ons. But quantifying that cost for people involved in the leasing process can help them continue to pursue the landlord's objectives in the future.

Although an occasional individual lease may materially sway a recovery factor, monitoring the long-term trends in recovery ratios is generally more meaningful. Understanding the financial impact of leasing tactics over time helps to establish parameters for current and future leasing plans. Because many add-ons require annual reconciliations, it is important to compare the actual results for the most recent year to estimates for the current year and to use that information in preparing budgets for the future.

Another outcome of managing recoveries is managing the rates charged to tenants. In the budgeting process, most landlords will calculate the amounts that a tenant signing a standard lease would have to pay for common area maintenance, real estate taxes, marketing, utilities and any other add-ons. These are often referred to as *quote rates*.

Tenants must manage their total occupancy costs and will usually negotiate their total rental obligation, which is the sum of fixed minimum rent, overage rent and add-ons. For example, a tenant expects to produce $250 psf in its store and is willing to pay 10 percent of its sales as occupancy costs. If add-ons are $15, that leaves only $10 psf for fixed minimum rent. If the landlord were able to reduce add-ons through the management of expenses and recoveries, the tenant would likely pay more in fixed minimum rent even though the tenant's total occupancy costs would not change.

Managing recoveries and related expenses in order to maximize rent will generally increase the value of the shopping center. Since rent and net operating income (NOI) often have a nearly 1:1 relationship—that is to say that rent flows directly to the bottom line—maximizing rent will increase NOI and, ultimately, value.

In most markets, tenants have competing retail venues available to them to locate a store. Landlords must also manage recoveries and quote rates with consideration to the rates offered by competing properties. Increasingly, regional shopping centers compete with community and power centers for the same tenants. This, too, has put pressure on landlords to manage add-ons and expenses.

ACCOUNTS RECEIVABLE

The most common method of monitoring accounts receivable is an aged receivable analysis ("aging"). This report groups outstanding tenant balances by the number of days the unpaid balance has been overdue. The headings for a typical aging are:

Tenant Name	Charge Type	Current Balance	Over 30 Days Old	Over 60 Days Old	Over 90 Days Old

The "Charge Type" column helps to segregate rents from add-ons and monthly charges from annual reconciliations. The "Current Balance" column usually sums up the charges billed in the month during which the aging is produced. Depending upon the billing practices of the landlord, this column could be misleading. For example, if a landlord bills May rents and produces an aging report on May 31, unpaid May rents might appear in the current column although they are probably 30 days if the shopping center leases require rent to be paid in advance on the first of the month. For this reason, as with any report, the users of the report need to be educated about how to gauge and assess the information presented.

Some landlords will also measure accounts receivable at a more "macro" level. One practice is to quantify how many days of revenue the outstanding receivable balances represent. This is accomplished by dividing a year's worth of tenant revenues, usually the current year's budget, by 365 and dividing the total accounts receivable balance by that result. For example, if a shopping center's annual tenant revenues are $1 million, then one day's revenue is $2,740. If the total unpaid tenant balances are $10,000, then accounts receivable are equal to 3.65 days of revenue. Performance benchmarks for this measurement are established internally, but indicators as low as 2.0 to 4.0 days can be found in the industry.

EXPENSE CONTROL

Landlords frequently separate expenses into two classifications: recoverable and nonrecoverable. Nonrecoverable expenses, of course, flow directly as a deduction from the bottom line. They might include professional fees such as those for legal service or repairs to the structure of the landlord's building. Most landlords will require third-party managers to provide separate reports on fees paid to the manager, whether recoverable or nonrecoverable under the shopping center leases.

Recoverable expenses are those for common area maintenance, real estate taxes and so on, which are reimbursed by tenant revenue. Over the last several years, many landlords have pursued programs and initiatives to reduce these expenses or to minimize increases from one year to the next. Therefore, an important component of monitoring expenses has become the analysis of expenditures over time and the success of programs to reduce expenses. If a landlord has several properties, this analysis is often presented as a cost per square foot so that performance can be compared among properties on a more equitable basis.

Another consideration in monitoring expense is following the guidelines established in both management agreements and tenant leases. Most management agreements provide that certain approvals must be secured from ownership if a proposed expense exceeds budget by some stated dollar amount or percentage. Compliance with the rules of those agreements is critical for any third-party manager. Additionally, where certain expenses are allowed as pass-throughs to the tenants, some tenant documents require that an annual budget be provided and that the tenant approve variances from the budget. Where this language is present, it is usually in older department store documents.

INSURANCE

Shopping center administration can support the landlord's risk management efforts by sound record keeping. As a rule, both contracts for service and tenant leases require that *certificates of insurance* be submitted to the landlord. These certificates are evidence that an insurance policy for a certain amount of coverage has been issued. Each certificate should be reviewed against the lease to ensure that the limits of coverage and carrier rating are correct. The shopping center administrator should also maintain a tickler file, sorted in order of the expiration dates of the tenants' and contractors' insurance, to ensure that all such required insurance remains in force.

Public safety officers at the shopping center will usually make a record of any incident that may represent a potential loss for the landlord. These incident records should be carefully maintained to be available in the event of an insurance claim or lawsuit. Similarly, preventive maintenance logs and inspection certificates should be properly filed and secured in case they are needed if a loss occurs.

BENCHMARKING

Benchmarking is the process of monitoring or measuring performance against some standard for performance. As most commonly used, the practice compares one entity's performance against that of another, as in a division of a company comparing itself to overall company results, or a company comparing itself to standards for its industry or a shopping center comparing itself to competing centers in the trade area.

As more and more shopping centers are owned and operated by publicly traded companies, a great deal of information about shopping center performance is becoming publicly available. Statistics such as occupancy, average rents, sales volume and sales productivity are regularly reported.

The availability of such information has made it possible for landlords to compare themselves to one another. Furthermore, the number of shopping centers included in these statistics has become large enough to be a very valid sample providing indicators of performance, or benchmarks, for comparisons of individual shopping centers.

Of course, care needs to be taken before comparing a shopping center to industry benchmarks. Perhaps the most important distinction is recognizing whether the data include results for regional malls, community centers, power centers, off-price centers or all of the above. Comparison of a power center's performance against the average performance of regional malls might be interesting but not necessarily meaningful. Understanding the definitions used to create a benchmark is also important. For instance, if one landlord includes theaters in its calculation of sales psf and another does not, a comparison between the two might be invalid.

But benchmarking does not need to be limited to comparison against the results of other landlords or managers. Internal benchmarking is a useful means of pursuing improvement in operating results. As an example, if accounts receivable averaged 4.0 days across ten different centers in the prior year, performance goals for the current year could be established requiring that all centers meet or exceed an average of 3.6 days—a 10 percent improvement over the prior year.

Reporting

FINANCIAL STATEMENTS

The basic financial statement package usually includes a balance sheet, an income statement and a statement of changes in financial position. The *balance sheet* is usually described as a "snapshot" of financial condition at a point in time, while an *income statement* summarizes the results of operations over a specified period of time. A *statement of changes in financial position* describes the reasons for differences between the balance sheet for one date and the balance sheet for an earlier date.

A balance sheet is presented in three sections, which are often stated as a formula: Assets = Liabilities + Owner's Equity. *Assets* are any owned physical object (tangible) or right (intangible) having monetary value. *Current assets* are those that can be converted into cash within twelve months. *Fixed assets* are less liquid and include things used in the operation of the business, such as buildings and equipment. *Liabilities* are the financial obligations of a business and are usually classified as either current or long-term. *Current liabilities* are obligations that must be met within twelve months; *long-term liabilities* are payable sometime beyond the next twelve months and usually include notes, loans or mortgages. *Owner's equity* is the owner's interest in the business after all other obligations are met, or the net value of the business to the owner.

The basic formula for an income statement is Revenue – Expense = Income. *Revenue*, for a shopping center, comprises the rents, add-ons and specialty leasing fees paid to the landlord. *Expenses* are the charges involved in running the business and do not generally include interest expense or depreciation. Income, or *net operating income* (NOI), is the difference between revenue and expense, sometimes called profit (or loss). NOI is often said to be before interest expense and depreciation if those items are not included in expense. Sometimes revenue, and therefore NOI, will exclude interest income as well.

Real estate investment trusts (REITs) use a measurement called funds from operations, or FFO. FFO equals net income (computed in accordance with generally accepted accounting principles), excluding gains (or losses) from debt restructuring and sales of property, plus depreciation and amortization, after adjustments for unconsolidated partnerships and joint ventures.

As stated earlier, the financial statements can be prepared using either cash basis or accrual basis accounting. Financial statements, particularly the income statement, are the landlord's "scorecard" for how the shopping center is performing.

CASH FLOW STATEMENT

Whether the shopping center's books and records are maintained on a cash or accrual basis, the landlord may require a cash flow statement or a cash flow analysis to be prepared from time to time. The *cash flow statement* presents cash inflows and outflows, netting out to available cash; a *cash flow analysis* is a projection of anticipated inflows, outflows and available cash. This analysis is essential for a landlord to plan distributions to partners or shareholders, to manage mortgage debt or to plan for major expenditures in the future.

VARIANCE ANALYSIS

Most landlords will require that actual financial results be compared to the budget or plan and that differences between the two be explained. *Variance analysis* is the explanation part. Good variance analysis describes the events or the change in circumstances that created a difference or that invalidated the original budget assumptions. Variance analysis must recognize relationships and trends. For instance, if the current year's average occupancy is higher than last year but the recovery ratio for CAM has dropped from 95 percent to 90 percent, the analysis must include an explanation.

Variance analysis explains both the "what" and the "why." For example, if a shopping center's NOI is less than budgeted for the same period, the analysis would have to describe:

- Which revenue sources were affected
- The impact of occupancy changes
- Which expenses were involved
- Whether the variance is temporary (timing), permanent or nonrecurring

Since occupancy and leasing are the primary drivers of NOI, any such changes would have to be further explained, to include:

- Changes in rental rates, whether for proposed or existing tenants
- Changes in the assumptions for renewals
- Changes in the assumptions for store closings

- Changes in the assumptions for new stores, whether location or timing

Detailed variance analysis is valuable when it provides adequate information for the landlord to change its plans or to take action correcting an unfavorable situation or capitalizing on a favorable one. If NOI is lower than budget because of unexpected store closings, the landlord will ensure that leasing efforts are focused on replacing those stores in addition to the planned leasing program. If specialty leasing revenues are better than plan because of unexpected demand, the landlord may add additional specialty leasing units to the center even though those units were not anticipated in the current year budget. If heavier than usual snowfall created an onerous increase in CAM expense, the landlord might choose to defer a different expense to the next year.

The contribution made by the shopping center administration through variance analysis or any other activity is to help the landlord protect its assets and maximize the value of its property.

Summary

The principal activities of shopping center management are to meet the landlord's objectives for the property and to secure the landlord's rights under the various documents of the property. Administration supports these activities. Through planning, monitoring and reporting, administration provides the means for management to be accountable to ownership. Through the implementation aspect of administration, management safeguards the landlord's rights under leases, reciprocal easement agreements, contracts and other documents. Thus, successful administration is critical to successful shopping center management.

Resources

The A.M. Best Company quantitatively and qualitatively evaluates the financial condition of insurance carriers and publishes ratings.

The International Council of Shopping Centers (ICSC) publishes *The SCORE*, a handbook on shopping center operations, revenues and expenses. In this publication, data for strip centers and enclosed centers are classified separately, and then further classified by size of center. *The SCORE* provides statistics at summary and detail levels.

Recommended Readings

Alexander, Alan A., SCSM. *Shopping Center Rent Administration: A Manager's Guide to Avoiding Cash-Flow Problems.* New York: International Council of Shopping Centers, 1990.

Alexander, Alan A., SCSM, and Richard F. Muhlebach, SCSM. *Operating Small Shopping Centers.* New York: International Council of Shopping Centers, 1997.

Fundamentals of Shopping Center Management. Audiocassettes. New York: International Council of Shopping Centers, 1983.

ICSC Keys to Shopping Center Management Series. New York: International Council of Shopping Centers, 1992.

The SCORE: ICSC's Handbook on Shopping Center Operations, Revenues and Expenses. New York: International Council of Shopping Centers.

This chapter was contributed by Kate M. Sheehy, Vice President, Lend Lease Real Estate Investments, Inc., Atlanta, Georgia.

6 | Marketing

Marcy Carter-Lovick, SCMD

Marketing may be the most misunderstood term in the shopping center vocabulary.

Definitions of marketing vary by type of center, by market and by the general philosophy of the center management firm and/or owner. The perception of marketing's role varies greatly by the perspective of the observer; retailers, center owners, consumers and the various disciplines of the center's management team—leasing, specialty leasing, development, construction, tenant coordination, operations and management, legal, accounting and security—all have differing viewpoints regarding the proper application and execution of marketing.

Marketing encompasses a diverse and extensive list of activities within the shopping center industry. Marketing is often defined as one or more of its many components—advertising, sales promotion, special events, media planning and buys, community and public relations, crisis communications, gift certificate sales, merchant relations, investor relations, leasing support, seasonal decor, retail sales associate training, customer service, visual merchandising and merchants' association activities are all included within the scope of marketing by many shopping center owners and management firms.

The implementation of marketing continues to change rapidly within the shopping center industry, as consumer behavioral changes and new technology intersect to bring both new challenges and new solutions.

Shopping center marketing is subject to both trends and fads as new ideas surface and old ideas are recycled by new generations of marketing professionals.

This chapter will examine the history of shopping center marketing in relationship to its current role, some of the challenges faced by marketing today, the role of the marketing director and the fundamental basis of marketing programs—the marketing plan.

To fully understand marketing's current role, and where it may be headed in the next century, a look back at its history may be helpful.

The "Roots" of Shopping Center Marketing

The first marketing programs—established in the middle of this century—were coordinated by a center's merchants' association. Merchants banded together in loosely organized groups to address those issues of common concern, such as security, common area maintenance and promotion of the shopping center, which were not addressed by the landlord in the center lease at that time.

In its earliest days, shopping center marketing was dominated by special events. The merchants' association board of directors, or the promotion director hired by the association, vied to be the first in its market to host the latest special attraction—activities and appearances which ranged from circuses and animal acts to fireworks displays and military bands.

As shopping center programs became more commonplace, those responsible for the marketing function began to use newspaper and radio advertising to support the calendar of special events.

The merchants' association also became more structured, with many organizations adopting a charter and bylaws to govern their activities. Landlords began to include a standard clause in the majority of leases, requiring the participation of center merchants in the association and establishing a set financial contribution for both the retailer and, in some instances, the landlord.

Cooperative advertising pieces became a dominant marketing tool in the 1960s, as the center retailers banded together to group their individual ads under a common banner, resulting in the familiar "box ad page," or behind a common cover page, thereby creating a multipage flyer or tabloid insert.

As center merchants reported success with these grouped efforts, landlords again responded by adding a cooperative advertising clause to many of their leases, requiring center merchants to participate in a specified number of cooperative efforts per year.

In the early 1970s, many landlords began replacing the standard merchants' association lease clause with a clause specifying the establishment of a common marketing fund to promote the shopping center. Merchants' associations were, and still are, required to file a tax return annually, paying taxes on any unspent funds, a requirement which often meant funds were spent at the end of the association's fiscal year on programs which might not have been considered under less "taxing" circumstances. Since marketing funds are not subject to the same tax parameters as merchants' associations, the new format was appealing to both retailers and landlords. The landlord also agreed to assume the administration and any resulting liability of the marketing funds and programs. The role of the retailer shifted from one of day-to-day administration and approval of all programming, budgeting and accounting—typically accomplished through a voting process—to one of adviser on the retail marketing environment.

With this shift, most promotion directors now reported to the landlord, often as an employee of the management firm for the center, rather than to the association board of directors. During this same general time period, the job title of the center's "promotion director" was changed to "marketing director," and the position's job duties were expanded to encompass such things as market research and strategic planning duties, as well as the implementation of special events and advertising.

During the late 1970s and early 1980s, cooperative advertising efforts continued to dominate center marketing strategies, becoming more and more "slick" as shopping center programs emulated the glossy catalogs and magazines produced by retailers. As the quality of these advertising vehicles increased, so did the costs of participation by the center retailers.

The mid- to late 1980s brought a backlash to these increased costs by center retailers. Retailers found that the increased costs were not always reflected in increased results for their individual shopping center locations. Cooperative advertising pieces fell out of favor, as shopping center marketing professionals sought other strategies to meet retailers' needs. Lease clauses changed once again, as many landlords eliminated the cooperative advertising clause, replacing it with a common advertising fund. The common advertising fund required center retailers to pay an additional charge of a specified amount that would be used to advertise and promote the shopping center as a whole. The common advertising fund differed from the marketing fund clause in the manner in which the funds collected could be used. Marketing fund or merchants' association dollars may be used to fund a number of different expenses, such as administrative expenses (salaries, rent, office expenses), seasonal decor, market research and public relations in addition to advertising and promotion. For the most part, advertising funds are earmarked for sales promotion, advertising and related expenses such as production costs of the advertising.

With the advent of the common advertising fund, shopping centers began to explore a wider range of marketing tactics. Budgets in the 1990s permitted a number of centers to utilize television, direct mail, premiums with purchase and long-term, sophisticated campaigns such as frequent shopper (loyalty) programs.

Funding Marketing Efforts Today

Although all leases vary significantly, *existing* shopping center leases may contain the following minimum requirements for marketing:

1. *Establishment of a marketing fund and/or merchants' association at the landlord's discretion.* If established, the merchant is required to pay a specified dollar amount to the fund or association. The landlord contributes to the fund or association on a specified matching basis, and may contribute "in-kind" services or supplies in lieu of a cash contribution. The contribution by both the merchant and the landlord is typically subject to Consumer Price Index (CPI) increases on an annual basis.

2. *Establishment of a common advertising/promotion fund.* The contribution by the retailer (and any matching contribution by the landlord) is typically based on an amount per square foot, tied to a sliding scale by size of space. The contribution is subject to CPI increases on an annual basis.

3. *Initial assessment.* The retailer is obligated to pay a one-time charge to fund the marketing portion of the grand opening of the shopping center. Some leases allow an initial assessment with the addition of each new department store and accompanying small shop space and/or with the renovation/remodeling of the center.

The funding of marketing is currently undergoing a major change. As retail profit margins are squeezed, retailers are subjecting all expenses to additional scrutiny. Lease-required marketing expenses have been one of the first cost items to be questioned, as many chains spend significant dollars to market their stores on a national and/or regional basis. Lease negotiations have resulted in decreased contributions for marketing, or the elimination of marketing clauses from leases. In some cases, retailers have negotiated for a "gross lease" with the landlord, in which the tenant pays one fixed amount, which is then allocated by the landlord to the appropriate expense areas.

The return to gross leases by some landlords creates a new chapter in shopping center marketing. With true gross leases, funds for marketing and advertising are no longer specified in the lease. Companies using this approach report a whole new methodology of funding for marketing. Center marketing professionals prepare a request for funding detailing the manner in which the funds will be used, and then petition the ownership for an allocation of a portion of rental income to fund that specific program. This approach ushers in a new era of accountability and innovation for marketing.

Today, with this new accountability, it's critical that the confusion over marketing's role be eliminated. While the *execution* of marketing should vary by the situation, all shopping center marketing has a common denominator in its fundamental role. Marketing's fundamental role is to *increase center value.*

Marketing's Contribution to Increased Center Value

Since center value is directly tied to the net operating income (NOI) for the center, marketing has to contribute to the achievement of the center's NOI. Marketing's ability to contribute to NOI can be categorized within three areas on the income side, and three areas of expense control, as outlined below.

Income:
1. Fixed minimum rent
2. Overage rent
3. Miscellaneous income

Expense Control:
1. Loss prevention
2. Elimination of landlord subsidies due to overspending
3. Elimination of additional landlord funding requests

Marketing can make a significant contribution within each of these areas. The impact of the contribution will vary with the circumstances of the specific situation.

Increasing Center Value Through Income

FIXED MINIMUM RENT

The area of fixed minimum rent (FMR) typically makes the most significant impact on the center's NOI. Marketing can make a meaningful contribution to the center's FMR in three key ways:

1. Driving sales growth to drive fixed minimum rental rates
2. Tenant retention (income preservation)
3. Marketing the center and its available space to key potential retailers (leasing support)

Driving Sales to Drive Rents. Since retailers can only afford to pay 10 percent* or less of gross sales in rent and additional occupancy charges, the sales per square foot achieved by the center are critical to rental rates. For example, a center achieving $300 per square foot in sales can support rents and charges of $30 per square foot, at a 10 percent occupancy rate. The higher the sales, the higher the rent that may be charged at that property. This principle is especially important when a center is approaching a time period with a significant number of lease renewals.

The following example illustrates the significant impact that a 3 percent increase in sales can have on fixed minimum rent and center value in a renewal situation. The example uses the following assumptions:

Mall shop sales:	$298 per square foot
Center sales goal:	3 percent
Rent to sales ratio:	9 percent
Renewing and/or vacant mall shop gross leasable area (GLA):	135,000 square feet
Assumed cap rate:	8 percent

*Ten percent has been a frequently used benchmark for occupancy costs (rent-to-sales ratio). In today's retail environment, escalating expenses and shrinking profit margins have placed additional pressure on occupancy costs, with many retailers now striving to reduce occupancy costs to 8 percent or less.

To project the impact of the 3 percent sales gain on FMR and center value, first calculate the sales per square foot gain.

3% × $298 per square foot = $8.94 per square foot (additional sales)

Next, multiply the rent-to-sales ratio percentage by the additional sales gain per square foot to determine the potential increase in rent per square foot.

$8.94 per square foot × 9% = $0.80 rent increase per square foot

The third step multiplies the potential rental increase per square foot times the available mall shop gross leasable area (GLA) to determine the total rental income gain.

$0.80 per square foot × 135,000 square feet = $108,000

In the final step of the process, divide the total rent gain from step 3 above by the center's assumed cap rate of 8 percent to calculate the increase in center value.

$108,000 ÷ 8 percent = $1,350,000 additional center value created

Tenant Retention. The unplanned loss of a shopping center retailer may be very costly to the center, in terms of both consumer and retailer perception, lost rental income and increased leasing expenses.

Marketing can play an important role in preventing unplanned vacancy. The first step is to ensure that each new retailer is launched at the center with the appropriate measures. This typically involves offering the retailer information and assistance in planning an appropriate grand opening/awareness campaign for the store/product line at the center.

The second key to tenant retention is the consistent monitoring of store sales performance, to identify any retailers who may be in danger of closing their location due to sales productivity issues. As retailers are identified, marketing can offer information and expertise in specific areas to help the retailer improve its sales productivity. Assistance may range from helping the retailer develop a marketing plan appropriate for the product line and the market to providing a list of local resources for visual merchandising talent and props.

The third area in which marketing plays a key role in tenant retention is that of goodwill. Stores that are profitable, but not meeting company goals, may be influenced to give the center an additional trial period if the retailer has a good relationship with the center owner/management company. The burden of relationship building often falls primarily on the local management/marketing team.

Leasing Support. Offering a merchandise mix consistent with the consumer's needs and desires is one of the keys to a successful shopping center. While some shopping center marketing personnel do have hands-on leasing responsibilities, most on-site marketing people can impact merchandise mix and NOI for the center by identifying key retailers needed to fill voids in the mix, communicating that need on a consistent, factual basis to the center's leasing team and then providing the marketing support needed to recruit that retailer for the center. In this instance, marketing support may consist of providing customized demographics and economic market facts, along with information on the center and its customers, in packaging appropriate for the targeted retailer. In addition, the importance of "curb appeal" in leasing cannot be overlooked. Marketing makes a significant contribution to leasing and the curb appeal of the shopping center through appropriate barricade treatments for vacant spaces, seasonal decor and color (banners, flags and/or flowers for planter beds) and professional communication (signs, brochures).

OVERAGE RENT

Overage rental income can be a significant factor for many mature centers. By lease, many retailers pay a specified percentage of their sales as additional rent to the center owner when they reach a predetermined level of sales. In centers with this potential opportunity, the marketing team has a clear picture of the way in which to contribute to NOI and increased center value. For every dollar in sales that an overage rent–producing retailer achieves over the benchmark, the center's value is increased. Marketing's focus on increasing sales for these retailers results in a direct contribution to the center's NOI.

In the following illustration, the impact of a 5 percent increase in sales for an overage rent merchant, and the resulting increase in center value, is calculated. The example is based on the following assumptions:

Annual breakpoint:	$480,000
Overage percentage rate:	6 percent
Projected annual sales:	$680,400
Projected overage rent:	$12,024
Assumed cap rate:	8 percent

In this example, the retailer is projected to achieve $680,400 in annual sales. At that sales level, this retailer will pay $12,024 in overage rent for the example year. If the retailer's sales can be increased by 5 percent over the projected level, to $714,420, the overage rent paid by the retailer will increase by $2,041, to a total of $14,065 for the example year. To determine the impact on center value of this increased overage rent, divide the increased overage rent of $2,041 by the assumed cap rate of 8 percent, which results in $25,512 in increased center value.

MISCELLANEOUS INCOME

Through the years, marketing has developed a real talent for creating miscellaneous income using the center common area. Marketing first experimented in this area in an effort to increase marketing budgets. Christmas tree sales on the parking lot, Easter and Christmas photo sales, kiddie trains and income-producing shows such as car shows, home improvement shows, arts and crafts shows, antique shows and travel shows have all been used in years past to supplement marketing budgets.

Marketing became so good at creating additional funding through these activities that they may be income areas for the center owner. For example, a car show with eighty autos at $100 rental income per car per day will generate total income of $32,000 in a four-day time period. Using an assumed cap rate of 8 percent, that $32,000 in additional income equates to an increase in center value of $400,000! In some companies, ownership pays the marketing fund or merchants' association a percentage of the income generated, as a commission for the creation of that income.

In many companies these funds continue to be an important contribution by marketing to the center's NOI, while some companies have shifted responsibility for miscellaneous income generation to the specialty leasing (temporary tenant leasing) area.

Increasing Center Value Through Expense Control

While marketing is typically not thought of as a key element of NOI on the expense side, marketing can make a contribution.

LOSS PREVENTION

Lawsuits resulting from the marketing program can be costly. Marketing can limit losses through careful attention to all local, state and federal laws and regulations governing contests, giveaways and activities. In addition, marketing personnel should require a signed marketing license agreement from all participants in any marketing activity, along with a certificate of insurance.

RESPONSIBLE FISCAL MANAGEMENT

Staying within the marketing fund budget is a basic, straightforward way to control expenses, thereby avoiding the necessity of a landlord subsidy to cover overexpenditures and the resultant negative impact on the center's NOI. The center's marketing team will need to closely monitor marketing income, as well as expenses, to ensure that funds are collected as projected. If the funds received do not meet projections, planned expenses will need to be reduced to remain consistent with the income received.

ADDITIONAL LANDLORD FUNDING REQUESTS

Requests for additional landlord funding for special marketing programs may be warranted in certain specific situations. It's important to remember that any additional funding provided to marketing by the center owner lowers the NOI for the center for the year in which the contribution is made, unless the marketing program funded can produce at least enough income to replace the funds contributed.

In the real world, it's very difficult to create a marketing program that can directly offset the additional funding on a short-term basis. Many of the marketing programs financed by additional landlord contributions in the past, such as holiday decor or awareness campaigns, have an indirect, long-term impact on the center's growth that is difficult to measure.

When considering an additional landlord funding request, it's helpful to project the income impact of the requested funds, and translate that amount to increased center value. For example, assume that a center is contemplating a new holiday decor package that will require an additional landlord contribution in the amount of $100,000. (At an assumed cap rate of 8 percent, that contribution is actually worth $1,250,000 in center value to the center owner.) The center's marketing director projects that the new holiday decor package will enable the center to achieve an additional 10 percent sales increase, over and above the projected sales that would occur without the new decor package. This 10 percent increase will mean an additional $31 per square foot, bringing center annual sales per square foot to $343. With a rent-to-sales ratio for the center of 10 percent and 20,000 square feet of vacancy, the 10 percent sales gain will translate to $3.10 in additional rent per square foot and an increased center value of $775,000. The increased rental income will not help offset the additional landlord expense though, since it will not occur until the year following the decor investment. The marketing director also reviews the impact the increased sales will have on overage rental income, which will occur in the same fiscal time period as the investment. He or she finds that eight of the center's retailers who are significant overage rent players are also peak-selling merchants during the holiday season. After factoring their various breakpoints, percentage rates and annual sales volumes, the marketing director determines that these eight retailers will pay an additional $30,000 in overage rent as a result of the additional 10 percent sales gain. With an assumed cap rate of 8 percent, the $30,000 translates to an additional $375,000 in center value—still far short of the $100,000 owner contribution, which equates to $1,250,000 in center value at the assumed cap rate. A discussion with the center's asset manager will be necessary to determine whether the owner will be interested in a two-year return on the investment, through the combination of lease-up and overage rent, to justify the additional expenditure.

The Marketing Plan

What can be done to ensure that marketing programs are properly focused on the most significant opportunities to increase center NOI and value? Marketing's best and most basic tool is the center's marketing plan.

The marketing plan is a comprehensive, written document detailing needed actions for the center. The marketing plan consists of five key parts:

1. The situation analysis
2. Identification of problems and opportunities
3. Goals and objectives
4. Strategies
5. Tactics

The most effective marketing plans are typically those which are developed with team involvement. An effective planning team will include not only marketing specialists, but representatives of the center's management/operations, leasing and asset management teams at a minimum, with additional disciplines represented as appropriate for the center's circumstances. For example, a center with a planned renovation/expansion would definitely want to include a representative from development and construction on the planning team when preparing the center's marketing plan. Ideally, the entire team is involved in the first three steps of the marketing plan preparation: situation analysis, identification of problems and opportunities and establishment of goals and objectives. With these three sections completed, the individuals directly responsible for the marketing of the center complete the planning process with the development of the center's marketing strategies and tactical plans. Some companies accomplish the first three steps as a part of the preparation of the annual business plan, with each department (marketing, leasing, operations) then producing a departmental plan encompassing strategies and tactics.

THE SITUATION ANALYSIS

The first section of the marketing plan—situation analysis—is a thorough review of all facts regarding the center, the market, the customer, the competition and the resources available to assist in the marketing of the center. During this part of the planning process, the marketing planning team should review all market research (both primary data gathered by the center itself—telephone studies, focus groups, customer intercept studies, etc.—and secondary data collected from the U.S. Census, Chambers of Commerce, state and local agencies, etc.) available for the center, a three- to five-year trend analysis of center sales, along with the current year sales report, an analysis of actual and projected overage rent, a list of lease renewals for the upcoming five-year period, center vacancies and the leasing depth chart for those vacancies, the center's occupancy costs analysis and evaluations of past marketing programs. During the situation analysis, asset management can provide input for the planning team on the owner's long-term strategy for the center. For example, an ownership strategy to hold the center for the long term, as opposed to a quick sale of the property, will make a critical difference to the planning team. Understanding the center owner's goals for the property as an investment ensures that the marketing plan developed is consistent with those goals.

PROBLEMS AND OPPORTUNITIES

During the second step in the development of the marketing plan, the planning team formally identifies problems (obstacles, challenges, threats or "blocks") facing the center, and opportunities that can be maximized to increase center value.

GOALS AND OBJECTIVES

Goals and objectives are a clear, written definition of what is going to be achieved for the center. Section 3 of the marketing plan specifies when these accomplishments will be achieved, but does not describe how they will be achieved.

Typically, the overall goal for the marketing plan coincides with the overall financial goal for the center. The overall goal is often expressed in terms of an increase within a specified time period for net operating income, or funds from operations (FFO). An example of an overall goal may read as follows: "Increase net operating income by 10 percent by December 31, 2000."

Objectives are a statement of the specific measurable achievements that will be undertaken to facilitate the achievement of the center's overall goal. An example of a marketing objective designed to support the example goal given above would be: "Increase mall shop sales per square foot by 10 percent by December 31, 2000."

Effective goals and objectives must be measurable, feasible, suitable, achievable, worthwhile and acceptable within company policy.

STRATEGIES

Section 4 of the marketing plan—strategies—is an outline of the approach that will be used to achieve the center's goals and objectives, given the specific set of circumstances detailed in the situation analysis. The strategic outline summarizes the general direction of the marketing program, but details are reserved for section 5 of the marketing plan—tactics.

An example of a strategy is as follows: "Increase cross-shopping for mall shops among department store customers."

TACTICS

Tactics are the detailed who, what, when and where of the marketing plan. Specifically, the tactics section of the marketing plan includes the center's calendar of advertising, sales promotions, special events, seasonal decor, merchant programs and community events, along with the budget necessary to produce those activities. The tactical section of the plan will include an advertising plan detailing both media buys and the creative message to be communicated, a merchant communication plan and a public relations plan.

Measurement of Marketing Results

The measurement of results from marketing plans and specific marketing programs has been an inexact and elusive science. Many long-term programs, such as awareness campaigns, can only be measured through costly research studies. And results measurement is often clouded by the fact that there are always many variables impacting sales productivity for center retailers at any one time. Even a "measurable" program's results may be attributed in part to uncontrollable factors such as the weather, an individual retailer's concurrent advertising or even something as simple as a public school holiday.

Technological advances, such as computerized daily sales reporting systems, have made the task of results measurement easier for shopping center marketing.

The "cost-to-sales" ratio is one of the most important barometers for shopping center marketing programs. Marketing professionals can use the analysis to determine the results of a particular program—i.e., what did it accomplish, and how much did it cost to achieve those results? A frequently used guideline, the cost-to-sales ratio, for an effective center program should be no greater than 0.25. In the following example, the cost-to-sales ratio is a very high 0.63.

In this illustration, a traditional gift-with-purchase program is planned. The premium will cost the marketing fund $5 per item, and will be offered to consumers for accumulated receipts totaling $75 or more. (The center's "normal" average purchase is $48; the required $75 expenditure to receive the free gift will generate plus-on-normal sales of $27 per participant.) The goal established for this program is to generate a total of $135,000 in plus-on-normal sales, requiring a response by 5,000 shoppers, each spending a minimum of $75.

Based on past experience, the marketing director projects a maximum of a 2 percent response rate for the program. Therefore, he or she will need to reach a minimum of 250,000 people with a message about the special offer a minimum of seven to eight times to achieve a purchase response from the required 5,000 people. In the example market, it will cost a minimum of $45,000 in media placement costs to reach 250,000 people at the required frequency. Advertising production and collaterals will cost an additional $15,000 for the program.

In total, this program will cost the center $85,000 to implement (premium costs plus media placement plus advertising production and collaterals) to achieve the projected $135,000 in plus-on-normal sales. Cost divided by sales delivers a cost-to-sales ratio of 0.63—far higher than the 0.25 or less benchmark.

With a thorough understanding of the cost-to-sales ratio, many marketing professionals have spent much of the 1990s searching for ways to increase sales at a reduced cost. "Shared" marketing programs and alternative funding sources are two of the primary approaches used thus far in the industry.

SHARED MARKETING PROGRAMS

Shared marketing programs have enabled centers to spread the cost of producing creative materials and collaterals over several centers. Shared campaigns can be very effective for groups of centers which are similar in type, mix, market and goals. Shared programs have been most successful for those programs which are more universal in nature, such as semiannual sidewalk or clearance sales.

By their nature, shared programs may be somewhat generic, requiring local customization to maximize their benefits for the individual center.

ALTERNATIVE FUNDING SOURCES

With the transfer of miscellaneous income from marketing to the owner, marketing has begun to explore new funding sources, such as trade-outs and "partnership" marketing.

Trade-outs, partnership marketing and cosponsorships have similar characteristics; the terms are often used interchangeably by the marketing team.

Trade-outs refer to those situations in which two parties exchange services or something of value, in such a manner that both parties benefit. For example, a local radio station may trade on-air time to be used by the shopping center at a later date for display space in the center during the radio ratings survey period. Both parties benefit, and no cash is exchanged.

In partnership marketing, two or more parties combine forces to implement a marketing program that will benefit all parties. In a recent example, a national credit card company partnered with a shopping center management firm to implement a holiday program in which gifts purchased with the credit card at center retailers would be wrapped for free. The program promoted the use of the credit card for purchases *and* encouraged gift purchases at center stores, so that both partners benefited equally.

Cosponsorships are only slightly different. All parties benefit from the program in exchange for some consideration in services or dollars, but cosponsors typically do not benefit on an equal basis. For example, a home improvement show sponsored by a shopping center may have several cosponsors, such as a local radio station, the local home builders' association, a regional shelter magazine, a local cable television channel or any number of other entities. The benefit to the cosponsors may be limited to exposure through a listing in event advertising and the cosponsors' association with the event.

Avoiding Common Marketing Plan Stumbling Blocks

Not all marketing plans are successful in the achievement of the desired results. There are a number of reasons why plans don't perform as intended. To facilitate the successful implementation of the marketing plan, be wary of the following common pitfalls, which can occur during the development and/or the implementation phase of the plan:

1. Key players on the center's team were not involved in the planning process.
2. Sufficient approvals by key executives and/or ownership were not secured.
3. The situation changed in some material way, making elements of the plan inappropriate.
4. Goals are not financially driven, or are inconsistent with the center's overall business/financial goals.
5. Strategies/tactics do not support the plan's goals and objectives.
6. Goals and objectives are not monitored on a regular basis.
7. Marketing is not held accountable for the achievement of the plan's goals and objectives.
8. The advertising/creative plan does not support the plan.
9. The media placement plan does not achieve market saturation with frequency and/or reach.

10. Marketing dollars are diverted from the agreed-upon plan to tactics which do not support the achievement of the plan.

The Role of the Marketing Director

While on-site staffing varies greatly by size and type of center, responsibility for the development of the center's marketing plan, as well as its implementation and the day-to-day administration of the marketing program, is typically assigned to the center's marketing director. Other titles may be used for the same position, such as marketing manager, director of retail sales or director of marketing.

In some instances, the marketing director may have a dual role, combined with center management duties. In other cases, a single marketing director may be assigned responsibility for a group of smaller centers in one geographic area. In larger centers, the marketing director may supervise a marketing secretary, an intern and/or one or more assistants.

SKILLS AND QUALIFICATIONS

With such a variety of responsibilities called for in shopping center marketing, what type of person is best suited for the role of marketing director? The marketing position requires an unusual combination of science and art. The development of the strategically correct marketing plan falls within the realm of science, while the effective supervision of the plan's implementation requires talents from the arts.

Many successful marketing directors have the ability to use both sides of the brain—they can make the switch from the technical, structured thinking necessary to correctly interpret research results and effectively translate those results into strategic plans for the center's long-term growth, to the creative thinking needed to communicate with creative resources and evaluate the output of those resources appropriately. Within the same hour of a typical day's schedule they may be called upon to write a press release on the latest fashion trends offered at center retailers and to calculate overage rent potential for those same apparel retailers. In many centers with an active merchants' association, this same marketing director often performs all accounting functions for the association.

Most successful marketing directors demonstrate good business sense, along with ample common sense. They have strong presentation/public speaking skills and very good "people" skills, with a proven track record in conflict resolution and sales. They are self-starters, good time managers and have a well-developed ability to "multitask." They find a business-oriented educational background and practical work experience in a related field very helpful.

A limited number of colleges and universities now offer a course curriculum that is shopping center specific. A business degree with an emphasis on sales and marketing is also an excellent choice. Many successful marketing directors have started with degrees in journalism, with an emphasis in public relations, and the liberal arts. Today, a number of shopping center-specific educational opportunities are also available to the marketing professional.

Marketing directors with prior work experience in retailing or sales-oriented positions have been particularly successful in the shopping center arena. A number of marketing directors have also entered the shopping center industry from marketing positions in hotels, banks, hospitals, department stores and convention and visitors' bureaus.

ICSC offers accreditation for those in the shopping center marketing field, with the designation of Certified Marketing Director, based on on-the-job experience and a comprehensive test of industry-specific knowledge. A senior-level designation is also offered to ensure continued professional growth.

THE MARKETING CAREER PATH

The career path for marketing directors can take any number of variations on three major routes. A marketing director may enter the profession as an assistant, assuming single-center responsibility as a marketing director when the appropriate experience has been gained. As the opportunity presents itself, the single-center marketing director may opt to:

1. Assume multicenter responsibility. Multicenter duties may be through a traditional position as regional marketing manager for a major shopping center owner, or through an assignment for a group of smaller centers within the local area in which the marketing director has primary accountability for marketing, while supervising one or more marketing assistants.

2. Move to another discipline within the shopping center industry. Many marketing directors have successfully advanced in their careers through a move to a shopping center management or leasing position.

3. Move to a larger, more complex center, or a larger market. As the marketing directors' skills and job-specific experience build, they may elect to change positions to continue their career development.

Challenges Faced by Marketing Today

Shopping center marketing faces a number of significant challenges as the new century approaches:

1. Changes in consumer shopping habits and behavior
2. Shrinking marketing budgets and increasing marketing costs
3. New technology requiring increased marketing sophistication
4. Increasing pressure to produce short-term, measurable results
5. Recruiting and retaining qualified marketing personnel

CHANGES IN CONSUMER SHOPPING HABITS AND BEHAVIOR

Marketing is challenged to find new ways to package the shopping experience. For some, the solution has been an increased emphasis on convenience or customer service, while others have found success with the new entertainment formats.

SHRINKING MARKETING BUDGETS AND INCREASED EXPENSES

New funding sources, new accountability and new marketing programs will be required to accomplish marketing's goal to increase center value.

NEW TECHNOLOGY

New technology in point-of-sale terminals, computers and the Internet will require increased sophistication and innovation by marketing personnel as they plan programs for the shopping center. New technology may provide the solution for shrinking budgets and increased costs. For example, database marketing programs currently being tested by several centers promise the potential of decreased communication costs as these programs reach maturity.

NEED FOR SHORT-TERM RESULTS

Many marketing plans are programmed to deliver long-term results, focusing on awareness, changes in consumer behavior and image (positioning). In today's investment arena of shopping center real estate investment trusts (REITs), mergers and acquisitions, short-term results are more in demand than long-term gains. Marketing must find new ways to shorten the impact cycle of programs, and/or create new short-term solutions to impact NOI.

RECRUITING AND RETAINING QUALIFIED MARKETING PERSONNEL

Position requirements and expectations may need to be refocused, as the labor market for highly qualified professionals becomes increasingly competitive.

Recommended Readings

Fraser, Kim A., SCMD. *Marketing Small Shopping Centers: How to Increase Retail Traffic and Sales.* New York: International Council of Shopping Centers, 1991.

Fundamentals of Shopping Center Marketing. Audiocassettes. New York: International Council of Shopping Centers, 1983.

ICSC Keys to Shopping Center Marketing Series. New York: International Council of Shopping Centers, 1993.

The Library of Shopping Center Marketing Forms. New York: International Council of Shopping Centers, 1992.

Maccardini, Rebecca L., CMD. *Merchants' Association or Marketing Fund: How to Make the Choice.* New York: International Council of Shopping Centers, 1988.

Reddington, Judith J., CMD, comp. *The ICSC Shopping Center Public Relations Handbook.* New York: International Council of Shopping Centers, 1992.

Roca, Ruben A., ed. *Market Research for Shopping Centers.* New York: International Council of Shopping Centers, 1980.

Shopping Center Niche Marketing: How to Find and Profit from Market Segments. New York: International Council of Shopping Centers, 1994.

This chapter was contributed by Marcy Carter-Lovick, SCMD, Principal, Carter Marketing Works, Southlake, Texas.

7 | Maintenance

Don Paul, CSM, RPA

Maintenance, as defined by Webster's dictionary, is "the act of maintaining; the state of being maintained; support; the upkeep of property or equipment." Maintenance is a necessary part of the shopping center business. However, many shopping center managers and operation managers (facility managers) view maintenance as a necessary evil. Management that disregards maintenance will eventually have nothing left worth managing. Shopping center managers need to change those views by demonstrating to owners just how important maintenance is to the overall success of the business. Management needs to develop a strong maintenance staff that understands how the shopping center functions and its interrelationship with retail tenants, customers, community and environment. Its style, location, climatic variations, and owner's philosophy largely determine the complexity of the maintenance of shopping centers. Maintenance is really part of the business. Maintenance can and does add value to the center.

Shopping Center Maintenance Goals

Management, through maintenance, must strive to ensure that the center's systems are running effectively in order to enhance the customer and tenant environment as well as preserve the owner's investment. It must strive to keep the maintenance functions behind the scenes so that customers and tenants can roam about the center without any annoyances, distractions or facility-related tie-ups. This goal is not based on a "wait till it breaks and then fix it" philosophy.

A well-run maintenance program addresses the following points:

- Maintains a proactive maintenance program
- Provides cross-training of maintenance employees to provide more flexibility in responding to center problems
- Emphasizes constant communication among all center operations, management and marketing departments, as well as ownership
- Constantly strives to identify areas in which greater efficiency and productivity can be achieved. Researches those areas and recommends appropriate actions to ownership
- Plans and develops a crisis maintenance management plan to be implemented in conjunction with the overall scope of the center's master plan

Landlord and Tenant Maintenance Obligations

In order to understand the responsibilities of the landlord, small stores and major department stores as they relate to the maintenance of the shopping center, management must first look to the leases and Agreements of Record such as declarations, reciprocal easement agreements (REAs), etc. These are the legal documents that the center manager must understand and abstract in order to be able to identify maintenance obligations of the landlord and tenant. The leases (which are between the owner and smaller tenants) and the REAs (which are typically between the owner and major department stores) outline and define those obligations in detail.

A typical lease would define the landlord's various obligations to maintain all of the common areas within and without the shopping center as they relate to the following categories:

- Heating, ventilation and air-conditioning (HVAC)
- Central plants
- Roof repairs
- Electrical repairs
- Interior and exterior lighting
- Plumbing
- Interior and exterior landscape
- Structural repairs
- Parking lot striping, lighting and pavement

- Equipment repairs to maintain the shopping center
- Sprinkler system
- Energy management system
- Alarm system
- Public-address/music system
- Sign repairs
- Seating/furniture of the common area
- All doors, including locks and hardware
- Snow removal
- Pest control
- Security and safety environment
- Elevators and escalators
- Rubbish removal
- Food court common area
- Truck docks

The center manager must keep in mind that while the list outlined above is extensive, it is important that he or she read, understand and abstract each and every lease between the landlord and tenants, as there are many exceptions. Typically, a center manager can use the following rule of thumb: if a maintenance function falls outside the tenant's lease line, then it is the landlord's responsibility to maintain that function, and the resulting expense is part of the common area operating budget.

Tenants' obligations are also spelled out within the body of the lease. A typical lease will require the tenant to maintain its premises, fixtures, signage, air-conditioning, lighting, storefronts, electrical system and plumbing in good repair and according to standards acceptable to the landlord.

The REAs will also define the maintenance obligations and responsibilities of each party to that agreement. Typically, an REA is between the owner and each of the major department stores and outparcels that are part of the shopping center complex. Under this agreement, the landlord typically is required to maintain all of the common areas surrounding the major department store/tenant building.

The Landlord's Accountability

The landlord, through its contractual obligations in the leases and REAs, must maintain a complete and detailed accounting of all the expenses that are chargeable to the common area budget. The center manager, with the help of his or her maintenance and administrative staffs, should keep detailed records of monies spent toward the maintenance and operation of the shopping center. At the beginning of each year, a budget that has been approved by the owner is the blueprint from which the shopping center is maintained, as outlined under the various contractual agreements. In addition to their rent, the tenants will pay additional charges on a monthly basis to cover the operating expenses of the shopping center. These tenants usually pay in advance. At year's end, they are either given an adjustment billing to cover the shortfall or receive a refund if the total expenses are less than budgeted. Below is a typical budget under which a center manager would operate his or her center:

Income
- Rental income
- Percentage rent
- Common area income
- Food court income
- Real estate tax income
- Utility income
- Other tenant charges
- Temporary tenant income
- Miscellaneous income

Common Area Expenses (subtracted from the total income)
- Administrative
- Janitorial/cleaning
- General building maintenance
- Interior and exterior landscaping
- Security
- Rubbish removal
- Snow removal
- Parking lot maintenance
- Payroll
- Employee benefits
- General insurance
- Professional services
- Utilities
- Real estate taxes
- Food court expenses

Net Operating Income

In the development of a net operating income statement, only items of income and expenses that are expected to occur in the annual operations of the shopping center should be included in determining the center's net operating income, as indicated below.*

Total Gross Income:
- Rental income
- Percentage rent
- Common area income
- Food court income
- Real estate tax income
- Utility income
- Other tenant charges
- Temporary tenant income
- Miscellaneous income

Total Operating Expenses:
- Administrative
- Housekeeping
- General building maintenance
- Landscaping
- Security
- Trash removal
- Snow removal
- Parking lot maintenance
- Payroll (including payroll benefits)
- Insurance
- Professional services (consultants)
- Utilities
- Real estate taxes
- Food court expenses

Foundation of the Maintenance Department

Each center's maintenance and housekeeping departments will vary in size and skill level depending on the size and complexity of the shopping center. Management must balance the requirement to maintain the building according to the leases, REAs and owner's standards with

---

* Net operating income is the gross income less total operating expenses.

the cost to operate and implement those systems. Staffing for the various functions can be divided into three categories:

- Totally staffed by in-house personnel
- Totally staffed by outsourcing the personnel
- A combination of the two

In determining the approach that management wants to take in staffing and implementing the maintenance and housekeeping functions of the shopping center, it is important to compare costs by evaluating in-house costs first. Consider the following criteria:

- Personnel staffing requirement (based on total hours needed rather than by number of forty-hour/week people)
- Employee benefits
- Cost of supplies and materials, including any up-front capital costs, with depreciation over three years
- Uniform costs
- Training costs
- Workers' compensation insurance
- Administration time involved in handling personnel matters and paperwork
- Manager's time involved in hiring and terminations
- Turnover
- Americans with Disabilities Act (ADA) compliance

Once you have considered these issues, you need to address some of the following questions:

- What is your core business or responsibility as the manager of the center? What does ownership want you to emphasize? Evaluate the time that is needed to accomplish these tasks.
- What is the employment/labor market in your area? Is there high or low unemployment?
- Are the tasks that need to be performed of a specialized nature or of an infrequent time frame? You could just pay for that service one time rather than carry the payroll year-round. For instance, do you want to buy and maintain snow removal equipment year-round to be used for just two or three snowfalls a year? Yet you may be in an area where snowfall is a major factor and where maintaining the equipment is a necessity, as there is a limited supply of companies that can

provide services to you because they are needed to maintain the major roadways.

- What will it cost in payroll dollars to hire the expertise to manage or oversee certain maintenance functions, such as landscaping, pest control and insecticide application?
- Is there growth opportunity for your staff, so as to avoid turnover?
- Is your company willing to train and develop the personnel at your site to keep up with the latest technologies?
- Does the location/market of your center prevent outsourcing companies from wanting to or being able to travel to your center?
- What are ownership's goals and objectives for the property?
- How do you balance the need to achieve the goals and objectives versus managing personnel?
- Is the property a real estate investment trust (REIT) or is it privately owned? Properties in REIT tend to be more income driven, thus ownership may demand that you concentrate on income-producing efforts rather than managing personnel.
- Do the size and the sales volume of the center allow you to maintain skilled in-house personnel and still focus on your core goals and objectives?
- Due to the high visibility of your property, may outsourcing companies price their services lower just to say that the center is their customer—a form of advertisement for them?

After you calculate the above numbers and dollars, you can determine which course of action to take. The most common approach is a combination of in-house staff and outsourcing of services. There is no one answer as to which services should be handled in-house and which services should be outsourced.

Tasks Performed in Key Maintenance Areas

JANITORIAL/CLEANING

One of the most defining areas that sets various shopping centers apart is the quality of the housekeeping at the center. To understand how to maintain a cleaning standard that is acceptable to the tenants and customers, management must have a detailed set of procedures for the staff to follow. Of utmost importance is the need for management to inspect daily the interior and exterior common areas before the center opens for business. Management must have a diligent routine of walking and inspecting the exterior grounds, truck docks, parking areas, back hallways, rest rooms, fountains, doors, windows, tenant storefronts and trash cans. This will assure the manager that the center is ready for customers and the environment is free of any hazards.

Also, management must provide tasks each day to the housekeeping staff. For example, daily tasks could include emptying all trash containers, clearing all truck docks of debris, cleaning all center door windows before 9 A.M., policing and picking up litter from the common area parking lot and cleaning all rest room fixtures. Nightly tasks could include scrubbing and mopping the center's common area walkways and food court floors, wiping down and cleaning all chairs and tables, cleaning all trash cans, pressure washing all entrance ways and removing all gum, drinks, spills and so on. Daily tasks in the food court could include washing and cleaning all tables and chairs within the seating area, checking and emptying all trash cans on a regular basis, cleaning and returning all food trays to the respective tenants and mopping all spills immediately.

GENERAL MAINTENANCE

It is also very important to check the operating status of all items within the center on a daily basis. Each maintenance staff member should have routines to follow. This will assure management that the building is being maintained and that no item is neglected. If operational problems are neglected, they can become safety hazards and/or liability issues as well as major expenditures. Following are suggested items the maintenance staff should have scheduled rounds to inspect and repair, among others.

Daily:
- Inspect rest rooms and make sure fixtures are running properly.
- Inspect and repair all door handles, hinges, glass, closures, etc., including public entrances and service entrance doors.
- Check and clean out all water fountains within the common area.
- Check for broken irrigation fixtures to prevent water waste.
- Check the parking lot for potholes, broken curbs, etc. Have security check the parking and building lights nightly to ensure that none are out and no safety hazards exist.

- Check for any safety hazards. These include broken tiles, torn carpet, cracks in the sidewalk, etc.
- When it snows, lay down chemicals at entranceways to prevent slips and falls each day. Change floor mats, as they become wet and dirty during heavy snowfall days.

Monthly:
- Check the roof for debris left by outside workers.
- Check all common area HVAC units and replace filters. Perform the preventative maintenance program as outlined.
- Check all fire extinguishers and smoke alarms.

LIGHTING

Planned lighting and group relamping maintenance programs provide the shopping center manager with cost controls and uniform lighting levels throughout the center. Most planned lighting and maintenance programs consist of three key elements:

- Scheduled group relampings
- Scheduled repair services
- Emergency response provisions due to security or lightning strike problems. (In many states, lightning strikes are serious problems. For example, lightning can hit the parking lot light poles and completely burn out a whole section of parking lot lights, thus creating a security issue for evening customers. Therefore, a backup system must be in place to respond to this crisis, such as an on-call electrical company, parts and materials in stock, or a company from which temporary lights can be ordered to supplement the regular parking lot lights until they can be repaired.)

It is important to schedule the mass replacement of aging and inefficient lamps before they fail. Within the center, the primary loss of light levels is due either to lamp lumen efficiency depreciation after the initial installation, to lamps becoming dusty, dirty and covered with grime or from poor maintenance or to failure to replace defective ballasts immediately.

The shopping center manager should keep in mind the many benefits of planning scheduled lighting maintenance programs. Through these programs, management can realize cost reductions, and budget projections become more predictable and easier to control. Additionally, planned services can be performed during nonbusiness hours to minimize disruption, and inventories of lamps and ballasts can be maintained at a reduced level to prevent breakage.

LANDSCAPING

Like the janitorial functions, proper landscaping maintenance can distinguish your shopping center from the rest of the competition. Yet if it is not kept up, the appearance of the landscape can have a deterrent effect on your customers.

Interior Landscaping. When evaluating your interior landscaping program, some of the basic elements to be considered are as follows.

- Potted landscape plants can define seating areas without developing permanent barriers. For example, plants and benches can create a seating area in front of a coffee shop to encourage customers to stay longer at the center as well as help tenant sales.
- Potted plants can be moved or removed depending on the season, the type of marketing promotion or the expanding merchandise units.
- Keep the plants clean and free of dust and insects. If you don't, the investment you made to upgrade the appearance of the center will be short-lived.
- Rotate plants on a regular basis. Don't overwater them. This will encourage roaches and other insects to infest the planters.
- Always use indoor plants that are able to survive in low-light areas.
- Avoid high and dense plants in front of storefronts, as this will block the visibility of the tenants' signs.
- Avoid using live plants in high hanging baskets, especially around railings in two-level malls. Permanent silk flowers can be installed that will still create the feeling of greenery. By installing permanent silk flowers in high areas, you can reduce labor time needed to water and care for them. You avoid the chance of leaking containers that could create slip-and-fall water spots on the walkways below.
- Seasonal flowers can be used to enhance certain events during the year. Poinsettias can be used at Christmas. Mums can be used to kick off springtime promotions. These are a great addition, especially after a long winter.
- Potted plants can be used to reduce liability by creating natural barriers around architectural designs and to signal changes in elevations within walkways.

• Caution: When buying and placing plant containers, be aware of ADA requirements. You do not want to create a traffic hazard for people going through the mall.

Exterior Landscaping. One of the first impressions that a customer has of your center is the exterior landscaping. The appearance and maintenance of your exterior landscape send a signal to your customers and tenants that your property is a place to come to and stay in awhile. It softens the feel of all the exterior asphalt in the parking lot. It can hide building flaws. It can announce mall entrances. It can provide color and greenery to an otherwise poor architectural design. But landscaping needs to be planned and maintained in a way that will not create liability or unusual maintenance problems.

Only consider those plants and trees that are common to the geographic region. You need to consider the weather conditions, the amount of rainfall and the amount of snowfall. Keep trees away from parking lot light poles. At nighttime, they can create liability issues. Avoid trees whose roots are shallow. These can cause eruptions in your parking lot and create additional liability issues from trips and falls. Avoid dirty trees, such as ones that create berries that may damage the paint on cars. Create barriers around tree islands so that snow removal equipment does not damage your landscaping. Keep trees pruned above eight feet to avoid dangerous limbs. Watch for dead tree limbs that can fall and injure customers or damage cars.

HEATING, VENTILATION AND AIR-CONDITIONING (HVAC)

While janitorial and landscaping services can set the standard for the appearance of your property, the quality of the environment which your customers and tenants experience depends on the quality of your HVAC maintenance program. In today's building design, conditioning the environment in the building is becoming a much more important aspect of building management. Issues such as "sick building syndrome," climate control for indoor plants and control of energy costs are all related to the maintenance of your HVAC system.

The type of HVAC systems within shopping centers is usually based on the age, location and type of building. For example, some centers have central plant equipment in which the air-conditioning and heating are controlled out of a central location and supplied to the tenants and common area through a piping system via chilled water or steam heat. In some areas, gas may be used for heating if it is available and cost-efficient. Some centers utilize individual package units, as opposed to a central plant, which provide the heating and air-conditioning for both the tenants and the common areas.

No matter what the system, there are a few basic items that every manager needs to keep in mind:

• The number one cause of air-conditioning compressor failure is dirty air filters. The second is loose belts.

• Replacing any HVAC equipment more than twelve years old is generally a good investment since you will have reduced maintenance costs and increased energy efficiency.

• Keep thermostats away from high customer traffic areas and inaccessible to employees. Everyone loves to play with thermostats and no two people have the same air-conditioning needs. An automatic energy management system is one alternative.

• Establish preventive maintenance programs for HVAC equipment. Regular maintenance pays off in reliable operations, fewer breakdowns and longer life. Evaluate your program from time to time and make any required modifications.

• Know the brand of your HVAC equipment. All brands have certain idiosyncrasies that require special attention in certain areas.

• If you are outsourcing, be sure the contractor is performing as contracted.

• Be aware of the pending Environmental Protection Agency (EPA) rules as they relate to the use of various refrigerants known under such brand names as Freon, Genetron and Isotron.

• Be willing to pay the price for quality HVAC preventive maintenance programs. There is nothing more disconcerting to a tenant or a customer than being too cold during the winter months or too hot during the summer months due to HVAC breakdowns.

ROOFS

Roof maintenance can be one of the most neglected aspects of shopping center management and ownership. The roof is out of sight, and oftentimes out of mind—until there is a roof leak. Not only are roof leaks unsightly, but they can increase your liability insurance due to slips and falls in the common area. How does a good shopping center maintenance program prevent and anticipate roof repair needs? By having someone walk the roof on a regular basis, all four seasons of the year. Some thoughts on roof maintenance and how to keep the major costs at bay follow:

- No roof bond or guarantee keeps water out of a building.
- The number one cause of failure is poor workmanship during installation.
- The number two cause of failure is inadequate maintenance.
- When making your routine inspections, note any splits, bubbles, low spots, blocked drains and new penetrations such as antennas, fan ducts, satellite dishes, etc.
- The roofing system is a major factor in the energy consumption of any shopping center.
- Roof drains need to be inspected monthly to ensure that they are free of debris to allow for quick drainage during and after rainfall.
- HVAC repair workers are one of the major causes of roof problems. They often do not pick up discarded tools, screws, trash and other types of materials that can wreak havoc on your roofing system, especially on a single-ply roofing system.

In summary, if you have an effective roof management program, you can lower your life-cycle roofing costs significantly. Your demand for emergency leak repairs should be drastically reduced. You should then be able to project your specific needs and budgets on an annual basis with very few surprises. You will require less labor and less money to perform the roofing management function over time.

PARKING LOTS

Besides the roof, the next most neglected area of shopping center maintenance is the parking lot. Yet the parking lot can be one of the center's biggest sources of liability and cost if it is not properly maintained. Daily inspection of the parking lot is needed and items of note should be attended to immediately, otherwise they can become major expenditures or result in major liability claims. Items that should be noted in an inspection are:

- Faded, broken or vandalized traffic signs
- Faded or hard-to-see traffic directional markings on the drive lanes
- Broken curbing and broken car stops that could create accidents and tripping hazards
- Potholes in drive lanes that need to be repaired before they become a major expense or create a liability

- Policing and picking up broken glass, bottles and cans daily can reduce wear and tear on the asphalt and can prevent customers from tripping over such items.
- Small cracks in the asphalt should be attended to immediately. These cracks should be cleaned out and sealed before they become major potholes.
- Parking lot striping should be done once a year, depending on the location of your center. Keep the striping and traffic directional signals easy to see

PARKING DECKS

As more and more shopping centers are expanding and renovating, parking space is at a premium. To meet parking space requirements specified in REA agreements with the tenants and to meet local code regulations, owners are adding parking decks. While parking decks allow for protection from weather conditions such as rain, heat and snow, they do present unique problems. As in the case of parking lots, lighting and safety concerns are uppermost in the minds of the customers and the tenants. Review lighting, patrols and call-box needs in this area. Traffic control signage should be highly visible and easy to read. Areas should be marked to help customers remember where they parked their cars. Pedestrian walkways and safety islands should be well lit and noted.

PARKING LOT LIGHTING

The perception of the safety of your parking lot at night is directly related to the amount of light that your parking lot light poles emit. Shopping center managers should constantly monitor the number of burnt-out lights in the lot at any one time. This should be done on a routine and scheduled basis each night. There should be detailed records of each pole and when the lightbulb and ballast were replaced. Simple maintenance procedures such as cleaning your light fixture lenses can increase light levels. To determine when to turn off the lights after the center closes, you must balance the need to save energy and dollars against the security aspect. Do you have restaurants that stay open later than center hours? Do you have movie theaters that have midnight shows, thus letting their customers out after center closing hours? If your customers and tenants feel safe and secure in the center parking lot, then they will feel invited to come into your center and do their shopping. This is your payback for the investment in the lighting and maintenance program. Higher traffic translates into increased sales for your tenants.

SNOW REMOVAL

Snow removal is a case in point which demonstrates how important it is to establish service contracts with the flexibility to meet local conditions and the unpredictable variation in weather patterns. Very few centers maintain their own snow removal equipment, due to the capital outlay and cost of personnel. Outsourcing the work, either fully or partially, is the typical practice among property managers. Planning ahead is the key. It is important to lay out the timing and procedures for when and how snow removal will be done, as well as where to dump the snow. Planning needs to be done in the springtime rather than a couple of months before the winter season. Prior to executing the contract, walk the property with your contractor. Identify existing curbs, signs, landscaping, speed bumps and damage in the parking lot. Contracts should note which roadways and areas should be cleared first and where to store the accumulated snow. Negotiate an agreement that is tailored to your locale and customer base. Develop a price that will provide for a standby fee plus an hourly rate on each piece of equipment. The contract should also specify an automatic response time, a minimum level of service under specified conditions and an additional price as directed. There may be a deal worked out with the service provider to store equipment on site in order to guarantee immediate and priority response time. Of course, this depends on the availability of space and agreements with the major department stores. Ultimately, the responsibility to know when to call in the equipment for snow removal lies with the general manager of the shopping center.

EMERGENCY GENERATORS

Emergency generators are typically located in truck docks and are fueled either by natural gas or diesel. The supply is usually contained either in a nearby tank if it is diesel, or in a direct line if it is natural gas. There should be a timer on the emergency generator so that it is exercised on a regular basis, specifically on weekly intervals. The tank should be checked on a weekly basis to determine its fuel level. Detailed written logs should be kept and, once a history is developed, regular prescheduled refills of fuel can be arranged with the local supplier. This is one maintenance task that the manager should personally perform to ensure that the scheduled log is being maintained and to prevent failure in times of emergency.

ELEVATORS AND ESCALATORS

Of all the maintenance tasks that fall under the manager's responsibility, elevator and escalator maintenance is among the most technical. Therefore, it is imperative that the manager deal only with reliable service companies. These companies should have access to and maintain an adequate supply of key parts on hand, as well as certified technicians to work on the mall's specific brand of equipment. Additionally, the manager must be assured that the service is capable and is staffed to respond to emergencies during business hours, as well as after the center closes.

Blueprints and Record Keeping

One aspect of maintenance is maintaining accurate and timely records of all maintenance functions within the shopping center. These records should be kept in an area that is easily accessible and free from obstructions. Limited access should be given to the completed logs and records. Some of the various types of blueprints and records that should be kept are as follows:

• The original shopping center "as built" blueprints will show the actual location of all the underground piping, electrical lines, sewer lines, etc. These blueprints should never leave the property, unless copies are left behind, in case of an emergency.

• Tenants' "as built" store plans should also be kept in a location with limited access.

• Completed maintenance logs of the various pieces of equipment within the center should include logs by in-house personnel and service functions that are outsourced. This record keeping helps project maintenance costs for budgeting purposes, for capital replacement and for scheduling work tasks such as relamping of the center's lighting.

• All manufacturer specifications and warranties also need to be kept and cataloged by type of equipment and manufacturer. This will help in parts replacement, insurance claims and repair support from the manufacturer.

Communications

When establishing a relationship among ownership, tenants, community and management of a shopping center, focus on one thing and one thing only: communications. What and how to communicate, and which form of communication the manager takes, are key. There is much more to the process than just the preparation of monthly reports to outline what has happened during the past month. The effective manager will make routine visits to the merchants in his or her shopping center. Talking with merchants about maintenance issues will give you better insight into how things are going, the type of problems they feel exist and their attitude in general. As far as the community is concerned, regular attendance at chamber of commerce meetings, involvement in task forces and attendance at monthly city council meetings are important parts of learning about the issues that will affect the property. The manager should be fully informed about the entire operation and environment of the center. The manager should be the most informed individual on the owner's team. This requires being aware of matters that will have an economic impact on the property, such as changes in health, safety, building and fire codes or the adoption of new building codes. A strong manager will keep current on all aspects of the shopping center's operations on a daily basis; know what the city planning commission is discussing and debating, especially on building matters; listen to tenants, customers, contractors and the community as a whole and relate relevant issues to the owner with an analysis; bring all operational liability issues to the attention to the owner, even if they aren't in the approved budget; and most important of all, inform ownership. Owners do not want surprises. When the owner is fully informed, he or she is then in the best position to provide management with meaningful and informed direction.

Special Maintenance Issues

There are a number of special maintenance issues that a manager needs to be aware of as they relate to the operation of the center:

1. *The Americans with Disabilities Act (ADA) Compliance Regulations.* The act, signed by President Bush in July 1990, is designed to extend civil

rights protection to persons with disabilities. The law is divided into five major titles that prohibit discrimination against the disabled in employment, state and local government services, public transportation, public accommodations and telecommunications. The two titles that have the greatest impact on operations and maintenance of shopping centers are public accommodations and telecommunications. Under public accommodations, persons with disabilities are to be provided accommodations and access equal to, or similar to, that which is available to the general public. Examples include ramps, curb cuts in sidewalks and entrances, installation of accessible door hardware, designated accessible parking spaces and so on. Telecommunication examples include repositioning public phones, providing volume control on phones and providing a cord at least twenty-nine inches long from the telephone to the handset.

2. *Roof management tools.* Infrared imaging can be used to locate wet materials within the roof system by providing a visual representation of heat radiated from the roof. Digital photography provides photographs of roofs that can be inserted into a computerized roof management system database.

3. *Refrigerant certification.* Make sure that your contractor is certified under the EPA certification test.

4. *Clean Air Act.* This relates to boilers on the property. The Clean Air Act was enacted to regulate and reduce air pollution. The Clean Air Act is administered by the U.S. Environmental Protection Agency. Is the source of workplace air located so that only clean, fresh air which is free of contaminants will enter the workplace?

5. *Clean Water Act.* This relates to storm water drainage and runoff of the shopping center's parking lot. Are there catch basins in place to contain contaminants?

6. *Occupational Safety and Health Administration (OSHA).* OSHA was created to encourage employers to reduce workplace hazards, to implement new or to improve existing safety and health programs, to develop mandatory job safety and health standards, to enforce these standards in the workplace and to maintain a reporting and record keeping system to monitor job-related injuries and illnesses in the workplace.

7. *Recycling.* Most states require recycling of paper and aluminum, but in the near future, most states will also require recycling of fluorescent lightbulbs and ballasts, as well as plastic hangers.

8. *Dry cleaners.* Any dry cleaning establishment on site must provide the owner of the property with certification that it is in compliance with all EPA and OSHA rules and guidelines. These are guidelines as they pertain to the removal of chemical waste from the property.

9. *Underground storage tanks.* Are there any on your property? If so, they must be identified to the Environmental Protection Agency and maintained in accordance with applicable requirements.

10. *Hazard Communication Standard (HAZCOM).* The goal of HAZCOM is to ensure that employers and employees know the specific hazards associated with hazardous substances and how to work safely with them. This is the most frequently violated OSHA standard. Such a system and a check-off procedure must be in place for each property.

11. The possible deregulation of utilities could create the following situations:

- Formation of brokers who will negotiate special rates for electricity, gas and water
- Major mergers of utility companies nationwide
- Regulated companies will most likely become large entities: those that generate the energy, those that distribute the energy (this should stay a regulated profit center) and those that provide customer services by maintaining local lines and reading meters and bills

Securing the Future

Maintenance in the shopping industry is more than just repairing equipment, fixing roof leaks and checking broken tiles. It is about securing the future of the asset, the shopping center, through a planned maintenance program. It involves the willingness to vigorously embrace innovation by thinking outside of the box and adapting the latest technology to develop databases which allow better cost control and cash flow projections for ownership. It means keeping up to date on the latest local, state and federal government regulations. It means setting benchmarks in order to search for the industry's best practices that lead to superior performance. Finally, it is a proactive process rather than a reactive one and is aimed at changing operations in a structured manner in order to achieve superior performance.

Recommended Readings

Advanced Shopping Center Management: Housekeeping. Audiocassettes. New York: International Council of Shopping Centers, 1985.

Advanced Shopping Center Management: Parking Lots. Audiocassettes. New York: International Council of Shopping Centers, 1983.

Advanced Shopping Center Management: Roofs. Audiocassettes. New York: International Council of Shopping Centers, 1983.

ICSC Law Library: Environmental Issues. New York: International Council of Shopping Centers, 1996.

Security and Safety: Issues and Ideas for Shopping Center Professionals. New York: International Council of Shopping Centers, 1995.

This chapter was contributed by Don Paul, CSM, RPA, Vice President of Business Development, SSC Service Solutions, Vairico, Florida.

8 | Security

Anna C. Northcutt

Property owners and/or managers have an ever-increasing obligation to provide for the safety of individuals invited to their property. Courts are holding property owners and managers responsible for activity occurring on their specific properties, for having an awareness of the criminal activity occurring in close proximity to their properties and for seeking to prevent criminal activity from encroaching onto their properties.

The past decade has resulted in significant changes in the perception of security and the realization that security must be an integral part of property management if the property is to remain viable. Security must be addressed whether the property is a neighborhood center, community center, power center or superregional shopping center. The security programs for each property may be different in their scope and implementation, but the initial development of a program is identical regardless of the property.

This chapter will focus on the essential elements in the development and maintenance of a security program; this information is applicable to all types of properties regardless of the location. Prudent property owners and/or managers will evaluate the security risk to their property and prepare to minimize the risk. Managers must realize it is impossible to control the actions of third parties and unrealistic to assume a security incident will not occur on the property. Documentation of security decisions will be invaluable during future litigation, which should always be anticipated. Included in this chapter are samples of security-related documents that may be helpful in the creation of a security program.

Risk Assessment

A security plan begins with a realistic assessment of the property and the surrounding community. Much of this information can be gathered by observation; however, property managers are frequently too familiar with the property to make an objective assessment, so it may be helpful to use a professional security consultant for the risk assessment. The consultant will prepare a detailed report based upon an objective evaluation.

The assessment should include a thorough inspection of the facility, including the back hallways, public rest rooms, maintenance and storage areas, electrical and telephone rooms, trash courts and public transportation corridors as well as the visible public common area. Each area should be evaluated to determine the potential for physical injury or criminal incident. Additionally, the facility will be evaluated to determine if liability situations are created because of structural features. Once a property owner or manager recognizes a potential problem there is an obligation to take corrective action. This statement should not suggest that "ignorance is bliss"; not being fully aware of the risks inherent in a property can be as damaging as being aware and taking no corrective action.

During an assessment of the property, local law enforcement should be contacted and the center general manager (GM) should meet the law enforcement commander for the area and seek to cultivate a long-term relationship. The meeting with law enforcement should provide the GM with several vital pieces of information—the perception of the center's vulnerability to crime, as well as actual information on recent criminal activity on the property and in the surrounding community. As a minimum, law enforcement information should be gathered on an annual basis; ideally, the meetings will occur on a quarterly basis, with information updated more regularly if needed. Some law enforcement agencies charge a fee for producing statistical information. This fee should not dissuade a GM from obtaining the information.

In addition to information that can be obtained locally, GMs should consider using a demographic research company. This type of research firm reviews the reported criminal activity at a specific address and compares that data to the criminal activity of the county in which the property is located and to the nation. An index number is assigned to specific criminal categories and indicates whether crime at the property is lower than, equal to or greater than crime in the county or nation. These reports generally cost several hundred dollars and will assist in determining the potential of crime at a specific site.

Once an assessment of the property is complete and the GM reviews the data, a realistic understanding of the security challenges facing the center should be apparent. The GM can then develop a security program appropriate to the property. Each property is different; therefore, each security program will be different, even within a large portfolio of properties. A security program can be as simple as documenting the assessment phase and determining no further action is needed. The GM of a strip center in a small community may determine, at the conclusion of the assessment phase, that security is adequately provided by local law enforcement and take no additional steps other than documenting the assessment process, including all conversations with law enforcement leaders. All reports produced during the assessment phase should be maintained as documentation for the GM's decisions.

On the other hand, a general manager may determine that a more complex program is required based upon the information obtained during the assessment. One of the most common enhancements to a security program is the addition of an on-site security staff. Once the decision to add staff has been reached, the choice of using either a contract or proprietary staff will need exploration. Before reviewing the merits of either contract or proprietary security, it may be helpful to understand more about private security.

Private Security

Private security predates most public law enforcement agencies and continues to grow at a phenomenal rate. The roles and expectations of private security and public law enforcement are quite different from each other. Security is responsible for the implementation of a comprehensive physical protection program. Toward that goal, security personnel are responsible for enforcing established procedures to accomplish the following:

- Serve as a representative of the owner, providing assistance to customers, merchants and employees
- Provide for the safety of customers, merchants and employees
- Protect the property and interests of the owner, customers, merchants and employees

Many cities have developed proactive community-based police programs, yet public law enforcement is often limited by declining resources and can only respond after an incident has occurred. These limited resources may not allow public law enforcement to routinely patrol shopping areas as a deterrent to crime, and it is therefore incumbent upon the property manager to provide an alternate form of protection for the property. Ways to encourage a law enforcement presence on the property are detailed later in this chapter.

Private security generally has two objectives:

- Crime prevention—successfully preventing incidents from occurring and thus eliminating the need for an arrest
- Order maintenance—a visible presence that allows people to work and/or shop without concern for their personal safety

Contract versus Proprietary

Once a general manager has determined that the presence of uniformed security officers is a necessary part of the center's security program, the question of using proprietary officers or contract officers will surely arise. There are a number of issues that may influence a particular choice. Does the GM want to increase the number of employees at the center? Are administrative support personnel in place to accommodate an increase in center employees? Does the GM want to shift the liability associated with security? Does the GM want to control who is hired and how training is conducted? There are advantages and disadvantages in selecting either type of security staff, and there is no right or wrong choice.

Proprietary officers are generally retained longer than contract employees. Many contract security firms have high turnover rates, meaning that every security position is filled with a new employee several times during a twelve-month period. The GM considering the use of contract security should require the security company to provide the turnover rate experienced by the company during the previous two years.

Recently a comparison was made between the security departments of six centers; three of the centers had proprietary security and three had contract security. The centers chosen were of comparable size and located in similar communities. A national security vendor with an excellent reputation was used at the three contract centers. The contract vendor provided employees with health care and vacation and sick days, benefits which are not always provided to contract security employees without substantial client contributions. The results indicated the proprietary centers experienced turnover rates of less than 15 percent, while the rates at the three contract centers were between 40 percent and 70 percent.

A by-product of longer retention is the ability of the security officers to become familiar with the property, the merchants and the customers. Recognizing that customer service is a major component of security, the more affinity the security officer feels for the property the more likely customer service will improve. In addition to the test referenced above, a separate test was conducted in 1997 on three proprietary security departments and three contract security departments. The contract security vendor was a national vendor with an excellent reputation. The test was designed to evaluate the actions of security personnel in a variety of situations, ranging from customer assistance to potential criminal activity.

The test was conducted without the knowledge of center personnel, approval to do so having been obtained from the corporate office of the centers' management company. The same test scenarios were conducted simultaneously at each of the six centers using actors and actresses of similar age and appearance. The test concluded that the proprietary officers were generally more responsive than the contract officers. Proprietary officers provided customers with greater service and responded more quickly to reported incidents. In one test situation, the contract employee directed a "customer" to a competitor's mall where, the security officer was sure, "they'll have what you want." A comment sure to cause the marketing director concern. To be fair, not all proprietary officers responded as expected. In one test situation, the proprietary officer remained generally unresponsive when a customer was locked out of a vehicle; the officer handed the individual a coat hanger and directed the person to a pay phone at the end of the hall. This was not the center's policy for vehicle assistance.

An advantage of using a contract security provider is that the burden of employee relations is removed from the center management staff. This is a major consideration, as staffing and employee problems can be burdensome without a strong administrative staff. Using a contract company clearly removes the burden of hiring, training and terminating an employee from the center staff. Additionally, the contract should provide for the immediate removal of any security employee when requested by the center management staff. The removal of problem employees may not be so easily accomplished within a proprietary department.

The monetary cost of security is essentially the same whether a contract company or proprietary staff is used, though when using a contract company there is often room for a substantial increase at the time of renewal. The amount and frequency of increases should be clearly defined in the initial contract. Unfortunately, some security companies submit an initial low bid and then request an increase at the time of renewal, recognizing that most GMs are reluctant to replace an in-place security provider based simply on a price increase. The contractor's final bid should include all items associated with the full security program—hiring and training employees, furnishing uniforms and equipment, as well as health benefits and/or other special incentives. These items must be clearly discussed prior to signing a contract. Without a clear understanding of what is being provided, a GM may be surprised to discover security officers have one pair of pants and two shirts and no sick leave or vacation time or health insurance.

A significant reason for using a contract company is the ability to shift or share liability. In order to ensure the contract company can meet this expectation, the GM should require at least $2 million of general liability insurance. Managers should be cautious when reviewing proposals from companies with only a few employees and/or assets directly related to the personal worth of the company's president. In more than one security incident, contractors have essentially signed the insurance policy over to a plaintiff, leaving the center on the hook for additional damages claimed by a plaintiff after an incident.

There is no right or wrong answer in terms of selecting either contract company or proprietary staff; each can provide excellent security service and each can lead to extraordinary aggravation. The selection of one type of staff over the other is often a matter of the personal preference of the center's general manager. It should be noted that several national property management companies use contract security with success, while other national companies chose to remain with proprietary programs.

It is the responsibility of the GM to ensure the best security possible is provided while simultaneously maintaining an appropriate level of cost. Regardless of the type of staff selected there are considerations and requirements common to both, the most important being the hiring and training processes.

Employee Hiring Considerations

Regardless of whether a contract company or a proprietary staff is used, specific requirements must be established for the individuals hired as security officers. When using a contract company, all hiring requirements should be clearly described in the contract and the GM should randomly review hiring packets to ensure contract compliance. As a minimum all security officers should:

- Have a high school diploma (or GED)
- Speak, read and write English (or the native language of the country where the center is located)
- Possess a valid driver's license from the state in which the property is located (there may be some exceptions, such as military personnel, students or persons living near a state line)
- Possess any licenses required by the city, county or state
- Be able to physically stand and/or walk for extended periods of time. (This can be verified at the time of the interview by inviting the applicant to walk the center with a current security employee—not a member of management. This "walk around" can provide additional insights into the applicant via casual conversation. More than once a GM has heard comments such as, "Whew, do you always walk this much?" or "It looks like it would be easy to get dates here.")

In addition to the basic hiring requirements all applicants under consideration should be screened for criminal history, drug use, a valid social security number and a clean driving record. All checks require a release form provided by the investigative agency. The screening conducted by an investigative firm generally costs between $50 and $100 and should be standard for all security employees. The applicant will complete a form providing his/her birth date, Social Security number, driver's license number and all residences for the past seven years. The checks requested will typically be completed within a week.

The criminal history check is critical and generally limited to the last seven years. The check will reveal all felony convictions and some misdemeanor convictions, depending upon the jurisdiction. Hiring managers of both contract and proprietary personnel often assume if an applicant has a state guard card or license no independent check is needed; this is a risky assumption no GM should make. In many states an individual can work with a temporary license while the state is checking criminal records and fingerprint files and processing the permanent application. In some states a check can take months to complete and in other states the check is limited to a local geographical area; a nationwide search may not be done. In recent years security officers working with temporary permits have been responsible for incidents that resulted in both the loss of life and property. Do not take this risk. The expense of conducting a criminal history check is nothing compared to the liability and the negative publicity associated with an incident involving a security officer.

In addition to the criminal history check, applicants should be screened for drug use. Drug screening should be a part of any security contract. This test is best performed by an independent medical lab. There are drug tests which can be administered on site and which work similarly to a home pregnancy test; urine is collected and exposed to a reactive agent which then reveals the presence of a particular drug. While this type of test is convenient and relatively inexpensive, it is not as reliable as a medical laboratory due to the error factor associated with nonmedical personnel performing the test and determining the results.

The social security number should be verified to ensure it is a valid number and is being used by only one individual. False, misused and/or multiple social security numbers may indicate the individual has exercised poor judgment and/or is involved in activities ranging from avoiding creditors to income tax evasion. Regardless, any anomalies in this check should be closely reviewed.

The applicant's driving record should be checked even if the person is not being considered for a mobile position. A driving history can provide valuable information on the maturity level of the individual. Are there multiple citations for reckless driving, driving while intoxicated or other moving violations? These may indicate a person who does not control impulsive behavior and who may not be suited for employment as a security officer.

A credit check is frequently considered and may reveal useful information; however, the law regarding the use of credit information imposes significant restrictions on both employers and investigators. A separate release form is required, and if negative information is revealed the applicant must be notified and given a reasonable opportunity to correct and/or explain the information before an employment decision can be made. These restrictions and requirements expose the center to the risk of an inadvertent error; therefore, exercise caution when requesting a credit check. Certainly, there are positions in which individuals regularly handle money, and these may require a credit check; however, in the case of a security officer, an informed hiring decision can be made based upon the interview, the drug screen, Department of Motor Vehicles report, Social Security number verification and criminal history check.

Training Considerations

LIABILITY DECREASES AS TRAINING STANDARDS INCREASE

After hiring the right person, training the new employee becomes the critical factor. The responsibilities assigned to a security officer may appear to be little more than common sense, but consider the expectations placed upon the officer. An officer is expected to be a representative of management, respond to emergencies, serve as a liaison with the police, firefighters and paramedics and provide customer assistance. It is vital the initial training be complete *before* the individual is assigned to patrol the property. Many security organizations hire an individual and provide four to eight hours of training, relying on additional training to be provided over the next twelve to eighteen months. Consider the possibility of an incident occurring before a particular module of instruction has been presented.

If a security contractor is used, ask what training is provided, or even ask to sit in on a *full* training session before signing the contract. A contractor may indicate that sixteen to twenty-four hours of training are provided; however, when the specific topics are identified it is not uncommon to see classes such as "insurance forms," "payroll" and "issuing uniforms" as a part of the training program. These topics are clearly not security training and indicate the actual time spent on security training is minimal.

A forty-hour training course, most of which is conducted on site, offers the new employee the opportunity to learn the skills necessary to be successful and the opportunity to become familiar with the management staff, the merchants and the physical layout of the center. The training should include both classroom instruction and the opportunity to *observe* patrol operations. A mistake often made is assigning a new employee to on-the-job training. OJT rarely is the best approach as employees can easily learn the bad habits of others. The on-site security director is usually responsible for training; this responsibility should not be delegated to others, though certain specific training topics can be conducted by line officers who have demonstrated proficiency in a particular skill.

Topics that should be a part of a training program are:

1. Legal issues, including the powers of arrest and the use of force
   - Officers have no greater power to arrest than any other citizen.
   - Officers should use only the minimum force necessary to overcome resistance.
2. Public relations, including customer service expectations, communication skills and handling aggressive or disturbed persons
3. Emergency response, including the use of fire extinguishers, first aid, locating lost children and handling bomb threats as well as natural disasters common to the area
4. Patrol operations, including expectations for both the interior and exterior of the center and the procedures for opening and closing the center
5. Shoplifting assistance
   - Ensure there is a written policy to facilitate officer training and to serve as a handout for the merchants. A sample policy and liability release form are included in this chapter.
6. Juvenile behavior, especially covering truancy and gangs
7. Third-party access
   - The access given to third parties for noncommercial expressive activity varies from state to state; it is essential the security staff is knowledgeable on this point.
8. Report writing
   - This is one of the most important aspects of training. The officers' written reports will often be the primary pieces of evidence during litigation. Officers must report only what they have observed or have been specifically told, clearly identifying the reporting party. Opinions have no place in a security report.

Consistency of performance expectations is essential to a well-run security department, and the center's commitment to excellence is often first communicated during the training phase of employment. Training topics must be addressed fully to ensure the newly hired officer can effectively perform his/her job. There are a number of training programs available which cost from a few hundred dollars to several thousand dollars and range from self-study workbooks to videotapes to computer-based instruction. Regardless of the method of instruction, it is important that the center or contract company have a specific training program which is consistently taught to all employees.

Taking the time to hire the right person and the time to provide an appropriate training lays the foundation to reduce exposure involving negligent or inadequate security. Training should not end with the initial training program; it is important to have continuing training to ensure new information is appropriately disseminated and to review policies which may have been discussed months before. It is a good idea to hold a training session prior to the holiday season to ensure all security employees are aware of the seasonal plans for off-site parking, anticipated crowds, change in operating hours and marketing promotions, and to remind the staff of the policies for assisting with shoplifters, third-party access and handling juveniles. Once the staff is hired and trained, it is important the daily tasks and expectations are continually available for review. This information is traditionally found in a policy and procedure manual.

Policies and Procedures

Policies are the guidelines by which the security officer performs his/her duties. A comprehensive policy and procedure manual should be available at every center, regardless of size and regardless of whether there is a permanent staff or supplemental officers during peak shopping periods. Absent written policies, the staff is forced to rely on common sense, and what may seem appropriate at the time of an incident may not always be reasonable or prudent upon greater reflection.

Earlier in this chapter the need for a customized security program, regardless of the center's size or location, was discussed, and while a GM may determine that no permanent security staff is needed, a policy manual is always needed. The policy manual should articulate the philosophy and expectations of center management on a wide range of security topics and clearly outline what is expected of the security staff. Policy manuals will vary in length and level of detail based upon the size of the center and the complexity of the security program. A security consultant may be helpful in preparing the manual. A well-written policy and procedure manual may take a significant amount of time to create and should be reviewed by a variety of disciplines within the management company to ensure all points of view have been considered. It should be written in a style and language that will be easily understood by the primary users—security officers. Finally, the manual should be reviewed and approved by corporate counsel. The completed manual should be available to all members of the management staff and all security officers should have a copy and be encouraged to review it. The manual should be routinely reviewed and updated to ensure it remains relevant to the center.

In addition to the policies and procedures manual, the following information should be made available to security officers and other staff members:

- Location of all interior and exterior fire sprinkler valves and the zones protected
- Location of all fire hose cabinets, hydrants, extinguishers, pumps and/or other equipment
- Location of all utility main shutoffs for gas, water, electricity and lawn sprinklers
- Location of all electrical rooms, mechanical rooms, roof access and the emergency generator
- Location of escalators, elevators and stairwells
- Location and designation of all exterior doors
- Location of trash compactors/trash courts, delivery zones and loading docks
- Parking lot zones designated by number or color
- Location and number of parking lot light poles and night lighting
- Location of electrical outlets in the center common area
- Employee parking area
- Evacuation plan
- Alarm system
- Center information, including map and open/close times

Security Duties

The primary duty of a security officer is to be a visible deterrent to crime while simultaneously providing customer service. This is most often accomplished via patrol. Security officers should move continuously throughout the property, aware of ongoing activity and alert to liability situations such as spills, damaged equipment or fixtures and/or the inappropriate behavior of individuals.

Patrol areas are frequently divided between the interior and exterior areas of the center. Patrolling the interior is more than simply strolling through the central common area of a property; it means actively observing every area of the center—the back corridors, telephone alcoves, utility room, storage areas, public rest rooms and maintenance areas—alert for sights, sounds or smells that are out of the ordinary. Officers should ensure areas off-limits to the public are kept locked to prevent unauthorized entry. Officers patrolling the center after hours should visually inspect merchant doors and/or gates to ensure all are properly secured; however, officers should not physically check each merchant door, as doing so may establish a duty to ensure the merchant space is secure and thus the center may be held responsible if a store is left unlocked and merchandise is missing. A significant portion of the interior patrol duty involves customer assistance; officers should be hired with that ability in mind, and the need to provide customer service should be continually reinforced to the staff.

Exterior patrol frequently involves a mobile patrol of the parking areas, though there are situations in which a fixed exterior patrol is appropriate. Mobile patrol is provided by either walking or by using bicycles, horses, automobiles or trucks. Officers circulate through the property alert for any unusual activity or areas which may need attention. Officers may also provide customer assistance, such as unlocking vehicles, locating vehicles and assisting with mechanical problems, which may simply mean calling an automotive service company. No mechanical service should be performed without prior training and a liability release form signed by the vehicle's owner or driver.

Whether on interior or exterior patrol, officers should be particularly sensitive to graffiti. The property owner/operator should ensure graffiti removal is a top priority. Graffiti significantly impacts the feeling of safety by individuals visiting the property and may be commonly interpreted as indicating the area is under the control of organized criminal gangs which pose a threat to those individuals not in the gang. Security officers should specifically look for graffiti during the first patrol of the day, which often occurs before 8 A.M.; discovering graffiti at that time gives the center an opportunity to remove the graffiti before the customers and merchants arrive. If there is no on-site security staff but an on-site management team is present, someone from the management team should have the specific responsibility to check for graffiti each morning. In the case of a center without an on-site management staff, a reliable merchant should check the center daily and immediately report graffiti to the person or company designated to remove the offensive markings.

Written Documentation

There are two types of documents often created by security officers— a daily activity report (DAR) for routine activities and an incident report for more significant situations. On the DAR, officers should record all activity, including customer service requests, when and where patrols occurred and the names and vehicle license numbers of individuals they assist in the parking areas. Unfortunately, many DARs contain only three entries—"on duty," "dinner," "off duty." During litigation often the first information requested by the plaintiff's attorney are the DARs and/or incident reports made regarding the allegation incident, and so officers must continually be reminded of the importance of what is written.

Activities reported on a daily activity report should by verified by a supervisor. Supervisors can verify patrol activity by either using random physical checks or by using an electronic watch tour device. Physical verification is an attempt to objectively verify an officer's activity and requires the supervisor to compare the officer's DAR against the assigned patrol area, other officers' DARs and a dispatch log, if maintained. Even then physical verification can never be completely reliable; however, there is a patrol verification method that is objective and reliable. The method is an electronic watch tour system which records, via a small wand or reader, the location of the area checked by an officer and the time the area was checked. A watch tour system is a computerized system which requires the placement of bar codes or electronic buttons, generally the size of a watch battery, throughout the property. These bar codes or buttons can be placed indoors or outdoors and are generally not noticed by the public. The electronic system allows the security officer while patrolling to make notations regarding an area via bar codes or buttons with preassigned meanings. Using this system, an officer on patrol can note any concerns electronically. At the end of the shift the scanned information is downloaded into a computer, where it is then available for review.

In addition to the daily activity reports, officers frequently prepare reports on incidents occurring at the center. Therefore, the writing ability of an applicant should be assessed during the hiring process to ensure reports are well written and accurately relate the facts. Reports must be timely—that is, prepared prior to a security officer's going off duty, even if overtime is required. Information must be recorded while it is fresh in the officer's mind. Reports should contain only the facts of an event and not the officer's opinion or speculation about the incident. Supervisors should regularly review and critique the officers' writing, otherwise the officers may become sloppy in the use of grammar and spelling or lapse into the habit of adding extraneous information to the report, which can be problematic should litigation occur. Supervisors should ensure documents are presentable for use in court, as this is where such documents may end up. Computer software programs are available which allow security reports to be prepared in a standardized format and result in more professional-appearing paperwork and, by extension, a more professional-appearing department.

Emergency Situations

One of the most challenging aspects of shopping center management is responding to emergency situations. If the center has an on-site security department, those officers will likely be the first responders. For centers that rely on public responders, emergency situations may present a greater challenge, as an emergency may be well under way before assistance arrives. Managers must prepare for incidents ranging from medical emergencies to facility emergencies to manmade crises to natural disasters. Emergencies often attract the media and can result in a negative portrayal of the center based upon a spontaneous comment from a security officer or a graphic photograph of the incident.

Every center needs a comprehensive emergency response plan. The plan should cover all anticipated emergencies and provide the response required of the merchants, the center staff and others expected to respond.

The center staff should ensure merchants are familiar with the emergency response procedures, and relevant information from the emergency response plan, with a customized evacuation route for each merchant, should be included in the merchant handbook. Local emergency responders (law enforcement, firefighters and paramedics) should be familiar with the center's emergency plan and should have detailed floor plans of the center that include utility shutoff points and other features that may not be readily visible or apparent to the public.

Notification of the merchants and customers during an emergency often presents a challenge. Center managers have several notification methods available to them: (1) memos delivered by the staff; (2) a merchant telephone tree that relies on merchants calling one another; (3) a public-address system; (4) a specific notification system installed at the center; or (5) an off-site notification system.

The delivery of memos is a method that is simple and inexpensive and can work for a small center in the case of minor emergencies such as a facility problem or anticipated bad weather. Centers relying on the delivery of memos should prepare them in advance and place them in an accessible location. This method has drawbacks—delivery may not be timely, as each merchant may want to discuss the incident as the memo is being delivered; production or distribution of the memo may be hampered by the availability of staff or equipment; and finally, a memo prepared in advance may not address the specifics of an emergency.

The telephone tree method places responsibility on the merchants to notify one another. Emergency notification is not the responsibility of the tenants. There is significant room for error when multiple individuals relay information, and the potential exists for one or more merchants simply to fail to notify those on the list.

The public-address system is efficient and can communicate a message quickly to everyone in the center; however, caution must be exercised in the use of emotionally charged language that may cause panic and lead to greater disruption than the original emergency. For example, rather than announcing, "A bomb threat has been received —everyone should evacuate," it is less disruptive to announce, "A facility emergency exists which requires the evacuation of the center; please leave the via the nearest exit and proceed to your vehicle. The center will reopen as soon as possible." Announcements intended for the public-address system should be prepared in advance and individuals reading the announcement should practice before using the public-address system. A confident voice instills confidence in others and helps avoid panic.

A dedicated emergency notification system can also be installed. This system can be expensive, and may require new wiring and additional telephone lines and/or equipment. It is reliable and can effectively and quickly carry a message to all merchants.

A cost-effective alternative to the installation of emergency notification equipment is the use of an off-site notification system operating over the existing telephone system within the center. In the event of an emergency an authorized individual calls a central notification site, where an operator verifies the authorized name and password and records the emergency message that will be immediately and simultaneously delivered to all merchants via the existing phone lines.

In addition to an emergency plan and a notification system, it is important to conduct an annual emergency exercise. An annual exercise ensures that the staff, the merchants and the public responders such as the police and fire departments are familiar not only with the property but with the skill levels and expectations of everyone responding in an emergency. (See sample scenario, p. 189.) This type of exercise is best conducted when the center property is not open to the public. The exercise should simulate an event occurring when the center is open and active, and security staffing during the exercise should reflect the staffing at the time of the simulated incident. Role players will make the exercise more realistic by portraying victims and/or suspects; volunteers can be found among the merchants, mall walkers and students. It is helpful to videotape the exercise; local law enforcement often will provide this service. The videotape will assist in identifying areas of the response that may need improvement. The annual exercise can be a marketing tool; local newspapers and television can be notified of the exercise and the center may receive positive publicity on the commitment to public safety.

Emergency situations cannot be predicted; however, emergencies can be anticipated and response plans prepared and practiced. Public response to a property after an emergency may depend largely on the professional response by the staff during the emergency.

Equipment

Equipment requirements vary among properties. Numerous factors influence equipment selection, including the size of the staff, location of the property and the relationship with local law enforcement.

CENTER EQUIPMENT

A GM may determine that to enhance customer safety and convenience additional equipment is required. Security equipment considered often includes closed-circuit television (CCTV), emergency call boxes, enhanced lighting and telephones. The equipment in this section, if installed, will be an integral part of the center's security program and must be kept operational. Service contracts should obligate the service provider to repair the equipment within four hours of notification.

Closed-circuit Television. CCTV is technology that can supplement an on-site security staff or cover an area not staffed via off-site monitoring and notification of local law enforcement. CCTV can effectively monitor areas such as back corridors, transportation drop-off points, video arcades, escalators and food courts and/or areas where slips and falls are likely to occur. Using CCTV places additional responsibility on the center staff to ensure the equipment is properly installed, monitored and maintained and that activity observed is responded to in a timely manner. Failure to perform any of these tasks may result in substantial liability. Prior to contacting a CCTV salesperson it may be helpful to use the services of a security consultant to determine the most effective use of the technology. A center manager should consider the following questions: (1) What do we expect to observe? (2) How do we expect to respond to what is observed? and (3) Is there sufficient manpower to monitor the CCTV equipment and respond to observed activities?

The use of CCTV will likely require remodeling the security office to accommodate equipment and the person monitoring the system twenty-four hours a day. There are service companies which monitor CCTV from an off-site location and direct security units to respond as required. An off-site monitoring service should be thoroughly investigated to ensure all equipment is appropriately monitored and maintained, the directed response is timely and a contingency plan exists in the event the regular mode of video transmission is disrupted.

The individual monitoring the cameras should not perform other tasks that limit the ability to observe the CCTV. Reassign duties such as answering telephones, handling walk-up complaints or processing security paperwork to ensure monitoring the CCTV remains the top priority. CCTV rarely reduces security costs and may increase costs in that additional personnel may be required to monitor the equipment and respond to incidents. CCTV can be an effective addition to a security program when implemented in a prudent and thoughtful manner.

Emergency Call Boxes. Emergency call boxes have long been installed in parking structures; however, some centers are now installing these devices throughout the property. Emergency call boxes allow an individual to contact security to request assistance, report a medical emergency or report a security incident. These devices are activated and security contacted when an individual presses the "call" button. The line can ordinarily be terminated only by security personnel; this ensures someone experiencing a medical emergency or security situation does not have to continue to depress the call button. CCTV can be installed so that when a call box is activated security not only hears what is happening but can see the area. Emergency call boxes are not generally misused; the public views these devices as a "911" call and reports of prank calls are rare.

Emergency call boxes are generally most effective when hardwired phone lines are used rather than other types of technology which may be disrupted by weather conditions or simply by the use of cellular phones. Emergency call boxes should be tested daily to ensure the devices are operating properly. Technology allows continual testing of the lines and any break or disruption of service is reported as an alarm. This is an effective way to ensure the system is operating properly; however, each device should be physically inspected by security personnel during routine security patrols. Late-night inspections ensure problems are reported to the vendor prior to the center opening and increase the opportunity for repairs to be completed before the public arrives on the property.

Emergency call boxes should be marked consistently throughout the property with signage indicating "customer assistance" or "security assistance." Bright colors and bold graphics help draw attention to the devices. Emergency call boxes provide customers and merchants with an additional method of contacting security and allow security to be a visible presence throughout the property.

Lighting. Lighting may not ordinarily be classified as a security device; however, lighting is one of most effective ways to increase customer confidence and deter criminal activity. Many communities require specific light levels for parking lots and other facilities, not only to ensure safety but to ensure the surrounding areas are not negatively impacted by light that may be too bright. Light readings should be taken regularly to ensure light levels do not fall below established levels.

Parking structures and stairwells painted bright white increase the available light from both natural and artificial sources. Lights should be inspected nightly, and those which are not operating properly should be replaced as soon as possible. Many centers have a contract with a vendor to replace parking lot lights quarterly rather than as specifically needed; this may result in a decline in light levels if an inordinate number of lights needs replacement before the vendor's scheduled visit. Managers must ensure there is always sufficient light on the property and should establish criteria, such as when a number or percentage of lights is nonoperational, for the service to be performed ahead of schedule.

Typically, light levels are significantly reduced when a center closes. Care should be taken to ensure there is sufficient light to observe activity. Older centers may not have the ability to activate specific sections of lights and are faced with the choice of the lights being either on or off. Dark parking lots may invite unwanted activity. There are times when a situation may require additional light and security officers should have the ability to activate the lighting system after hours. Lighting is an effective tool and can enhance the property and improve customer confidence in shopping after dark.

Public Telephones. Public telephones can play an important role in a center's security program. Centers with an on-site security staff may configure the telephone system so that individuals can access security from any public telephone in the center by dialing *11 or some variation. Even absent an on-site staff, well-maintained telephones ensure the public has access to emergency services. Many centers restrict incoming calls to the public telephones to control loitering or criminal activity. Like the graffiti removal program, someone must be responsible for regularly checking the telephones to ensure they work properly and that problems are reported to the telephone company.

STAFF EQUIPMENT

Selecting the proper equipment for the security staff, whether proprietary or contract, is an important decision. The security officer is often the only representative of the center seen by the public and the image conveyed by the officer is often the perceived image of the center.

One of the most effective security tools is the security uniform. Many centers have moved away from the "blazer and slacks" uniform toward one which mirrors the uniform of local law enforcement and tends to evoke greater confidence and respect from the public. Regardless of the color, the uniform should fit well and always appear clean and fresh. Proprietary departments may either purchase uniforms or use a rental service. The primary drawback to purchasing uniforms is eventually having a stockpile of uniforms that often can only be donated to a charitable organization. Using a rental company gives the flexibility to change uniforms as needed; moreover, changing uniform color can often give a boost to the security program. It is not uncommon for merchants and customers to assume additional staff has been added when the uniform has changed. Any change in the security uniform is likely to make security much more visible— for a while.

Apart from uniforms, another important security tool is a radio. This section will not discuss the various types or models of radios; however, the center or security contractor should purchase a reliable product that can be serviced and/or repaired quickly. Security should have a separate channel and/or frequency depending upon the size of the center and the other functions using radios at the center. Multiple functions using the same channel or frequency can be disruptive during routine incidents and disastrous during an emergency. Officers should be equipped with lapel microphones and earphones to ensure radio traffic is secure and not broadcast to the entire center.

Additional equipment which may be appropriate, depending on the location of the center and the training of the officers, includes handcuffs, pepper spray and first-aid equipment. There are situations which require security to confront combative individuals and handcuffs may be necessary to prevent injury to security or others until law enforcement arrives and takes control of the situation.

Pepper spray is a defensive weapon. Often just the threat of being sprayed controls the situation. Prior to using any equipment, officers should be trained by a qualified instructor, who can be located through law enforcement contacts or private security training schools.

First-aid training and equipment are appropriate not only for the security staff but for all members of the management team. A medical emergency can happen at any time and prompt attention may make a significant difference in recovery. The public expects uniformed personnel to provide assistance, including first aid. Security officers should be trained, certified and carry a cardiopulmonary resuscitation (CPR) mouth shield and latex gloves. Officers should be instructed to wear gloves whenever providing first aid; this simple precaution may prevent the transmission of blood-borne pathogens such as HIV and hepatitis.

Assessing the Security Program

Once a security program is established it must be regularly reviewed to ensure it remains appropriate to the property. A security audit should be comprehensive and take place over an extended period of time, ensuring the property is thoroughly reviewed. A written report should be prepared and include not only what needs improvement but areas which are working well. Because an audit may be requested during litigation, it is wise to protect this information as an "attorney/client privileged communication" by having the reports requested by and addressed to the center's attorney. Whether this designation will preclude the information from being released is a matter for the court; however, without taking this step, the document will surely be released.

Public Relations

The security program of a center should be marketed as any other positive aspect of the property. Exposure to the security program can be subtle, via photographs of security in routine center advertising, or by placing security service information in the center brochure. There are creative ways to market security. One center's recent holiday campaign produced radio spots in which various individuals told what they enjoyed about the center; included were merchants, customers and a security officer. The officer identified herself, how long she had worked at the center and why she enjoyed her job. As a result of the commercial the public was aware of the center and that there was an on-site security staff. Personal safety continues to be one of the public's major concerns, and center managers should not be reluctant to inform people about security at the property. A word of caution—never imply or state that more security services are available than regularly are.

On-site security officers should meet the merchants, and customers and merchant employees should be regularly reminded of the services provided by security. Merchants should be invited to meetings at which security information is presented by either the on-site security staff or invited lecturers such as members of law enforcement, the Secret Service (which handles counterfeit bills and credit card fraud) or others with security or crime prevention information of interest to the merchants.

Local law enforcement personnel realize they cannot ensure public safety by working alone and welcome the assistance of a professional security staff. Security directors should meet regularly with local law enforcement and fire department leaders; in the absence of a security director, another representative of management should meet with law enforcement leaders to ensure an ongoing relationship. A center can do a number of things to encourage local law enforcement and fire departments to be a part of the center's security program. Frequently, members of these departments are eager to train at facilities within the community, and both law enforcement and fire departments should be invited to train at the center. These departments should have floor plans of the center and should receive regular updates. Law enforcement personnel may visit the property if it is made convenient; for example, by providing several parking spaces near a primary entrance designated as "law enforcement vehicles only." The spaces may also discourage law enforcement officers from parking near the curb and/or on the sidewalk, which may cause customers to suspect some criminal activity has occurred. A sign can be placed on a table in the food court which reads, "Reserved for on-duty law enforcement"; this may encourage law enforcement officers to eat in the food court more often. These ideas are simple, yet may encourage law enforcement personnel to visit the center more often during operating hours. Moreover, these signs serve a second function of informing the public that law enforcement is regularly on the property.

Centers may want to assist local law enforcement more directly and can obtain more bang for the buck by contributing to specific programs or projects. Rather than contribute $500 to the general fund of the Police Officers' Association, contribute toward the purchase of specific equipment such as protective vests or bicycles for the bike patrol or new equipment for the police gym. One center contributes money toward the production of police trading cards, which are distributed by police officers to children in the community. Each card has a picture of a police officer and facts about the officer and department. In return for a relatively insignificant contribution, the center's logo and name appear on every trading card.

Summary

Security is an art, not a science, and each property must be approached as a unique environment. Individuals visit properties where they feel secure and comfortable; a well-balanced security program contributes toward those positive feelings. It is hoped this chapter has provided specific information on developing and maintaining a viable security program.

Assisting with Shoplifters: Sample Guidelines

The apprehension and detention of shoplifters are not the primary roles of security. Security officers only become involved in such situations at the request of merchant employees and respond to provide assistance only, as set forth below.

Security officers may not make arrests in cases of shoplifting from a store—only the store employee who actually witnessed the shoplifting may make an arrest under that person's citizen's arrest powers. If the store clerk sees the theft and elects to make an arrest, he/she must also be the complainant when law enforcement arrives.

In order to make an arrest the store clerk must have kept the suspect under constant visual observation and must be certain the items taken were not returned to the rack, passed to an accomplice or discarded in some other manner.

When security is contacted to assist with a shoplifting arrest the merchant will be asked if the police have been called and if the merchant intends to press charges.

Security officers may become involved if the suspect leaves the store and enters the common area; however, this involvement shall be limited to observation of the situation. If requested by the merchant employee, the security officer will keep the individual under observation in the common area until the merchant employee makes contact with the suspect. The merchant employee, making the arrest, will ask the individual to return to the store.

Security officers will not chase a suspect through the center. Security officers will not physically detain or restrain a suspect unless the security officer witnessed a crime and is personally making the arrest using his/her citizen's arrest authority.

If the suspect attempts to leave the center and ignores a request to accompany the merchant employee back to the store, the officer will not attempt to stop the suspect. The officer will follow the suspect and obtain a physical description of the suspect and/or any vehicle which may be involved.

Security officers will not pursue any suspect off the property.

If the suspect does accompany the merchant employee to the store, in the interest of safety the officer may remain until law enforcement personnel arrive.

Security officers will not search a suspect. If a weapon is suspected, the officer may conduct a pat-down of the person.

SUMMARY

- Security officers have no greater arrest power than any private citizen.
- The crime *must* have been witnessed by the person making the arrest.
- The merchant employee must have constant visual contact with the suspect.
- No physical restraint or detention will be made by the officer unless the officer is making the arrest for a crime he/she witnessed.
- No pursuits through the center or off center property are permitted.

Authorization to Assist with a Citizen's Arrest: A Sample

Officer(s)_____is/are hereby requested to assist

_____with the citizen's arrest of _____.
(Name and position)   (Name of person being arrested)

The person requesting assistance is an owner/agent of the _____

_____. In consideration for providing assistance with the
(Name of merchant store)

citizen's arrest, the undersigned, on behalf of _____,
                                                 (Name of merchant store)

agrees to indemnify, defend and hold harmless the owner of _____

_____ and their agents, servants, employees, partners,
(Name of center)

lenders, officers, directors, shareholders, parent and/or subsidiary

corporations and/or affiliates ("Indemnitees") from and against any

and all claims (whether or not meritorious), loss, damage, injury, lia-

bility, cost and expenses (including attorney's fees) ("Claims") arising

out of or in any way connected with the arrest of the above-named

person, including Claims caused by the concurrent negligent acts or

omissions, whether active or passive, of the above-named Officer(s)

or Indemnitees.

Annual Emergency Exercise: A Sample Scenario

Location:	ABC Center Middletown, CA
Date:	Sunday, February 1, 1999
Time:	0800–1000 Event 1100–1300 After Action Review
Emergency:	An earthquake at 4 P.M. on a Thursday; a fire in the food court and a minor collapse of the facade on the southwest corner of the center
Public agencies:	Middletown Police and Fire Departments
Role players:	Center mall walkers and students from Middletown Community College primarily from the drama and public safety departments
Publicity:	Photographer from the Middletown Daily News
Planning committee:	A. Brown—General Manager B. Green—Marketing Director C. Black—Operations Director D. White—LT. MPD E. Jones—CPT. FPD F. Smith—Middletown College
Narrative:	The exercise is designed to simulate an earthquake occurring on a Thursday afternoon which then results in a small fire in the food court and the collapse of a portion of building facade. All employees ordinarily on duty Thursday at 4 P.M. will be on duty at the time of the exercise.
	The merchants have been notified and approximately 25 percent are willing to participate

in the event. Participation wil include closing their space and evacuating the center if necessary.

The volunteers from the community college and mall walker organization will act as customers. Some "customers" will "suffer" health problems such as breathing difficulties and heart problems, others will be "injured" by the fire, the falling facade and the evacuation.

The police and fire departments have committed resources to this exercise and the exercise will serve as a training exercise for those organizations. A police photographer will videotape the event for review.

The staff will be assessed on their ability to (1) maintain radio contact, (2) activate the emergency notification system, (3) contact public agencies, (4) assess and minimize damage to the center, (5) respond to the fire, (6) clear and secure the area of the damaged facade, (7) evacuate the center as necessary, (8) provide first aid and (9) respond to media inquiries.

After the event the committee will meet to assess the event and prepare the after-action report.

Resources

American Society for Industrial Security (ASIS)
1625 Prince Street
Alexandria, VA 22314
703-519-6200
FAX 703-519-6299
Organization for security professionals

Berkey Research
910 Carmel Mountain Road, Suite D
San Diego, CA 92129
619-538-5920
FAX 619-538-5996
Full-service consumer research services and mystery shopping

CAP Index
20830 Valley Forge Circle
King of Prussia, PA 19406-1130
610-354-9100
FAX 610-783-5705
Provides information on reported criminal activity within a specific geographical area

Center Security Management (CSM)
31921 Camino Capistrano, Suite 312
San Juan Capistrano, CA 92675
949-581-0832
FAX 949-458-6851
csmtgco@aol.com
A security consulting firm specializing in the shopping center industry, providing forensic review and expert witness testimony as well as developing site-specific security programs

Community Alert Network
255 Washington Ave., Suite 105
Albany, NY 12205
800-992-2331
Emergency notification system which does not require special equipment

PPM 2000
10216 124th Street
Suite 500
Edmonton, AB TSN 4A3 Canada
888-776-9776
FAX 403-448-0618
Develops and sells security reporting software

ProvenImage[SM]
31921 Camino Capistrano, Suite 312
San Juan Capistrano, CA 92675
949-581-1359
FAX 949-458-6851
ProvnImg@aol.com
A scenario-based evaluation process that uses role players to assess the performance of center security personnel

Security Law Newsletter
2125 Bancroft Place NW
Washington, DC 20008
202-337-2700
FAX 202-337-8324
Review of pertinent security cases

Recommended Readings

A Guide to Writing a Shopping Center Security Manual. New York: International Council of Shopping Centers, 1988.

Security and Safety: Issues and Ideas for Shopping Center Professionals. New York: International Council of Shopping Centers, 1995.

This chapter was contributed by Anna C. Northcutt, the owner of Center Security Management, San Juan Capistrano, California. She is also a partner in ProvenImage[SM], a firm which evaluates the performance of security officers and assesses effectiveness of on-site security programs.

9 | Risk Management and Insurance

Robert Nelson

This chapter begins with one basic concept. Every claim experienced by your center eventually hits the bottom line. Professional risk bearers (aka insurance companies) do not create wealth. Indeed, they must take in premiums that exceed their claims payout by approximately 20 percent. While the insurance vehicle may smooth out the bumps, ultimately the cost of noncatastrophe loss is borne by the entity that produces it.

Understanding the fundamental principles of risk management is a tool all key shopping center personnel should possess. It is involved in security, maintenance, engineering, marketing, leasing, construction and general management.

Loss costs play a lead role in the common area maintenance (CAM) charge hit parade. In addition, an unprotected exposure can result in the economic destruction of the center. It is, therefore, incumbent on you to understand and respond to your responsibilities as a risk manager.

Risk management can be broken down into five steps:

1. Identify
2. Reduce, eliminate, avoid, minimize
3. Assume
4. Transfer
5. Monitor

To address this concept in a real-world scenario, assume the role of risk manager. You have the task of making risk management decisions regarding the purchase of a regional mall. The center was built in 1974 and is located in southern California. A review of past claims indicates a serious assault in the nonpublic area and a relative frequency of parking lot incidents, including purse snatching and one abduction and assault.

Risk identification is the first step. Because of space constraints, limit your analysis to three serious risks. Most of you recognize that asbestos was a widely used building material in 1974. The location cries out *earthquake*. Loss history clearly indicates security problems. While you could identify many more risks, take these three and walk through the additional risk management steps.

Remember, Step 2 is to reduce, eliminate, avoid, minimize.

Asbestos can be eliminated by removing it entirely. Since much of it is in occupied tenant space, a phased abatement (removal of asbestos-containing materials as leases expire and tenant space is vacated) may be more practical. Having a good operations and maintenance (O&M) plan in place will minimize the chance of a premature release.

Security has many Step 2 possibilities. Since you have notice of prior problems, the owner must take reasonable action to prevent further incidents. This might include:

- Surveillance cameras
- Police substation in center
- Liaison with police
- Roving patrol in parking lot
- Portable police substation in parking lot
- Guard towers in parking lot

It is imperative that a specific plan be developed and carried out for your center.

Since your building was built in 1974 it does conform to California's 1973 building code, which designated earthquake construction requirements. Additional retrofitting was not considered by the current owners because of its multimillion-dollar price tag.

To speed this up, combine Steps 3 and 4 (assume and transfer) and apply them to each peril:

1. *Asbestos.* You decide on a phased abatement program. All common area asbestos-containing materials will be removed within the first year. Since asbestos-in-place insurance coverage is readily available for

a premium of $30,000 annually, you might purchase a $10,000,000 limit of coverage for bodily injury, property damage and third-party business interruption.

2. *Security.* Even if you take all the steps indicated in the list on the preceding page, you still have a major exposure that must be insured. Broad liability coverage with substantial limits must be obtained. In addition, leases, construction documents, special event programs and vendor and security contracts must be drawn to transfer as much contractual responsibility as possible away from the center.

3. *Earthquake.* The previous owner had self-insured this major peril. He had a sizable mortgage which was equal to the current value of the center. Since the lender had not required earthquake coverage, the owner had opted not to carry it. Since your owners have a substantial cash investment, your decision is quite different. Here are three options:

1. Totally assume the earthquake risk
2. Purchase a $10,000,000 limit of coverage with an annual premium of $150,000 (your center has 500,000 square feet, so this would be $0.30 per square foot)
3. Purchase full earthquake coverage with a limit of $70,000,000 and an annual premium of $400,000 (the additional CAM charge will be $0.80 per square foot)

Stop! Make your decision.

Some center managers might opt for the $10,000,000 limit. But now, consider this fact. The center in this example was in Northridge, California, and after the 1994 earthquake it was a pile of asbestos-containing rubble.

This is not intended to imply that maximum transfer is always the solution. However, when dealing with catastrophic perils (earthquakes, floods, hurricanes, etc.), the option must be seriously weighed.

Finally, risk management programs are a moving target. They must be monitored carefully to be sure they meet the requirement of a constantly changing environment.

The Policy

Since the policy is an agreement between you and a professional risk bearer, it must be closely reviewed and—yes—read through. When you tackle this, it is a good idea to have an insurance professional explain any confusing language. Having a basic knowledge of how insurance policies are structured makes reading them a little easier.

ELEMENTS OF AN INSURANCE POLICY

Most policies contain five sections. They are:

1. *Declarations.* This section gives the named insured, policy dates, location and other pertinent information that identifies specific data to given exposures.

2. *Insuring agreement.* This part is critical because it sets forth the carrier's obligation and spells out what exposures are insured.

3. *Definitions.* Explanations of issues such as who is a "named insured" and who isn't would fall into this section. Understanding the meaning of critical terms is essential to analyzing a policy.

4. *Exclusions.* Although you have a broad insuring agreement, exclusions can eat away at your perceived protection. You should have a firm understanding of how they affect you and why they are used.

5. *Conditions.* This section establishes the ground rules between you and the company. They spell out preagreed procedures for reporting claims. Since you have specific duties when a claim arises, it is best to know the rules of the road.

Hopefully, these hints will aid you in the exciting adventure of policy reading.

PROPERTY INSURANCE: WHAT IS INSURED

Obviously, risk managers insure buildings. Asking a group of real estate professionals to define what a building is may seem a little silly. But wait—are freestanding signs, retaining walls, wall-to-wall carpets, building equipment and parking lots part of the building? Remember reading the policy? The "building" is what the policy defines it to be. You cannot accurately value your building unless you completely understand how the policy describes it.

The building definition can include all of the above, so to arrive at a proper value, you must be aware of your policy provisions.

Income Protection. Maintaining an adequate income flow after a major loss is principally based on *rental income insurance.* Under many forms, the loss is defined as paying rent, less noncontinuing expenses, for a period of time during which the owner could reasonably be expected to get the property back to its original condition and ready for reoccupancy. An extension of the provision for six months, or even a year, is generally available. It should always be purchased.

Business interruption insurance reimburses you for lost profits. It applies to income derived from nonrental sources, such as the operation of a parking garage.

Personal Property. Valuation of this item is often badly handled. The actual cost to replace furniture, fixtures and equipment may far exceed its book value. Coverage to replace personal property should be based on a realistic appraisal of its real value.

Tenants' Improvements. Handling of this item is tricky. For example, ask yourself, "When do tenants' improvements become the property of the owner?" In most cases, the lessor acquires ownership when the lease is terminated, or on the date of installation. Responsibility for insuring tenant improvements should be clearly spelled out in the lease. If the tenant is to insure the property, the owner should be named as an additional insured on the policy.

Methods of Insuring

You still find the wording "fire, extended coverage and vandalism" in leases. This is "named peril" coverage and is quite limited in scope. Property coverage should always be written on an "all risk" basis. To further clarify the intent in certain areas, you may wish to specify "all risk including earthquake, flood and/or wind."

Two valuation methods are used. They are "replacement cost" and "actual cash value." *Replacement cost coverage* provides for replacement of damaged property with materials of like kind and quality without regard to depreciation. (Yes, you really do get a new building when an old one burns.) Replacement cost should normally be written. *Actual cash value* may be used if the insured building will not be replaced. Actually, if you decide not to replace a property you would receive actual cash value even if you *had* purchased replacement cost coverage. Actual cash value is defined by the insurance industry as the "cost to replace, less depreciation." If the building is older and has not been kept up, the amount of depreciation can be significant.

Stipulated or agreed amount coverage is critical. Securing it requires you to submit values to your carrier with an explanation of how they were arrived at. It can be the result of:

- A professional appraisal
- A replacement estimate by a reputable contractor
- Updating values on newer buildings
- New computerized appraisal software

You and the insurance carrier should agree that the values used are correct and that no coinsurance penalty will be applied. Historically, insurers wanted to encourage "insurance to value." To do so they offered lower rates for insuring to higher percentages of actual replacement cost; 100 percent coverage received the lowest rate. To keep the insureds honest, a coinsurance provision was added to the policy. This clause, simply stated, said that if you have underestimated your property value it will be appraised at the time of loss. If the replacement cost was double the original estimate, and you had used 100 percent replacement cost rates, you would have had a partial loss reduced by 50 percent. Sounds complicated, but there should be no coinsurance provision in your program. The stipulated amount should always be used.

Most property policies exclude loss resulting from building code enforcement. While you would get new for old, the cost of bringing an unsprinklered building into conformity with a code that required sprinklers would not be covered. Your exposure in this area should be closely evaluated and an adequate limit of coverage should be purchased to pick up this shortfall. It is commonly a percentage of the building value.

Pollution is both a property and liability exposure. While some cracks are appearing in pollution exclusions, it's best to assume your basic insurance program offers virtually no realistic coverage in this area. Insurance products have improved dramatically in recent years. Broad coverage is available to cover toxic cleanup, bodily injury, property damage and even business interruption. Having a clean Phase 1 assessment (an environmental assessment involving a historical review of occupancy and use of the subject property and adjoining premises, combined with a visual inspection of the site) does not mean you are out of the woods. This noninvasive technique has a significant margin of error because no attempt is made to penetrate the surface to check for evidence of pollution.

Types of Insurance Policies

LIABILITY COVERAGE

After restrictive endorsements like the pollution exclusion were added to the comprehensive liability policy, its name was changed to the *commercial liability policy*. It still offers broad protection against claims for bodily injury, personal injury and property damage. Personal injury is coverage for items like libel, slander, unlawful detention or wrongful eviction. Since the specific forms vary, you should carefully review your own policy provisions.

Umbrella liability policies provide excess protection over commercial liability, auto and employer's liability limits. There is normally some coverage included in the umbrella policy that is not picked up in the primary policy. Things like nonowned aircraft, advertisers' liability and care, custody and control coverage may be included subject to a self-insured retention (which is similar to a deductible) of $10,000 to $25,000.

Many risk managers might be tempted to say, "We don't own any cars so we don't need automobile coverage." But what about employees using their personal vehicles on company business . . . hired security patrols . . . rented cars? It is very important that you include coverage for nonowned and hired cars, in addition to any owned autos, in your umbrella policy.

Professional errors and omissions coverage is carried by property managers, asset managers, investment advisers, real estate brokers and virtually every professional you come in contact with (even insurance brokers). It covers breach of a professional duty which results in loss. Property managers are often accused of overselling the attributes of a center. Lawsuits normally occur after you sue a tenant for back rent. The cross-complaint usually alleges that the tenant's failure was directly related to overambitious representations made by the property manager.

Directors' and officers' and general partner liability policies cover negligence in the performance of those officials' respective duties. Since directors assume individual liability, a key feature is picking up this exposure. Never sit on a board of any kind without reviewing the directors' and officers' coverage carried by the entity.

Employment practices liability is probably the fastest-growing coverage in today's litigious world. Protection is available for a broad range of claims, from wrongful termination to sexual harassment. It is now available to most firms regardless of size.

Workers' compensation and employer's liability represent one of the oldest forms of social insurance. The basic principal is that an injured worker should receive continued compensation for payment of medical expenses if injured on the job. In exchange for this protection, the employee gives up his or her right to sue his or her employer for work-related injuries. In addition to statutory coverage (benefits required by the state), employer's liability coverage is carried to handle cases that breach the exclusivity remedy of the Workers' Compensation Act. The exclusivity remedy restricts an injured employee from seeking redress except under the applicable section of the Workers' Compensation Act.

Workers' compensation policy rates are high and are directly influenced by losses. Since most serious workers' compensation claims cover an extended period, the carrier must estimate the eventual cost, called reserving. Constant review of workers' compensation reserves is a big help in cost control.

OTHER TYPES OF COVERAGE

Boiler and Machinery. Historically, steam boilers were always insured separately. A significant portion of the premium was the cost of highly skilled professional inspections. Machinery breakdown coverage is available on conveyors, heating, ventilation and air-conditioning (HVAC) systems, electrical panels and other center equipment. It is prudent to assess your exposure and secure quotations to evaluate effectively the assumption versus transfer decision.

Employee Fidelity and Crime. This could be more accurately described as employee *in*fidelity coverage. It covers financial loss suffered by an employer resulting from dishonest acts committed by employees. Unfortunately, these incidents are not rare. It should be noted that the profile of a dedicated worker (spends long hours at the job, does not take vacations, is highly trusted, etc.) may also be the profile of the successful embezzler. If you suspect a problem, proceed with caution. Secure advice from professionals before making any charges. Should you decide to hire an employee with a history of dishonesty, the risk, should a repetition occur, is yours. The fidelity bond will not extend to a person who you know has a history of dishonest acts.

Cash and Securities coverage is available in crime policies. If major amounts of cash are handled, you may wish to insure this exposure. Protection against depositor's forgery (the altering of your checks) covers a fairly common occurrence.

Surety Bonds. Surety bonds are not insurance. They are a financial guarantee that specific contracts will be carried out. Bonding contractors on significant projects deserves serious consideration. Provided the owner fulfills his or her obligations, this guarantees that the project will be completed as planned at the agreed cost. It does not guarantee timeliness, but would normally cover financial penalties (liquidated damages) for construction delays.

Risk Transfer Through Contract

A center owner's first line of defense is the protection provided in leases, construction contracts and special events and public area agreements.

Leases should be carefully drawn, by real estate legal specialists, to provide maximum protection for the owner. In addition to the broadest permissible "hold harmless" wording (which varies from state to state), it should clearly spell out the risk being assumed by the tenant regarding damage to stock, furniture and fixtures, equipment, tenant's improvements and business interruption. Full coverage on these items should be purchased by the tenant. All tenant carriers should waive their subrogation rights (the right of a party who has paid a loss on your behalf to recover from a responsible third party) against the owner/manager. Often a dual waiver (a waiver under the owner's property insurance policy) is inserted which stops the owner's property carrier from recovering against a negligent tenant.

Owners normally assume responsibility for claims arising out of their negligent management of the common area. Tenants should assume full responsibility for liability claims occurring in their space, or arising from their activities in the common area. Certificates naming the owner as "additional insured" must be secured from all tenants. Evidence of specified property insurances should be included. Tenants should stipulate their coverage is primary.

Construction generates serious exposure to risk. Before a contractor comes on the premises, certificates evidencing adequate coverage and naming the center as an additional insured should be in hand. The certificate should stipulate that the contractor's coverage is primary.

Securing proper protection for special events is not as simple as it sounds. The key is giving your insurance broker ample time to investigate all aspects of the proposed event to develop the proper level of protection.

Transferring risk through contract is simply a method to establish responsibility up front and avoid costly coverage disputes when a major loss occurs.

Claims

An insurance policy is just a piece of paper until a claim occurs. It is at this point you find out if it works. Liability claims are common in centers. From slips and falls to assault cases, there is a wide range of third-party activity. The key to successful claims handling is the initial contact and report.

Center managers should develop a claims manual for their properties. It should outline basic procedures for all personnel, and assign specific responsibilities. For example, most major fires occur at night. Since the policy (remember the "conditions") requires a reasonable effort to protect the property from further damage, someone must be assigned that task.

Never admit liability. While this may seem obvious, it is consistently a problem. Use a good incident report form and secure every piece of information you can. Take pictures of the site, the surroundings and the potential claimant. Secure names, addresses and statements from all available witnesses. Report serious injuries immediately.

A separate written plan should be developed for handling catastrophic events. These may be earthquakes, hurricanes, tornadoes, floods, bomb threats and other serious security problems like a gunman loose in the premises. Your plan should be discussed with local police and fire officials so they know what your response will be in a major emergency.

Selection of Professional Support

From reading policies to designing effective indemnity agreements, shopping center managers normally require the assistance of a trained professional. Selecting the right support person is critical to a sound risk management program.

If your firm is large enough you may hire a full-time risk manager. Most companies, however, do not fill this post on a full-time basis. Should you fall in this latter category, the following steps may be useful:

1. Select a representative group of brokers, agents or direct writers to interview.

2. Ask each selected firm to explain, in a one-hour presentation, why it should be selected to provide this service.

3. Pay particular attention to the firm's knowledge of the shopping center industry; staff size and markets it works with; available services, especially a dedicated claims professional; and in-house loss control, which can act to give you direct support.

If this sounds like you are hiring a professional service team, it should, because you are.

All too often, the selection of a broker is based on price alone. Most brokers can deliver a competitively priced package. Without the proper support, you won't maintain the low cost. Claims will ultimately be paid for in higher premiums.

Just imagine that you are selecting your new attorney or certified public accountant. Approach the hiring of an insurance professional in the same way.

Conclusion

Before closing, it is most important to emphasize one of the most significant shortfalls in the shopping center industry's risk management agenda. There is very little training of on-site personnel. Unless a concerted effort is made to train these people in risk management, effective loss control will be very difficult. On-site sessions that convey practical, useful tools should be conducted regularly.

In recent years, the buyer of insurance has enjoyed a soft market. Insurance rates are low and coverage is readily available. Unfortunately, this condition usually does not persist for much more than a ten-year cycle. Competition forces prices to an unrealistically low level, profitability drops compared to other industries and capital moves to more attractive climates, resulting in a short supply of "capacity." Since insurance companies are regulated primarily on a ratio of premium to surplus, any shrinkage in carriers' net worth (assets minus liabilities) reduces their ability to absorb new premium writings.

One fact that gives cause for alarm is the loss of four major carriers recently. Some familiar names have disappeared via the merger route.

When and if the next tight market arrives, be prepared. Have a good loss history built on good risk management techniques. Have a professional in your corner who can access the whole marketplace. Your staff must be trained to respond effectively in all situations.

Build the base now—it will pay big-picture dividends.

Recommended Readings

Security and Safety: Issues and Ideas for Shopping Center Professionals. New York: International Council of Shopping Centers, 1995.

Understanding Insurance Vocabulary. New York: International Council of Shopping Centers, 1987.

This chapter was contributed by Robert Nelson, Senior Vice President, Sedgwick James, Inc., San Francisco, California.

10 | Crisis Management

Alan A. Alexander, SCSM, CPM

Crisis management is one of those areas of responsibility that shopping center managers must all be ready for at any given moment, but hopefully will never have to put to use. Many shopping centers are open up to twenty-four hours a day and subject to all types of emergencies and crises.

With any luck at all, it is possible that a manager will go through his or her entire career without having to face any sort of serious crisis. On the other hand, managers cannot take the chance that a crisis will come up and not be ready to deal with it. The downside of not being ready can be severe property damage, injury to customers, tenants, employees and subcontractors and/or the death of someone on the property.

While most shopping centers carry liability insurance to cover them should there be a liability claim, there are none that would not prefer to prevent a crisis situation or minimize its effect rather than let the insurance company deal with a serious injury or death after the fact.

Likely Crisis Situations

Before you can put together a crisis management plan you should have some idea of the types of crisis that you are likely to be faced with. There are man-made crises and natural disasters. Typical man-made crises include bomb threats, fires, robberies, burglaries and assault. Natural disasters can also include fire, in addition to earthquakes, floods, tornadoes, hurricanes and, in some states, volcanic eruptions.

It is critical that you are aware of the types of situations that you are likely to encounter and that you have a realistic plan in place to deal with these situations.

Shopping Center Types

This topic will be approached from two points of view. Larger shopping centers are generally staffed on a full-time basis during all hours that the property is open to the public. Obviously, with on-site staff it is more likely that someone will be available to deal with the emergency almost immediately. On the other hand, smaller shopping centers are quite often managed from a central office, and there may not be a representative available on-site, or even available on short notice, to take charge of an emergency situation. Because of these differences, the following outline of an approach to crisis management will be considered from the perspective of both types of shopping center.

Shopping Center Location as a Factor

Obviously, the location of the shopping center will help determine the types of crisis that the center will likely encounter. On the West Coast, earthquakes are much more likely to occur than in the Midwest. On the East Coast, you are more likely to find hurricanes than on the West Coast. Flooding is common on coastal properties and in river valleys. Crime can occur in any environment, but it appears that urban locations are more likely to experience this type of problem than their suburban counterparts.

It is also necessary to be aware of the immediate environment. Are there conditions in the trade area that may suggest a higher degree of risk than in other areas? Take, for example, a shopping center in the middle of a known gang territory. It might be a good idea to employ a walking security force during the hours in which problems are likely to occur, and have a close working relationship with the police or county sheriff's office to help with any problems that may come up.

If you are located next to a major sports stadium you may experience problems after a big game. If you are next to a mass transit station you may have problems during peak commuting hours, both in the morning and in the afternoon. In order to do a complete job of crisis management you must fully understand the environment in which you operate.

Preparation

There are three basic entities that can be a great deal of help in putting together an effective crisis management plan. The local police department will come to your shopping center, walk the site with you and make suggestions for safety and security. The local fire prevention arm of the fire department will do the same, but more from the fire and explosion point of view. Finally, your insurance carrier will conduct an annual inspection of the shopping center and can be a great source of suggestions for handling all types of crisis. In many areas there is an office of emergency preparedness that can provide excellent information on various types of emergencies and how to deal with them. Many times this agency will have brochures to share with your staff and your tenants.

The shopping center owners will provide the guidance for any crisis management program, but the on-site management and/or third-party management has the responsibility to point out the likely situations and, where helpful, make suggestions as to the most effective crisis management plan for each shopping center.

While most owners are generally very concerned with safety and security and good crisis management, it is generally felt that the large institutional owners show the greatest interest and require detailed plans for dealing with likely crises. You can learn a great deal by studying the detailed approach of these institutions.

A manager should consult legal counsel on the importance of complying with procedures which have been adopted and disseminated. A failure to follow these procedures could have serious consequences in the event of litigation.

Security's Role in Crisis Management

Virtually every regional and superregional shopping center has a security staff. They are not there because the center has experienced security problems, but rather as a preventive measure and as a management tool to deal with potential problems, emergencies and crises.

Having staff members—i.e., security—on site provides the public with an additional comfort level while shopping in the center, and also relieves management of the need to be monitoring, on a direct basis, the everyday activities of the center relative to potential problems.

However, smaller shopping centers and even medium-sized shopping centers that have not experienced any security problems are reluctant to add security due to the high cost when allocated over the smaller square footage. When you do not have the luxury of on-site, full-time security, you should devise ways to keep informed of and have a quick response to problems when needed. Particularly in small shopping centers with no on-site staff, it is very effective to involve the tenants and site contractors in the crisis management plan to increase the chances that a crisis will be identified early and be brought under control before there is additional damage or injury.

Emergency Equipment

Most shopping centers do not have the space to keep a full complement of emergency equipment. However, each crisis management plan should have a list of the likely equipment that may be needed and where it can be found. Emergency generators may well be needed on short notice. Rather than calling around when others may have the same need, it is a good idea to identify a source and make arrangements on an "as needed" basis. You should know where to hire security officers on short notice. You may need to know how to get a window boarded up immediately, or the location of the nearest hospital emergency room, or which personnel or contractors can deal with an open 220-volt line immediately, with a broken water main on short notice or with a stuck elevator with a full load on immediate call.

If you do have emergency equipment on site, it should be checked on a regular basis to be sure it is in serviceable condition. Every six months is not too often, especially for flashlights, emergency first aid kits and fire-fighting equipment such as fire extinguishers.

Putting Together the Crisis Management Plan

Once information is gathered from the police, fire department, insurance carrier, tenants, owners and any other sources likely to contribute, the manager may go about drafting a crisis management plan. The following list contains topics that may be covered in the plan, with a brief description of each topic:

- *Statement of purpose.* The purpose is to identify likely emergencies, provide realistic steps to deal with various types of emergencies, provide a listing of proper agencies and personnel to deal with emergencies, steps to be taken to return the property to normal operating conditions, procedures to deal with the media in emergency situations and dealing with the paperwork to wrap up the emergency. This plan is for management and ownership and will not be shared with the tenants. A separate plan will be suggested for the tenants of the shopping center.
- *Types of emergencies to be covered.* This section should outline the likely emergencies to be dealt with at the specific shopping center. While you cannot cover every emergency, if you have a good plan it will very likely help even with emergencies that you did not anticipate.
- *Members of the emergency procedures team.* The emergency procedures team should be clearly defined. In large regional centers the first report most often goes directly to security and then passes along up the line from there. After-hours crisis situations should have a very specific calling order. Some malls have an emergency beeper that goes with a different person each night, ensuring that someone is always available through that beeper. A shopping center in Uruguay has a designated management person available by phone 24 hours a day and a designated management person on site during every hour that the shopping center is open.
- *Listing of emergencies and actions to be taken.* Each type of likely emergency should be listed along with the suggested action to be taken.
- *Listing of persons to be notified and/or called in case of emergency.* This listing will outline who is to be called first, who is to be called second, and so on, under various circumstances. This portion of the plan should be set up for easy substitution of names or titles. No matter the calling order, the center manager should be notified in all emergencies once the primary members of the team have been notified. In centers where there are no on-site personnel, it is very likely that the first call should go to the police or fire department, and only then should the main office of the management company be contacted. Most often the insurance company for the shopping center will want to be notified at the earliest possible time, but this reporting is usually left to the upper management rather than the person first responding to the crisis.

• *If emergency equipment is to be kept on site, the types of equipment, amounts of equipment and location of the equipment should be included in the plan.* If emergency equipment and supplies are not to be stocked on site, the items that are likely to be needed should be listed along with the sources for those supplies. It should be remembered that twenty-four-hour phone numbers should be obtained for getting these supplies, as a crisis can happen any time of the day or night.

• *Instructions for documentation of emergency actions taken.* This section should cover the insurance company's requirements for documentation, as well as the shopping center owner's requirements. It is a good idea to document action taken, monies spent, instructions given by the police or fire department, instructions given by management to tenants and customers and, where appropriate, photos taken or videotape recorded for future reference. It should be noted that during an emergency management can usually disregard any budget constraints and spend reasonable amounts of money to resolve the crisis without fear of being in violation of any management agreements. It may also not be necessary to get bids for services and/or materials under emergency conditions. However, if you have done any advance work on identifying sources of emergency supplies, it may be presumed that you would have tried to factor in the best price as well.

• *Dealing with the media.* This will be discussed at length later in this chapter, but very specific instructions should be outlined and all personnel fully aware of the company's position on dealing with the media. This is a much more sensitive area than you might suppose if you have never gone through the process.

• *Returning the property to normal conditions.* Once the emergency is over, it is critical to return the shopping center to normal operations as soon as possible. This section should deal with the need to meet police, fire department and insurance company requirements and then, at the earliest possible time, to return the shopping center to its normal look and full operation to eliminate the curious from coming to look at the damage.

• *Evaluating the situation after the fact.* There should be a procedure for evaluating the emergency response after the fact. This is a time to look for meaningful changes to the policies and procedures; to evaluate what went well and what did not happen as planned. It is not an opportunity to criticize personnel or to place blame. The purpose of this evaluation is to make sure that the next time the property is faced with an emergency situation, the staff is better equipped to handle it and any deficiencies are corrected.

In addition to an emergency procedures manual for the shopping center personnel, a tenant manual may also be prepared for the tenants of the shopping center (see pp. 216-217). This need not be a complicated or expensive document, but rather one that is prepared on the computer so it can be easily updated and distributed and handed out as needed. It is important to note that much of an emergency procedures manual can be used for various shopping centers, but the details should be specific to each shopping center, reflecting every unique condition that should be considered.

This manual will change slightly depending on the type of shopping center involved. Where there are either security personnel or management personnel on site during business hours, most calls will be directed to their attention. However, in smaller centers without on-site staff, the first calls may well go to the police and/or fire departments and then to management. Tenants should be instructed whom to call, depending on the situation.

Evacuation Plans

Generally, one of the more important details of a crisis management plan is that of evacuation of the property. A small strip shopping center is fairly easy to evacuate. The tenants are either instructed to exit through the front entrance, the rear door if they have one, or the closest exit depending on the type of shop. Usually, a small center has little problem with evacuation onto the parking lot.

However, a multilevel shopping center may well have thousands of customers and hundreds of employees to deal with in an emergency situation, and careful consideration has to be given to how they should exit and where they should go should an evacuation be necessary. Most often the police and fire departments can be of some help in working out an effective evacuation plan.

Another major consideration when creating an evacuation plan is who will make the decision and under what circumstances. In the past, the landlord would have to make the decision when to evacuate the center. Bomb threats were especially difficult, as they were most often a hoax. Today, however, most centers tell the tenants what the situation is and let them decide if they want to evacuate, except in situations where evacuation is clearly the best alternative.

In any case where it is necessary to evacuate the customers from the center, it is generally held that this should be done in the most "low-key" fashion consistent with the situation to avoid a panic in which more people may be hurt than would be from the primary problem.

Dealing with the Media

The larger the shopping center and the larger the disaster, the more likely the media will cover the situation and want information and/or interviews. The media should never be ignored. If you do not help them with their reporting, they are likely to find another source that will, and that source may not provide accurate or timely information, thus causing the shopping center problems in the future. It may seem to the novice that granting a media interview is an easy thing to do. Just sit down, cover the facts and answer the questions. If that were all there is to it, it would, in fact, be quite easy to do and almost any staff member could do it.

However, the media may be looking for an indication of wrongdoing, negligence or malfeasance and they feel compelled to report such findings to the public. The purpose of good media management is not to hide any problems, but to know when to answer a question and when to leave it to the corporate counsel, the insurance company, the shopping center owner or other personnel more familiar with such situations.

Only one person should be assigned the job of working with the media. That person may be a senior management member, fully briefed by knowledgeable personnel on how to handle an interview and supplied with a package of facts and figures on the shopping center to share with the media. Generally, such packages include the size of the center, the number of shops, the overall value of the center, staff size, ownership information, year of construction, and so on.

Dealing with Specific Emergencies

The following sections outline some of the more common emergencies along with suggested actions to be taken. However, it is recommended that the final plan worked out for each individual shopping center be developed with the local authorities, the company counsel, the insurance carrier, the shopping center owner, tenants of the property, all staff members and the local emergency preparedness office. The more input you can gather before finalizing the plan, the less likely that any important points will be missed.

EARTHQUAKE

One of the major dangers in an earthquake is from falling objects. In the planning stages the buildings should be inspected for items that are likely to fall in an earthquake, and they should be secured. Hot water heaters are a common problem, along with tenant signs that are not bolted to the building and interior space heaters strapped to the ceiling or wall. Any item that can be stabilized with reasonable effort should be tightly secured.

It is generally accepted that anyone who is indoors at the time of an earthquake should find something sturdy to get under—either a doorframe, a large desk or even a large sink. If people are outdoors at the time of an earthquake they are advised to move away from the buildings to avoid anything that may fall off. Great care should be taken to avoid fallen electrical power lines.

FIRE

Generally, shopping centers are reasonably well protected in case of fire. Many have installed sprinkler systems and have fire extinguishers on hand, while restaurants are required to have specialized equipment for range fires. The majority of centers are served by well-trained fire departments.

Additionally, you may want to implement an inspection program to be sure that heating systems are properly maintained, and that merchants do not have inadequate electrical cabling or noninspected gas or electrical equipment in their stores.

You should also inspect doors and windows to be sure that they open and operate as they should. Safety exits should not be barred so that they cannot be used in an emergency. Materials should not be stored in emergency exit lanes and all lighted exit signs should be in proper working order.

It is helpful to invite the fire department to walk the shopping center with you to discuss other fire safety precautions and, in some cases, make suggestions to tenants about improving their fire readiness.

ELEVATOR EMERGENCIES

While many smaller shopping centers do not have elevators, some have a second story for offices, and many larger, multilevel centers may have more than one elevator. Telephones in elevators are often hooked up to the elevator maintenance company on a twenty-four-hour-a-day basis. Elevators should be inspected regularly and under a service contract to assure that they are in good working order at all times.

While contacting the fire department in an elevator emergency might be considered to be a good idea, the best source of help, if it is immediately available, is the elevator service company. It fully understands the equipment and how to get someone out of the elevator when it malfunctions.

Communicating with the people stranded in an elevator during the emergency will help them get through what is a very stressful situation for most people. Just telling them what is going on and what has been done to get them out should help relieve some of their anxiety.

FLOODING

Flooding is more likely to cause property damage than injury or death, but flash floods can be life-threatening. If your shopping center is in a potential flood area, precautions should be made for emergency sandbag protection and evacuation plans developed.

Tenants, maintenance personnel and management personnel should be advised to be extremely careful in flooded buildings, as the potential for electrical problems in floor outlets is quite high.

If specific areas of the center are low or if there are basement locations, it might be a good idea to have emergency pumps on hand or available.

MEDICAL EMERGENCIES

You may have heard horror stories about someone who has come to the aid of an injured or sick person in a medical emergency and then was sued because the action taken was not the correct procedure. This is not likely to happen, due to more recent "Good Samaritan" legislation, but it is important to know what to do until properly trained help can get to the person.

You should know where to get the quickest response in a medical emergency. Many communities have emergency medical mobile units, which are available by calling 911. In other areas the local emergency room in the nearest hospital is the best source, but in any case you need to know which to call.

If a medical emergency happens in a store space and you are called, you should know just where your responsibility lies and what the appropriate action should be. A tenant's corporate office should advise the on-site tenant staff as to whom to call in this situation. Mall management can offer suggestions. Most major centers have first aid kits in the security office, but do not attempt anything beyond emergency first aid.

HURRICANES

The main source of problems in shopping centers during a hurricane is that of roof collapse. Fortunately, hurricanes are generally tracked as they move; this will give you some advance warning and a chance to evacuate the building. There is also the opportunity to prepare by securing items that may blow around and hurt someone, and by boarding up or taping windows.

During a hurricane people are advised to stay indoors and seek a secure place such as a basement to stay until the storm has passed.

TORNADOES

Tornadoes occur mostly in the southern and central United States, but there are few states that do not have some risk of being hit by such severe storms. Generally, tornadoes hit with little or no warning, and this makes them harder to deal with than hurricanes.

CRIME

There are many types of crime that you may have to consider in your shopping center. These can include rape, drug dealing, burglary, riots, gunfire, gang activity, fights, vandalism, robbery, family abuse, child abduction and hostage situations.

If someone is successfully mugged in the parking lot and security is not increased or other safety measures are not taken, the incident may be taken as an invitation for the next mugging.

Lighting is generally considered to be one of our best deterrents to crime, and should be high on the priority list for your shopping center.

If you have a small center without security, you can often get the local police to do several drive-throughs a day, giving your center a police presence. If you are experiencing a problem at a specific time of day, such as unruly teenagers after school lets out, you can ask for a special police patrol or add a private guard at the hours needed.

It is often helpful to issue a three-call system to all tenants, whereby designated persons each call three additional people. If a shoplifter is noticed in one store, all stores can be quickly notified through the three-call system of their presence in the center and other merchants will be put on the alert. If security personnel are present in the center, they often carry either a pager or cell phone and can be called to assist. While most security guards are there for the common areas, many will help if there is a problem within a specific store space. There can be serious liability for false arrest, and security guards should not be casually placed in that position.

Merchants should be encouraged to report any crimes to management and management should keep track of such reports to spot any trends that may be stopped by proper action. Keeping the merchants informed as to any ongoing problems, such as gang activity, will allow them to take precautions as well. While there is a concern on the part of some shopping center owners that keeping the merchants informed of criminal activities may cause undue alarm, it is generally held that keeping them informed will allow them to take precautions and will also lessen the potential liability on the shopping center owner's part should a similar problem come up in the future. It should be noted that once a system for notifying tenants is in place, there may be liability for the landlord's failure to inform the tenants.

The Tenant Kit and Emergency Procedures Manual

It is a good idea to issue a tenant kit and emergency procedures manual to each tenant in the shopping center. The table of contents could be developed along the following lines:

I. Building Information
   A. Building address, office and emergency telephone numbers
   B. Management and maintenance
   C. Moving-in procedures
   D. Tenant identification/directory listings
   E. Space designations
   F. Shopping center hours/after-hours entry
   G. Building security
      1. Security guard's telephone
      2. Tenant space security
      3. Theft/break-in
   H. Safety procedures
      1. Fire alarm boxes
      2. Fire exits
   I. Keys

   J. Building services and facilities
      1. Maintenance requests
      2. Heating and air-conditioning
      3. Trash pickup
      4. Mail delivery
      5. Employee parking
      6. Construction approvals
      7. Sign approvals
   K. Holidays
   L. Rental payments
   M. Marketing activities
   N. Rules and regulations
II. Emergency Procedures
   A. Fire protection
   B. Medical emergency
   C. Explosions
   D. Earthquake
   E. Suspicious objects
   F. Bomb threats
      1. Bomb threat checklist
   G. Criminal activity

The tenant kit and emergency procedures manual may be prepared on a computer and updated as new information is received. Generally, it can be given to each new tenant as soon as the lease is signed, provided to each new store manager as changes come about and reissued as new information becomes available.

The combining of emergency procedures (crisis management program) with the tenant kit and building operations manual takes away some of the concern that it may have the effect of alarming the tenants about dangerous or undesirable conditions. This makes the emergency procedures manual a part of keeping the tenants informed without indicating specific situations or concerns.

Counsel should provide appropriate disclaimers for procedures, manuals and kits.

Summary and Conclusions

Crisis management is one of those activities that you must be fully prepared for and hope that you do not need. Remember to work out the final plan for each individual shopping center with the local authorities, the company counsel, the insurance carrier, the shopping center owner, tenants of the property, all staff members and the local emergency preparedness office. The more input you can gather before finalizing the plan, the less likely that any important points will be missed.

Many of your management activities are repetitive and predictable, but many of the likely crises that you may face come with little or no warning. You should be prepared to go from normal functions to emergency operations and back to normal with a minimum of confusion and misdirected activities. We would all like to think we would be cool and controlled during an emergency situation, but there are often conflicting demands inherent in the situation, there are many needs that must be met at the earliest possible moment and there will be those that will be there after the fact to evaluate how we handled the situation. By fully understanding the situations that you may possibly be faced with and having an advance plan for those situations, you are much more likely to be able to deal with them in a calm, professional manner and, as a result, be able to minimize the risk to people and the shopping center.

You should first fully understand the types of crises that you are likely to face in any given shopping center. You should then prepare a plan to deal with those events that will be as realistic and effective as is possible. However, once you have devised the plan, it will not be of much value if you have not fully informed those who will implement that plan in the event of the emergency as to how the plan will work and what their role may be in implementing the plan. Training is essential for the staff and tenants that will be involved in the plan.

Your plan should include the necessary preparations for emergencies, the appropriate action to be taken during an emergency and, finally, procedures for getting the property back to normal as quickly as is practical after the emergency has passed.

No matter how complete your planning or how well you execute the plan during an emergency, there will be things that you could have done better, so it is important that you evaluate those activities after the fact to better prepare for the next crisis. This objective analysis is meant to help you to improve your response and not to punish those who may not have performed exactly as you hoped they would.

Your ability to deal with crisis situations will enhance your shopping center by providing the best possible level of response and providing the maximum protection for life, limb and property. The reduction of potential liability for the owners is an added benefit.

Recommended Readings

Alexander, Alan A., SCSM, and Richard F. Muhlebach, SCSM. *Operating Small Shopping Centers.* New York: International Council of Shopping Centers, 1997.

A Guide to Writing a Shopping Center Security Manual. New York: International Council of Shopping Centers, 1988.

Guide to Writing a Tenant Manual. New York: International Council of Shopping Centers, 1987.

Security and Safety: Issues and Ideas for Shopping Center Professionals. New York: International Council of Shopping Centers, 1995.

Shopping Centers and the Media: Crisis Communication. New York: International Council of Shopping Centers, 1994.

This chapter was contributed by Alan A. Alexander, SCSM, CPM, Senior Vice President, Woodmont Real Estate Services, Inc., Belmont, California.

11

Redevelopment and Renovation

Joseph P. Cilia, SCSM

During the life span of every shopping center there will come a time when the center must be renovated, expanded, reconfigured or redeveloped. Unless there are extraordinary circumstances, such as when the construction is a major redevelopment with a very high vacancy rate, the construction work will be accomplished while the center is open and operating. Maintaining the center's operation and profitability during the construction requires planning and constant supervision of the changing impact on the property as the construction progresses.

Renovation/Expansion/Reconfiguration/Redevelopment

RENOVATION

As centers get older, even well-maintained centers need updating. A tired-looking center is a target for sales decline and an invitation to competition. As tenant leases expire and stores renovate or are replaced, the new store look needs the appropriate mall setting to feature the store. The best-looking stores can be lost in an old, tired center. Renovations can include new floor and wall surfaces, addition of skylights, fountains and complete redos or additions of rest rooms and other amenities. Roofs, parking lots and lighting are usually addressed at this time with upgraded lighting and restriping.

EXPANSION

Expanding a shopping center is usually done in conjunction with the addition of an anchor tenant. An anchor tenant is a major store (usually a chain store) having substantial economic strength and occupying a large square footage, such as a major department store branch. The new anchor provides the customer draw and provides the support for increasing the gross leasable area (GLA), allowing the addition of new stores (new uses) or expansion of existing stores. Anchor stores will usually have large advertising budgets, and the stores' locations are generally identified in the ad, which increases customer traffic.

RECONFIGURATION

The configuration of a shopping center is the layout of the stores and the common area connecting the various stores. Strip centers are usually configured in a straight line or "L" shape, allowing passing traffic to view all the storefronts; anchor tenants are given prominent locations and act as a draw to bring in the customers; parking lies directly in front of the stores and rarely continues around the back and sides.

Malls traditionally are two strips of retail stores with anchors on each end, all connected by an open or enclosed common area. Larger malls might be in a cruciform (cross or X) pattern reaching out to the anchor tenants. It sometimes becomes advantageous to reconfigure the layout. This is done to:

- Accommodate new anchors
- Compensate for the loss of an anchor
- Improve parking lot configuration
- Add a level
- Change the use or image of the center

Reconfiguration is usually difficult and can involve relocating multiple existing tenants, changing the parking layout, reworking access and ring roads (roads that circle the mall) and relocating utility lines. If a level is added, it may require enhancing (strengthening) columns and supports in common area and tenant locations to accommodate the weight load of the new upper level.

REDEVELOPMENT

Redevelopment is usually a more comprehensive action and may include renovating, expanding and reconfiguring a center. Redevelopment looks at the entire center. It provides an opportunity to change the marketing direction of a center (targeting a specific customer your center is trying to attract) to meet a changing market area (the area surrounding a shopping center from which the center draws its customers). A center that once served an older customer may now be faced with a younger customer influx that requires different stores, more entertainment facilities and different amenities, such as family rest rooms (a securable separate bathroom which can usually accommodate a stroller and has diaper-changing facilities).

Redevelopment is also used to recycle a center that has lost its anchor tenant or is unable to meet new competition in the market area. Examples include a traditional center which previously housed a large department store and numerous smaller tenants. The loss of and inability to replace the anchor would normally adversely affect the other tenants. This center might be a candidate for redevelopment into an:

- Entertainment complex with theaters, restaurants and related retail
- Off-price center, which sells branded merchandise at lower prices
- Outlet center, consisting mostly of manufacturers' outlets selling their own brand at discount

Getting Started

The earlier a property manager can get involved the better. When discussions are being held involving planning the renovation/expansion/reconfiguration/redevelopment (hereafter referred to as renovation), ask to be included in these meetings. Show an interest, ask questions. This is especially important when they are held on site. Remember, your input counts; decisions that are made can affect future operations and common area maintenance (CAM) charges and the profitability of the center. For example, the impact of materials selected, such as glass railing, can add significantly to cleaning and repair/replacement costs.

This is the time to bring up any additions or changes you have been trying to make (wish list). If you were always having to run all kinds of extension cords to install holiday decor, get those electrical outlets installed with the renovation; it is almost always less expensive than doing them as an add-on later. If you are contemplating adding seasonal or temporary carts, get the phone conduit and electrical outlets in as part of the new floor. It is very difficult and expensive to come back and rip up floor material and run these lines. This is true for hose bibs (water faucets) that are needed by housekeeping and many other similar items that you need but were too expensive or difficult to install separately.

When new GLA is created, the leasing can be affected by different factors that are part of the construction:

- The amount of frontage (total linear feet exposed to the mall customer common area) retailers want to maximize the exposure and visibility of the store
- Depth of the store; the space should be deep enough to house the selling area and stockrooms, if required. This factor works with frontage; it is hard to lease a store 150 feet deep with only 15 feet of frontage.
- Impact of utilities and ductwork passing through the store; a 4 foot by 4 foot floor-to-ceiling shaft in the middle of a 600-square-foot space can greatly decrease the marketability of a tenant space
- Access to service corridors and delivery facilities; the retailer with a 3,000-square-foot toy store does not want to accept deliveries and take out trash through the front of the store. This would disrupt the selling floor and customers and greatly limit the time frame for deliveries. Appropriate accommodations for deliveries of stock and removal of trash would enhance the store's ability to produce and would reduce damage to common area floors and surfaces.

MEET THE PLAYERS

In most cases the planning meeting will include the construction or development wing of the company, the asset or senior management, the architect and the general contractor. Ask to see the site plans and drawings to get an overall idea of the scope of the project and its impact on the day-to-day operations of the center. You may be held accountable for the viable operation of the center during construction and will need to know the scope of the work and the players who will be on site. Get emergency phone numbers of contractors and key subcontractors. Make sure they have numbers for you and key people on your staff and where they can be reached. The architect and general contractor are key players, and their cooperation is essential in minimizing impact on day-to-day operations.

ASK QUESTIONS

The sooner the better, ask questions about:

- Floor and wall surfaces being used
- Door hardware

- Skylights/glass railing
- Fountains
- Additional rest rooms and their location
- Elevators/escalators
- Interior/exterior landscaping
- Lighting changes
- Heating, ventilation and air-conditioning (HVAC) changes
- Energy management systems
- Parking lots/decks
- Security equipment
- Plans for trash removal
- Food court deliveries, fixtures and tray wash
- Delivery location and circulation
- Temporary barricades and walkways
- Construction schedules
- Configuration of new GLA that will be available to lease (lease plans). Location, location, location—three of the most important words to a retailer. Every tenant wants a prime location with high visibility. The more highly visible locations, with the right size, frontage and configuration, you can create, the greater the return on the leasing and profitability.

This is obviously only a partial list, but the idea is to find out as much as you can about the project. These items will impact future operations of the center and its profitability.

Communication

One of the most important factors in the renovation process is communication—communication on all levels, from keeping senior management informed on the progress of the project to letting housekeeping know what will be included in the next day's demolition. Whether you are dealing with a corporate development office or directly with the contractor, you have to know the schedule, the timetable of what activities will happen when. Many times there are different teams or subcontractors working on different parts of the schedule on different timetables. It is very possible that these activities can conflict or overlap—for example, one crew working on a sidewalk in an area that requires limiting access to the center, while a demo (demolition) crew needs to close an adjacent area, both working on their own schedule—at the start of the Memorial Day weekend. Obviously, something has to be changed, but unless the parties communicate, there could be serious problems.

Communication is needed between center management and:

- Senior management
- Corporate construction/development personnel and consultants (architects, engineers, traffic, signage, etc.)
- General contractor/subcontractors
- Center staff: cleaning, maintenance, marketing and security
- Public/governmental agencies
- Tenants of the shopping center
- The community
- Customers

SENIOR MANAGEMENT

Whether you deal directly with the owner, corporate office or regional supervisor, it is important to keep them updated on the project; let them know of any problems or delays. If you are controlling the budget for the project or portions of it, keep them advised of any pending or threatened cost overruns or significant savings. Document conversations on scheduling and progress with the contractors; a summary worksheet showing status on construction, leasing and tenant activity, if applicable, may be helpful. Minutes of regular meetings with the contractor should be kept and used for follow-up at subsequent meetings.

CORPORATE CONSTRUCTION/DEVELOPMENT PERSONNEL

In larger companies, there may be a whole department or a key person assigned to construction and development; some projects may employ a construction manager. That person will generally hire the architect, project consultants and general contractor; coordinate permits and governmental approvals; and, in most cases, will also oversee the construction budget. As noted earlier, it is very important to get involved with this department as early as possible. It is advantageous to have input into the design, materials used and work schedule. Attending progress meetings allows you to have firsthand knowledge of the status of the work schedule and interject important site information relative to the center's needs. You are then in a better position to convey data back to your staff, the tenants and ultimately the customers.

GENERAL CONTRACTORS/SUBCONTRACTORS

The general contractor will have a project manager, site engineers, foremen and other personnel on site, depending on the size and scope of the project. There should be weekly job meetings to go over work schedules, coordinate different operations and examine center impact conditions. Unless the center has been closed for the construction effort, you will need to watch the impact on day-to-day operations closely. The contractor has a job to do and a schedule; you, as manager, have the obligation to assist, but must reduce negative impact on the operation and sales revenue of the property. The safety of the center's employees and customers must be guarded and risk reduced as much as possible. Public safety should always be addressed as each phase is discussed in the meetings. Public safety is a primary responsibility of the general contractor and he or she should not be relieved of it.

CENTER STAFF: CLEANING, MAINTENANCE, MARKETING AND SECURITY

Key center staff should attend the weekly construction meeting. This usually includes your operations manager, security director and marketing director. They will be able to relate what is discussed to their individual areas and have needed input as to possible problems and solutions. The firsthand knowledge acquired will assist them in conveying the needed input to their respective staffs, the tenants and the customers.

PUBLIC/GOVERNMENTAL AGENCIES

No large-scale project can be accomplished without the input/approval of local public and governmental agencies. This includes zoning boards, building departments/inspectors, fire marshals and other offices, depending on location. Key personnel in the departments noted should be kept in the loop; significant changes in plans should be reviewed. Many times code requirements for certain municipalities may differ from state or federal requirements. When the project includes additional tenant spaces, the tenant must also submit plans and obtain permits. If numerous tenants will be under construction, the building department should be advised so that the workload can be handled in a timely manner. You should obtain as much information as possible for incoming tenants so that plans will be processed by the agencies more smoothly. Different cities have special requirements that may be more stringent than the state's; for example, some municipalities restrict the use of combustible materials in storefronts in malls, may have special exiting requirements for stores over a certain size or may require rest rooms for employees/customers, including Americans with Disabilities Act (ADA) compliance.

TENANTS

Before renovation begins, all leases and REAs will have to be reviewed, necessary REA and lease consents obtained and documents amended, as needed.

During any renovation it is important to keep the tenants informed not only of the scope of the project but the timetable and the different phases before they impact the center. All the tenants want a better, more productive center. It is your job to let them know that the dust, noise, inconvenience and, in some cases, disruption of business is in the short run and the benefits are long term. An additional anchor and more or better parking and facilities are a plus. When a center is already doing well and the renovation includes an expansion, there are always questions regarding more competition for existing stores. There should be a tenant kickoff meeting and update sessions. Use marketing statistics that will show the benefit of three more shoe stores when you already have five. Creating a positive attitude is very important because it is passed on to the store employees and from them to the customers. This is the time to hold tenants' hands and let them vent to you. No tenant wants a construction crew ripping up the floor in front of its store or limiting access to the nearest entrance. Explain to the tenant that you will work to minimize the impact during center hours; offer additional signs and directions for customers for the best alternative access.

THE COMMUNITY

Before the announcement of a major project to the public, it is beneficial to lay the groundwork with the surrounding communities. Integration, participation and presentations at social and political organizations help ease the acceptance of changes that will occur, and questions and objections to the project can be anticipated and addressed. This is the time to "sell" the benefits of the project to the community and political leaders. Communities are always concerned about impacts on their lifestyle, such as additional traffic congestion, parking and security. A plan should be formalized to address these concerns.

CUSTOMERS

Experience shows that most customers are curious about construction work in progress. They want to be in the know about what new stores and services will be at "their" center. It is important to have proper signage with an architectural rendering of what the finished project will look like. Tell the customer why you're doing the construction (to make room for a new department store, food court, etc.). The construction effort should be included in any advertising or promotions.

What the customers don't want is to be or feel lost or dead-ended in a section of the mall under construction or to be lost in a parking lot that is ripped up. Signage is critical; it should be easy to read and have directions or arrows to follow. Customer service personnel may be needed to help the customers get to a destination they want and back to their cars. Temporary store directories would be helpful. Customers need to know that you are looking out for their safety with proper barricades. Nothing will turn off a shopper more than to walk into wet paint or trip on a partially finished floor that has not been properly barricaded or signed. When customers know what is going on, they feel like they are part of the process, and absorbing any inconvenience the construction may have imposed on them is a lot easier.

Surviving the Construction

As the project progresses and the disruption to the daily routine intensifies, the more communication and follow-up are necessary. The weekly meetings with the corporate office people (development, asset management, architect, contractor, etc.) should be supplemented by short at-location meetings with the general contractor and relevant subcontractors. Just as the various members of your team have different responsibilities, so do those on the contractor's. The contractor's teams are each working on its own schedule and their combined impact might have a negative effect on center operations. Get to know the members of the construction team; let them meet your team members. At some point, each of their schedules is going to affect your team; for example, night or early morning construction crews will affect your security coverage and cleaning schedule. It is hard to have a scrub crew come in to find a large section of the floor being jackhammered. With advance knowledge of the construction schedule, your housekeeping supervisor could use this opportunity to arrange other assignments.

DAILY WALK-THROUGH

Each day the center manager or a designated representative should tour the common areas of the center prior to opening to the public to ensure that the center is accessible and safe for customers and employees. This should be done early enough to correct any problem situations that may occur before the center opens to the public. The general contractor should also assign someone to accompany center management, someone with the ability and authority to make any necessary changes. In large projects where there are big on-site staffs, as many staff members as are available should attend the walkthrough. Among other things, the management team should be looking for:

• Conditions that might affect public and employee safety, including trip hazards, low clearance areas, open work sites which customers, especially children, might wander into, tools and electrical equipment left accessible by work crews. A plugged-in handsaw can be an inviting toy for a small child who has wandered away from his or her mother.

• Cleanliness—has the work area been swept, spills wiped up? Are customer rest rooms clean, up to housekeeping standards? With large construction crews, unless specific areas are set up for them, they will use the public rest rooms to clean up, change clothes, etc. During lunch and breaks, many construction crews will bring their own food in and eat on-site, in common areas and corridors. Provisions must be made for trash removal and some guidelines established on cleanliness.

• Security should be reviewing current work relative to opening and securing the center. Many times a day, construction workers will leave an entrance door blocked or a wall to the outside open that will have to be secured for the night to prevent access. Traffic control should be reviewed—are portions of the parking lot inaccessible, or has parking striping been altered? Will roadwork require traffic control personnel?

• Marketing should review changes in common area traffic flow; is additional signage needed? Are there directional or informational signs that need to be added? If any tenant storefronts or signage become blocked, additional freestanding or blade signs may need to be added. Will media need to be updated on the project status?

• The operations manager might be looking for benches or seating that may have been displaced or need to be relocated. Interior landscaping may need to be moved to safety or removed for various stages of the project. Has interior/exterior lighting been impacted? Will temporary lighting have to be installed? Are emergency lights still operable/tested? If there is an evacuation system or public address (PA) system, is it operable? Or will a temporary procedure need to be set— for example, assigned staff with bullhorns?

Usually there is only minimal construction occurring over the weekends and holidays. It is important, however, to do a second walk-through on Friday afternoons to ensure that the construction effort has not left any problems for the operation to handle during the weekends, which are usually busier with customer activity. It is also important that emergency numbers for the contractor be updated so someone can be reached to respond to an emergency over the weekends and holidays.

Weather factors should also be considered and any forecasted conditions, such as high winds or heavy rains, should be reviewed with the contractor. Usually during construction, materials are stored on site, and partially secured construction materials can become a hazard during high winds and storms. Local specialized conditions such as flooding, tornadoes, lightning and other conditions and their potential impact should be reviewed on an ongoing basis by monitoring weather reports.

PUBLIC SAFETY/INSURANCE

The safety of customers, visitors and employees at a shopping center is always a primary concern during any construction effort; additional care must be taken to safeguard them. As previously noted, safety and accident prevention should be an important part of meetings with the general contractor and during the daily walk-through. The need to look out for safety issues should be conveyed to all on-site personnel— security, housekeeping, maintenance, marketing. Any accidents that do occur should be reviewed for causes and what could be done to prevent future similar incidents. Many companies require that a safety committee be formed, chaired by the center manager. The committee would review accidents/incidents, investigate causes and suggest and implement remedies that would help prevent future accidents.

When accidents do occur, it is very important to follow company claims procedures. Claims made by individuals should be documented. In most cases your insurance carrier or claims representative should be notified as soon as possible after an accident. The general contractor should also be notified immediately so that he or she can review the accident site and prepare any documentation that may be required. Pictures of the scene should be taken and become part of the file. The general contractor, the tenant contractor, the tenant and all subcontractors must have commercial general liability insurance policies in place with the agreed-upon limits. The center should be provided with certificates documenting coverage for blanket contractual, personal injury, bodily injury and products/completed operations (see chapter 9, "Risk Management and Insurance"). The center owner, management and other related entities on site should be listed on the policy as "additional insured." These certificates should be logged and expiration dates checked; replacement certificates should be obtained when the policy expires. The certificate should also include a provision that additional insureds receive at least a thirty-day written notice prior to cancellation or termination of policy.

EXPENSES/BUDGETS

There is usually a construction budget that is different and separate from the budgets administered on site. General costs of plans, consultants, site work and hard construction costs are included in the construction budget. There is, however, an impact on the site-management expenses caused by a major project. There are additional costs associated with housekeeping, security, maintenance and marketing that should be discussed with the ownership so that bills can be properly processed to the correct account. In addition, there needs to be a detailed and fair allocation between construction-related expenses and normal common area expenses that are being passed on to the existing occupants of the shopping center. In some cases there is a trade-off of expenses, since not all normal expenses are generated. If interior landscape is removed during the construction period, the service contract and replacement expenses will not be incurred during that period.

Tenant Construction

Included in most renovations is the construction of additional gross leasable area (GLA). This will generate the need for new tenant construction in the newly created space. In addition, the relocation of existing tenants within the center may be required. Moreover, new tenants moving into spaces that have been vacated by tenants whose leases have expired may wish to renovate the existing store.

In order to ensure a consistent quality and look, the landlord usually establishes a set of criteria that the tenant's construction must adhere to. These standards are often defined in a "Design Criteria" manual or a similar document. This resource provides general and specific information relative to the center and what is required of the tenant, information that is needed by the tenant's architect and general contractor. The lease will include details of what is considered "Landlord's Work" and "Tenant's Work." Landlord's work can include providing basic connection points for utilities and plumbing, or installing demising walls or sheetrock. The landlord in some cases may give the space "as-is" to the tenant, and in other cases may build out a "vanilla box" for the tenant. Some landlords will also give the tenant a tenant allowance (TA) to build the space or provide rent concessions, including free rent, for a period of time.

Tenant Design Criteria

The design criteria manual for a center might include the following elements.

DIRECTORY
- Property location, including actual address, town and location relative to nearest large city
- Description of property, such as: a two-level regional mall anchored by two department stores and 75 specialty stores, located on 86 acres with a GLA of 875,000 square feet
- Landlord/developer's name and address, name of mall manager/tenant coordinator
- Contact at Building Department; fire inspector and utility contacts

GUIDELINES FOR STORE DESIGN
This section might include criteria for storefronts, signage, ceilings, interior finishes and merchandising. The amount of input into these factors can vary from company to company and by type of center within a company. Each tenant is usually required to submit detailed floor plans with samples of the different materials and colors to be used for floors, walls, ceilings, fixturing and storefronts. Local building and fire codes can also affect the materials selected. Plans usually must be approved by the landlord's corporate design manager.

MECHANICAL, ELECTRICAL, PLUMBING AND STRUCTURAL CRITERIA

In addition to visual store design, the tenant is required to submit detailed plans for HVAC, electrical design and requirements, plumbing fixturing (rest rooms, sinks) and layout, including fire protection (sprinklers/smoke detectors).

RESPONSIBILITIES OF TENANT/LANDLORD

This section outlines what is included in the location; for example, concrete floor slab, demising studding (steel supports located around leased space where sheetrock/walls will be attached) or connections to the site for electric supply or water source and drains. It spells out specifically what the landlord must provide and what the tenant must supply. This is usually also spelled out in the lease and amendments (changes) to the lease. In many cases, the landlord will provide plain cement floors, demising studding, empty conduit for electrical supply and access to sanitary sewer lines and vent connections. If the space was previously occupied, it may be turned over as the previous tenant left it. In most cases, the existing space must be demolished before new work can start. Sometimes, depending on design, some walls, HVAC and plumbing can be reused. This is usually addressed in the lease. In some centers, usually strip centers, the tenant is provided with a "vanilla box." This is a space that is partially demolished/constructed to provide ceilings, sprinklers, electric service and branch circuitry, HVAC system, storefront, basic walls and floor for the tenant to finish. It resembles a big empty box. The amount of build-out support in this area depends on the landlord's policy and what is negotiated in the lease.

In general, the tenant is usually responsible for the architectural design, demolition of existing store interior, floors, ceiling, storefront/doors/gates, painting/wall finishes, displays/fixturing, HVAC system, electrical and telephone systems, sprinklers, plumbing systems, alarms and all associated costs plus any filing fees, permits and taxes.

Timetable

The leasing department or manager will negotiate a tenant lease. As part of this process, the site is reviewed with the tenant. A lease outline drawing (LOD) is prepared for the tenant, showing the demised space and its relation to the center and adjacent spaces. Electrical, plumbing, HVAC and waste line entry points are identified. Existing partitions or fixturing is usually not shown. If the space was previously occupied and plans for that tenant are available, they would be provided at a later date. It would be wise on the tenant's part to have its architect, as well as bidding general contractors, measure and inspect the site. Once the lease is signed, the landlord will perform any work that he or she has agreed to perform and then turn the space over to the tenant. This turnover should be documented in writing and sent by certified, return-receipt mail to the tenant. This date will become the tenant's possession date and is the commencement date for the allowed tenant work period. The work period is the time the landlord gives the tenant to construct the store, usually without paying rent. This period can be anywhere from 60 to 180 days or more. It is important to document the possession/commencement date because it is the usual date that the clock starts ticking on the construction period. Most times the lease includes language that the tenant will start paying rent on the *earlier* of (1) the date the tenant opens for business, (2) the end of the construction period or (3) a specific date in the future.

During the construction period, the tenant must have the plans for its store reviewed and approved by the landlord and local municipalities, obtain permits, secure bids and hire a general contractor, build the space, stock it and open. This free-rent period should be limited and have penalties for exceeding limits to ensure the tenant will proceed in a timely manner and comply with the landlord's requirements.

In summary, the process is as follows:

1. The lease is negotiated and signed.
2. The landlord completes any work he or she is required to do under the lease.
3. The space is turned over to the tenant for construction.
4. The tenant has its architect draw up store plans and submits them to the landlord for approval.
5. The tenant submits plans to required municipalities for approval.
6. The tenant hires a contractor to build the store.
7. Construction of the store begins, along with inspections by the landlord and municipalities.
8. The store is completed and stocked with merchandise.
9. The store opens and the tenant starts paying rent.

Quite often, more than one item listed above may be occurring simultaneously. Requirements may be different for different landlords and different municipalities. Plans may get backed up by the reviewing agencies for municipalities; this is especially true when a major expansion, involving many new tenants, is in progress. Sometimes the services of a local expediter is desirable. The expediter is familiar with the code requirements and usually knows what the municipality requires. This can save numerous resubmissions and time.

Other Details

ENVIRONMENTAL ISSUES

Perhaps the best method of handling the following environmental issues is to have ongoing programs that meet the established governmental guidelines. During construction these problems may be amplified and can cause delays in the construction schedule and additional expenses. Numerous environmental issues may arise during construction; these include, but are not limited to the following:

Asbestos. Asbestos is a natural mineral that was processed into a fibrous substance and was once widely used as a fire retardant and insulation material. Its use has been mostly discontinued because some forms of the processed material have been found to be harmful to humans when exposed to the lungs. The fibers can cause respiratory ailments. Asbestos was sprayed on columns and beams as a fire retardant. Asbestos fibers were added to floor tiles, roofing material, insulation on piping and other applications during construction. There are very definitive and sometimes expensive prescribed methods for removal and disposal of this material. Before any construction begins, a complete survey of the property should be conducted and a plan established for any material that may have to be removed or encapsulated. Contingency plans should be established for any hidden asbestos that may be discovered during the project. Many leases have specific language relating to asbestos found in tenant locations and the responsibilities of the landlord. The removal, disposal or encapsulation should be carefully documented and records kept for future use. In general, the owner of the property is responsible for the proper removal and disposal of the material. This issue should be reviewed by both legal and insurance sectors of the company.

Underground Storage Tanks. Underground storage tanks used to house materials considered hazardous, such as gasoline or oil, are subject to strict regulation with regard to testing, inspection and replacement. Older tanks tend to deteriorate and seepage into the soil can occur. The cleanup and disposal of hazardous contamination can be expensive and disruptive to the site. Tanks that are no longer being used should be inspected, cleaned and removed or properly abandoned; this may include filling with sand or cement. Proper procedures must be obtained from municipalities (city, state, federal). It is important to maintain documentation as to dates and the procedure followed. Underground tanks that remain in use should be tested and replaced as required by governing laws. The best time to accomplish replacement and removal of tanks located in paved areas (parking lots) is when major paving is being done and the lot will be disrupted anyway.

ADA REQUIREMENTS

The Americans with Disabilities Act (ADA) is federal legislation that extends civil rights protection to people with disabilities. It includes various requirements and standards relating to accessibility of buildings to the handicapped (Title III, Public Accommodations). This law can have far-reaching and expensive implications for shopping centers, particularly when they are being renovated. Your architect and contractor should be fully familiar with this legislation and any stricter local codes that might affect your property. Examples of the requirements under this law include the number of handicapped parking spaces, curb cuts, ramp inclines, heights of telephones, audible alarm systems, aisle widths and handrails, to name just a few. A compliance survey should be conducted and plans established and documented.

Recommended Readings

Altoon, Ronald A., FAIA. *International Shopping Center Architecture: Details, Concepts and Projects.* New York: International Council of Shopping Centers, 1996.

The ICSC Guide to Renovating and Expanding Shopping Centers the Smart Way: Ideas from Industry Experts. New York: International Council of Shopping Centers, 1996.

Winning Shopping Center Designs 1997. New York: International Council of Shopping Centers, 1997.

This chapter was contributed by Joseph P. Cilia, SCSM, General Manager, Simon Property Group, Roosevelt Field Mall, Garden City, New York.

12 | Legal Issues

Colin M. Gromley, Esq., and
Kevin M. Walsh, Esq.

In a complex and competitive retail environment, the shopping center manager is called upon to handle an increasing variety of problems and address an expanding list of issues. The ownership of the center will want to contain its costs and hire a shopping center manager who is capable of identifying and (ideally) resolving many of these issues and problems on his/her own.

The variety and complexity of legal issues involved in the ownership and operation of a shopping center can be daunting. While a shopping center manager cannot be expected to replace the ownership's legal counsel, it is incumbent upon a good manager to be able to identify a problem, take steps to limit the adverse effects of the problem, and take steps to avoid a recurrence of the problem. The following is a discussion of some of these issues and recommendations as to what a shopping center manager can do to avoid certain legal problems and to minimize the adverse effects on the shopping center and its owner.

Environmental Issues

While there are significant environmental issues involved in the acquisition of raw land and construction of a shopping center thereon, particularly the potential existence of hazardous materials in the land and in building materials, the shopping center manager will likely not have direct involvement in these issues during the acquisition and/or construction phases. However, additional significant issues can arise after the shopping center is constructed, is leased to tenants and is open for business to the public.

There is a plethora of environmental laws, rules and regulations on the federal, state and local levels that govern so-called hazardous materials. Perhaps the best known is the Comprehensive Environmental Response, Compensation and Liability Act (CERCLA), commonly known as the Superfund Act, which includes detailed definitions of "hazardous substances" and establishes rules for determining who is responsible for cleaning up (or remediating) a site which has been contaminated by hazardous substances. Examples of hazardous substances are dry-cleaning chemicals; gasoline and other petroleum-based products; and asbestos. The focus of all these governmental requirements is to protect the environment and the public's interest therein, and to impose the burden of cleaning up a site contaminated by these hazardous materials on the identified "responsible party(s)." Various governmental agencies are charged with overseeing compliance with these laws (for example, the Environmental Protection Agency—EPA—and its state-based counterparts).

Certain hazardous substances occur naturally (for example, radon gas emissions or certain radioactive materials at a shopping center). These will invariably be the shopping center owner's responsibility. Additionally, environmental concerns generally arise in three other ways: (1) contamination by the landlord/owner or its employees, agents or other related parties; (2) contamination caused by a tenant or its employees, agents or other related parties; or (3) contamination caused by a third party (for example, a gasoline leak from a nearby service station which migrates onto the shopping center site). While a tenant's lease may apportion cleanup obligations to the tenant, and contracts or other relationships with occupants or other contracting parties may seek to shift the liability in connection with hazardous substances away from the landlord, the shopping center manager should know that, generally speaking, environmental laws will ultimately impose an obligation on the landowner (i.e., the landlord) to clean up its land. Remember, the focus of most environmental laws is to *protect the public and the environment.* Therefore, a shopping center manager must take reasonable steps to monitor the condition of the shopping center property in order to quickly identify contamination and to limit the effects thereof.

For example, the manager should monitor the discharges from restaurant tenants and take reasonable efforts to ensure that grease traps are working properly; if there is a dry cleaner or other user of chemicals on the property, the manager may want to see monthly reports from that tenant evidencing that potential hazardous materials are being properly stored and disposed of; if there is a gasoline service station on-site (or even nearby), the manager will want to keep an eye out for signs of a leak (dead vegetation, a petroleum smell from the ground, soggy soil). While the shopping center manager is not expected to be an all-seeing watchdog over any contamination that occurs, he/she must be aware of the potential costs associated therewith and must make efforts to quickly identify contamination, and also to identify the person or persons who caused the contamination, in order to preserve the owner's rights to pursue recovery of the cleanup costs from the responsible person. It will do the owner of a shopping center no good to discover that a dry cleaner contaminated its site if the discovery is made ten years after the contamination occurred, when the dry cleaner is long gone and out of business.

AIR QUALITY

In our litigious society, another area of concern for the shopping center manager is the interior air quality of the shopping center. The most obvious and most publicized current issue involves tobacco smoke. The key issue for the shopping center will be the health cost to persons inhaling secondhand smoke. Again, various governmental agencies regulate this area, often on a county-by-county basis. Many counties require that all buildings with public access be smoke free, and it will be incumbent upon the manager to educate him/herself on the particular legal requirements governing his/her center.

Whether the law in a particular jurisdiction requires a smoke-free environment, the manager may want to consider (in consultation with ownership) imposing uniform rules to make the shopping center smoke free, and to institute policies for dealing with offenders. This will involve educating the center staff and any security personnel in enforcing a nonsmoking rule. At a minimum, the manager should consider establishing permissible smoking areas at the property, which are adequately vented and away from the main common areas.

RADON GAS

Radon is a colorless, odorless gas produced naturally in certain areas of the United States. It can accumulate in enclosed areas and be extremely harmful. Different state laws impose different requirements on landowners with regard to radon. Florida, as an example, has specific rules addressing radon (for example, leases must contain a specific provision, identifying to the tenant that radon potentially exists in the leased premises). In any center where radon is a potential risk, the shopping center manager should take steps to ensure proper venting of the enclosed areas.

VOLATILE ORGANIC CHEMICALS

Volatile organic chemicals, which are airborne contaminants and can be found in carpets, cleaning supplies and even building materials, pose another health risk in shopping centers and are strictly regulated by state laws. Again, the manager should take reasonable steps to minimize the risks associated therewith. This includes selecting a reputable cleaning company to clean the common areas and establishing criteria for the cleaning performed by tenants.

FAULTY, INADEQUATE OR OBSOLETE HEATING, VENTILATING AND AIR-CONDITIONING SYSTEMS

In connection with the heating, ventilating and air-conditioning (HVAC) systems at a shopping center, the shopping center manager should first understand what type of system he/she is dealing with. Many centers have rooftop units servicing a single tenant or a group of tenants, while other centers have central HVAC systems, utilizing either chilled water or some other mechanism to provide cooling. The type of system and the possible sources of "unhealthy air" will impact the maintenance program the manager ultimately implements. Whatever the system, the shopping center manager will want to institute a maintenance program that ensures, to the extent possible, that all filters are cleaned and regularly replaced, that the system is maintained free of bacteria, fungus and other substances which create "unclean" and therefore unsafe air, and that the system is maintained to minimize breakdown. While most leases allocate at least some of these burdens to the tenant (particularly for the tenant's leased premises and tenant-specific rooftop units), the shopping center manager will still want to oversee the maintenance of the entire system, whether through monitoring each tenant's compliance with its lease or otherwise.

FEDERAL CLEAN AIR ACT

The shopping center manager should be aware of the Federal Clean Air Act (the Clean Air Act). The Clean Air Act provides, among other things, that as of 1995 manufacturers of air conditioners and other appliances are prohibited from producing equipment that emits ozone-depleting compounds; for example, chlorofluorocarbons (CFCs). Generally, for shopping centers constructed after 1995, and therefore presumably containing HVAC equipment manufactured after 1995, the shopping center manager can presume that its HVAC system satisfies the Clean Air Act requirements on CFCs. However, older units which utilize CFCs are another matter. The Clean Air Act prohibits individuals and entities from knowingly venting CFCs into the atmosphere. Therefore, if the HVAC system is leaking these compounds, the manager must take immediate and reasonable steps to stop the leak and do so in a manner that limits or prevents any further discharge into the atmosphere. Failure to do so can result in significant penalties.

Upon discovery of any type of leak, the manager must initiate corrective action within thirty days of discovery, through a technician qualified to perform maintenance under the Clean Air Act. Record keeping and monitoring of compliance with the Clean Air Act is paramount to reducing a risk of action by the EPA.

OTHER ENVIRONMENTAL MATTERS

In addition to so-called hazardous substances, the shopping center manager must be aware of and be prepared to deal with other environmentally sensitive issues. Underground storage tanks (USTs) are designed to hold various types of liquids or other substances. USTs are a major source of potential problems. In the shopping center, USTs typically contain petroleum-based products, such as heating fuel. Most states have established regulations for registering storage tanks and requirements for remediation of spills. Additionally, the EPA requires that, by December 1998, all USTs and related piping have spill and overflow prevention equipment and also that the USTs be protected from corrosion. To satisfy the latter, the UST system must either be constructed of noncorrodible material (for example, fiberglass), contain an interior lining or contain cathodic protection.

It is not uncommon in an older shopping center site for the ownership to be unaware of the existence of USTs that were installed before the current ownership acquired the property and were not discovered during the due diligence phase of the acquisition. Many USTs were installed before states established the registration procedures, and it is therefore incumbent upon a center manager to be aware of the possibility of USTs and to keep watchful eye for telltale signs of leaking. As with most environmental law requirements, ignorance will not be a defense against liability for contamination.

WETLANDS

The U.S. Army Corps of Engineers regulates all aspects of waters in the United States, including rivers, lakes and streams. Included in these areas is the control of sites called wetlands. Generally speaking, wetlands are areas inundated or saturated by surface or groundwater to the extent that they support vegetation typically found in saturated soil. There is an enormous body of law governing wetlands and the ability to alter them. Of particular concern to the shopping center manager will be the rules governing the dredging and filling of wetlands. Any type of dredging or filling of wetlands requires a permit by the U.S. Army Corps of Engineers, and likely requires additional compliance with applicable state law. Therefore, before undertaking any type of construction activity at the shopping center (for example, expanding a parking lot or the buildings in the center), or before permitting any tenant or other entity (for example, a utility company installing a utility line) to do the same, the manager must be certain that the proposed activity will not disturb a wetland. If the activity will or could reasonably be expected to impact a wetland, the manager must obtain (or require the party performing the construction to obtain) the requisite permits and must apprise the appropriate agencies and follow whatever regulatory requirements they may impose. Again, the bottom line is that the owner of the property is ultimately liable for compliance with wetland regulations.

ASBESTOS

The Occupational Safety and Health Act (OSHA) is intended to create safe, healthful working conditions. Among other things, OSHA requires employers to evaluate the hazards associated with using chemicals in the workplace and to communicate the existence of these hazards to employees, tenants, contractors and other persons likely to come into contact with them. There are extensive disclosure requirements under OSHA in connection with the potential exposure to asbestos. This is of particular concern where there is planned demolition and/or renovation of a portion of a shopping center in which asbestos and asbestos-containing materials (ACMs) might be disturbed. These OSHA requirements are in addition to the EPA's requirements under the various environmental laws. As the guidelines for dealing with ACMs differ from state to state, the shopping center manager should consult with an environmental expert to determine the extent to which state law differs from the federal regulations and what additional measures must be taken.

Security

Perhaps one of the most serious and sensitive issues facing a shopping center manager is that of security at the shopping center. Regardless of who is ultimately liable for a particular criminal act, the entire center will suffer if the public perceives the center as an unsafe place.

LIABILITY FOR THIRD-PARTY ACTS

When a crime occurs, the crime victim may sue everyone with any relationship to the shopping center in an effort to recover damages. This will include the owner of the property, any security company, the management company and any tenant potentially involved. The ultimate allocation of liability will hinge on several factors, including the terms of the particular lease (if a tenant's premises is involved); the actual physical use and control over the area where the crime occurred; and the relationship of the parties involved. The manager must be alert to the fact that, because the landlord generally exercises control over the common areas of a shopping center, the landlord may be liable for injuries or other damages that occur to a customer, tenant, employee or other person as a result of criminal activity in these areas, regardless of actual "fault" on the landlord's part.

A major factor in determining whether the landlord (or any other party) can be held responsible for criminal activity is determining whether that party has the duty to protect the victim and fails to take reasonable steps to do so. Unfortunately, this seemingly basic legal principle is applied in different ways by different jurisdictions and it is therefore impossible to establish absolute guidance criteria for the manager. For example, some jurisdictions impose a duty only to protect against criminal acts that the landlord knows or should know are occurring or are about to occur. Other jurisdictions impose a duty on the landlord to protect against criminal activity which is "foreseeable." While tests of the foreseeability of criminal activity vary from jurisdiction to jurisdiction, most are based either on an analysis of prior similar incidents or on the totality of the circumstances. In a shopping center, the prior similar incidents test turns on specific past criminal activity at the center. The test involves evaluating the risk of future criminal activity by knowing and evaluating past (particularly recent) criminal activity, not only at the shopping center, but also in the surrounding area. The totality of circumstances test evaluates all circumstances that would (or should) lead the landlord to anticipate criminal activity. These circumstances could include poor lighting, high crime in the surrounding area, the architectural features of the shopping center and other factors. Generally, conditions that make criminal activity possible (or increase the likelihood of crime, or enhance the ability to conceal crime) can lead a court to conclude that it was reasonable for the landlord to foresee criminal activity and that, therefore, a duty exists to provide for the safety of the shopping center users.

Finally, the shopping center manager must be aware of potential voluntary undertaking liability, pursuant to which a landlord is deemed liable where no duty to protect the victim otherwise exists. This liability arises where the landlord or its agent or employee voluntarily takes certain actions not otherwise required by or imposed by law, and in so doing fails to act with reasonable care. For example, when a landlord hires a security guard in order to patrol the center, and such guard performs his/her duties negligently, the landlord may have liability. Negligence may involve a variety of issues (for example, untrained guards, too few guards, insufficient equipment or the creation of a reliance on such services by third parties, including tenants and their employees).

Unfortunately, there are no easy or absolute answers to shopping center security. Procedures that are sufficient in order to avoid liability at one center may not be sufficient at another center and may generate liability for the landlord in the event of injury or loss to a customer or tenant. It is vitally important, therefore, that the manager understand and analyze each situation and the circumstances at his/her center, develop a systematized procedure for addressing security concerns and document this procedure.

First and foremost, the manager should analyze his/her center and factors that impact security, and the potential need for additional security. Factors to consider include:

- Have there been more frequent incidents of crime at the center or a particular store?
- Is there an increase of crime in the trade area?
- Do store sales indicate fewer sales are produced in after-dark hours?
- Do customers express concerns about safety?
- Have insurance premiums increased?

In order to implement an appropriate security program, the manager will also need to investigate alternatives available to address potential problems. This will include an analysis of state or local requirements; review of documentation with tenants or other entities with rights in the center; review of insurance provisions applicable to the center (including the landlord's and the tenants' coverages); analysis of the qualifications of alternative security personnel and the competency of such personnel; understanding the center's relationship with local law enforcement authorities; and the physical characteristics of the center.

The potential response to a security issue is as varied as the issues to be addressed. The manager will be faced with many choices:

- Whether to hire security personnel or to employ an independent security firm
- Whether to install security cameras or other equipment
- Whether to establish or increase security patrols; if so, when, how often, in what areas
- Whether to change the physical aspects of the center (limit access to the roof; remove vegetation to increase visibility; close off dark corners in obstructed areas; alter traffic patterns to make quick access and exit more difficult)

Other factors come into play in making these decisions. A prime example is the shopping center budget; the tenants may protest if their common area maintenance charges increase, even if the increase is a result of the landlord's efforts to provide a safer shopping environment for the tenants' customers.

Whatever decisions are reached and whatever type of security plan is implemented, the manager should understand that security is a fluid process and must be constantly monitored. The manager must continue to analyze the effectiveness of the security measures taken while staying abreast of new developments in the security area, including developments in the applicable law.

If an incident occurs, regardless of where in the center, the manager should review the elements of the causes and effects of the incident. Document the incident, but be aware that records which indicate a breach of the security procedure may point to a fault by the owner and will be damaging to the owner in any type of litigation. For this and for other reasons, the security personnel at a center should be trained, not only in security procedure, but to deal with the victims of crime.

The shopping center manager should discuss the security needs of the center with counsel, the owner's insurance representative, local law enforcement authorities and any other professional involved with the operations in the center in order to devise a security plan. Once implemented, the next step is adequate training and monitoring of security personnel.

Easements

The existence and necessity of easements at a shopping center must be understood by the manager. Generally, an easement is a nonpossessory "interest in land" of another. Tenants will usually request a nonexclusive easement to use the common areas of the shopping center; most landlord lease forms grant only a revocable right to use the common areas, as such areas may exist from time to time. The landlord wants to limit the rights of others in the center and preserve the ability to make changes to the center if it so desires. In the shopping center, it is not unlikely that one or more of the department stores or other anchor stores will own their building and, possibly, the land thereunder. In this scenario, there will likely be (or need to be) what is known as a reciprocal easement agreement (REA) between the department or anchor store and the landlord, in order to create reciprocal rights and obligations to each other. For example, one party may be delegated the obligation of maintaining the entire common area or parking area, even though a portion of such area is located on the other party's property. (Most likely, the landlord maintains and the department store contributes to the cost of the maintenance.) While the shopping center manager will not likely be responsible for drafting these documents, he/she must be aware of their existence and the impact they have on the center.

Generally speaking, an easement will give the beneficiary of the easement the right to access the easement area and to undertake certain actions on the easement area. At the shopping center, the two most likely areas of concern for the shopping center manager will be easements for utilities and for ingress and egress.

Shopping centers and the tenant spaces therein need to be served by various utilities. Many of the utilities will be supplied by utility companies or by the county or other local government. Each supplier of a utility will require an easement for the installation and ongoing maintenance of such utility. It will not be uncommon for the representatives of the local utility company to deal directly with the shopping center manager in connection with the easements. The manager must be aware that, if not already in place, the easements should be narrowly crafted to limit the utility company's rights in the shopping center property. For example, if a local cable company requests the right to install cable on the shopping center property, the manager should inquire as to what other properties are going to be served by the cable; whether the cable will be buried in the ground; who will be responsible for maintaining the easement on an ongoing basis; if the rights are intended to extend to aboveground facilities; if the utility company is attempting to obtain rights to install additional equipment in the future; and other related issues. The more expansive the rights given to the grantee of the easement, the more burdens are imposed on the shopping center, thereby restricting the owner's ability to utilize its land in the future.

Every tenant and every department store and anchor store at the center will want to ensure that its customers have continuous access to the shopping center. Therefore, it is likely that the center is either subject to one or more easements creating the access drives, or that the ownership will be requested to grant such easements. Again, while the shopping center manager will likely not be the draftsperson of such documents, he/she may be the recipient of a request for a change to the easement, or there may be a situation where the easement has to be altered temporarily or permanently. In such event, the manager must make certain to identify the obligations to the holders of any easements, in order to implement alternatives to continue to satisfy the requirements of the easements.

The issue of easements will also arise where there is construction at the center. A tenant that is responsible for constructing all or a portion of its leased premises may request an easement in order to place construction materials and vehicles on a portion of the owner's property. In this instance, the shopping center manager should take steps to ensure strict compliance with the terms of the easement. For example, the building materials should be stacked only in the permitted easement area and the recipient of the easement must be required to maintain and secure the easement area. Also, the holder of the easement should be responsible for ensuring that no liens are placed on the property encumbered by the easement. Finally, the shopping center may need an easement from an adjacent property owner or anchor store if the owner determines to expand the center. The shopping center manager can assist in obtaining any of the easements by establishing positive relationships with these other property owners.

Another area of shopping center operations involving easements will be for the drainage of water and creation of detention ponds.

Many centers are designed to have surface water drain to detention pond areas, either on the shopping center property or located nearby. The owner will often need easements to permit such drainage (and to maintain the drainage facilities) from the major tenants or from adjacent landowners. The shopping center manager will want to make certain he/she is aware of the center's obligations for these drainage systems and any rights that the landlord may have with respect to the use of the drainage system, whether a tenant is required to contribute to the maintenance costs thereof, or if the landlord has the right to require that another party maintain or repair the drainage system.

Bankruptcy

The filing for bankruptcy protection by any party involved with the shopping center can have immediate and significant consequences to the shopping center ownership and the manager. Generally, if a tenant files bankruptcy, there is an automatic injunction stopping legal actions against the tenant. Therefore, if the manager knows or suspects that a tenant has filed a bankruptcy, he/she should inform the landlord immediately and, collectively, they should determine whether to cease any kind of collection efforts that may be under way against the tenant.

Bankruptcy laws often permit a bankrupt tenant to continue operating within a specific prescribed set of rules and obligations, theoretically in a manner consistent with the tenant's lease. However, the manager must be aware that tenants are often given wide latitude in complying with the bankruptcy rules. For example, the lease may require a tenant to operate with full stock and staff in accordance with its operations on a national basis, but the bankruptcy court may not enforce this obligation against the bankrupt tenant in a store where the tenant is, in effect, holding liquidation sales and operating with a skeleton crew and reduced inventory. The focus of the bankruptcy court will be to protect the lease as an asset of the bankrupt estate, for the benefit of the tenant's creditors generally.

While the shopping center manager will not necessarily be directly involved in the bankruptcy process, the manager can take actions in order to protect the owner's interest. For example, the manager should take prompt action to ensure that each tenant is remaining current on its rent and otherwise satisfying the terms of its lease. A late payment of rent, particularly on a recurring basis, is often an indication of financial or other problems for a tenant. Making certain that rent is timely paid, or if not, that notice of default is promptly sent, can reduce the amount of outstanding receivables the landlord will have in an event of a tenant bankruptcy. Additionally, if the manager can identify in advance a financially troubled tenant, he/she may be able to assist in negotiating a termination of the tenant's lease and release of the tenant's space before the tenant files for bankruptcy, in order to minimize the damages to the owner and the shopping center.

The manager should also be aware of the general marketplace and communicate with ownership to understand the financial status of tenants, particularly national tenants. Finally, he/she should be familiar with the "going out of business" or liquidation sale regulations in the location of the center; these regulations may be useful in stopping a debtor or potential debtor from putting ads for going out of business or other types of sales in its windows and thereby detracting from the appearance of the center, as well as raising concerns of other tenants and customers as to the viability of the center.

Insurance

Another area of particular importance to property owners and managers is to make sure they have adequate insurance coverage, that vendors/contractors providing services to the property also maintain adequate insurance coverage and that tenants comply with the insurance requirements in their leases. The manager should be aware that leases may require the tenants to carry specific types of insurance coverage, plus additional coverage as may be "reasonably required by the landlord." Depending upon the owner's requirements, the types of coverage the owner may require from a third-party management company include: (1) comprehensive crime (or fidelity bond) insurance; (2) workers' compensation; and (3) any other insurance that may be required to comply with applicable federal, state or local law. The types of coverage that may be required of vendors and contractors providing services to the property include: (1) workers' compensation; (2) employer's liability; (3) commercial general liability; (4) comprehensive automobile liability; and (5) umbrella liability, depending upon the requirements of the property owner and the type of service being provided.

COMPREHENSIVE CRIME INSURANCE

Coverage for theft by an employee can be covered under either a comprehensive crime policy or a fidelity bond. The policy or bond is between the insurance company and the insured and provides coverage if an employee of the insured wrongfully takes money. The policy or bond reimburses the insured for the sums taken, subject to a deductible. The limit of the policy or bond should be determined based upon the insured's exposure, such as whether employees have access to cash or bank accounts.

WORKERS' COMPENSATION

Workers' compensation is required by law in most states and was established to provide benefits for injured workers without determination of liability. Workers' compensation generally is the employee's only source of recovery against its employer if the employee is injured on the job. If a shopping center (or management company) employee is injured as a result of his or her employment, the workers' compensation insurance will pay medical expenses; wages for lost time; and an award for loss of use. Benefits differ state by state; however, lost wages are usually paid based upon a percentage of the average weekly wage with a cap such as two-thirds of the weekly wage up to $300 per week.

VENDOR'S AND CONTRACTOR'S INSURANCE

The shopping center manager should ensure that all vendors/contractors providing services to the property maintain adequate insurance coverage so that in the event the vendor's/contractor's employees are negligent, the vendor's/contractor's insurers will pay the claim. If vendors/contractors fail to maintain adequate insurance coverage, the property owner may end up having to pay claims filed against the vendor/contractor by virtue of its status as owner of the property where the injury occurred. Vendors/contractors should maintain workers' compensation insurance in compliance with the laws of the state where the center is located. As part of the workers' compensation policy, the property manager and vendors/contractors should maintain employer's liability coverage that insures against common law liability for accidents and other claims that are distinguishable from obligations that are imposed by the applicable workers' compensation law. Not all employees are covered by workers' compensation; for example, farm employees and domestic servants are not covered, and each state mandates what category of workers are and are not covered. Those employees who are not covered by workers' compensation may sue their employer, and it is the employer's liability portion of the workers' compensation policy that will defend the lawsuit. Provided the damages result directly from an employee injuring him/herself in the course of employment, the employer's liability portion of the workers' compensation policy will also defend suits that are filed by spouses and children of the injured worker. Examples of the types of claims covered by the employer's liability portion of the workers' compensation policy include: (1) damages caused by a third party; (2) care in loss of services; (3) consequential injury to a spouse or relative of the injured worker; and (4) actions brought against the insured in a capacity other than as an employer, such as a product manufacturer.

COMMERCIAL GENERAL LIABILITY INSURANCE
Commercial general liability insurance insures the insured for bodily injury or property damage to third parties. It also covers the insured's liability for completed operations, such as claims for bodily injury or property damage caused by his/her completed work. One of the major reasons for completed operations coverage is that it has a separate liability limit versus the limit for general operations.

COMPREHENSIVE AUTOMOBILE LIABILITY
Comprehensive automobile liability covers the insured's liability for any accident involving a vehicle driven by its employee while on company business. It also covers all owned, non-owned and hired vehicles.

In instances where there is a greater exposure for bodily injury or property damage, the property owner may want to require that vendors/contractors obtain an umbrella liability insurance policy. As evidenced by its name, umbrella insurance acts as an umbrella over the primary policies such as the employer's liability, commercial general liability and automobile liability policies. For example, if an auto accident occurred on the property in which several people were seriously injured, the cost of the claim could exceed the coverage required under the automobile liability policy. If an umbrella insurance policy is in effect, it would cover the amount of the claim exceeding the coverage required under the automobile liability policy, but such coverage would only be up to the limit of the umbrella insurance policy.

Sample Language. The following language may be used as a model for insertion in agreements to be entered into between vendors/contractors.

Vendor's Insurance. Vendor shall provide insurance coverage, at its sole cost and expense, in the following minimum amounts:

(a) workers' compensation, as required by the law of the state in which the Property is located;

(b) employer's liability covering bodily injury:
by accident, $500,000 each accident;
by disease, $500,000 policy limits;
by disease, $500,000 each employee;

(c) commercial general liability insurance with a limit of $1,000,000 per occurrence, $1,000,000 general aggregate, including coverage for bodily injury, property damage and completed operations;

(d) comprehensive automobile liability covering all owned, non-owned and hired vehicles with a combined single limit of $1,000,000;

(e) at the option of Owner, umbrella liability insurance covering (a) through (d) with limits of up to $5,000,000.

All insurance policies shall be issued by companies and in forms satisfactory to Owner and shall expressly provide that the insurance company or companies shall notify Owner and Property Manager in writing at least thirty (30) days prior to any alteration or cancellation thereof. Owner and Property Manager shall be named as additional insureds to the above policies and each policy must stipulate that such insurance is primary and is not in addition to, or contributing with any other insurance carried by or for the benefit of Owner and Property Manager. Certificates of insurance evidencing the above must be delivered to Property Manager prior to the commencement of any work.

Again, required limits and associated deductibles require a tenant-by-tenant and vendor-by-vendor analysis based on use, services provided, financial status, claims history and such other factors as the property owner and manager deem necessary.

SUMMARY

The types and the amount of coverage that the third-party property manager should carry and that which should be required of vendors/contractors providing services to the property should be established by the property owner in consultation with the property manager and their respective risk managers or insurance agents. Except with respect to the workers' compensation policy, the property owner and the property manager (if a third-party management company) should be named as additional insureds on policies that are maintained by vendors/contractors providing services to the property. The purpose for requiring that the owner and property manager be named as additional insureds on such policies is that if a claim is filed due to the negligence of the insured party and one of the additional insureds is named as a defendant in the lawsuit, the additional insureds can turn the matter over to the insureds' carrier, thereby saving the cost of the defense and the payment of the claim.

Employment Issues

The purpose of this next section is to address some of the issues in the area of employment law which a manager may face on a day-to-day basis in the operation of a shopping center. This is by no means a comprehensive analysis of the law, and the manager should consult with counsel to address specific issues, particularly since many of the employment-related issues are governed by federal and state law. The purpose here is to acquaint the manager with some of the issues he/she may encounter, including sexual harassment; the Family and Medical Leave Act; the Occupational Safety and Health Act; and the Americans with Disabilities Act.

SEXUAL HARASSMENT

Perhaps the most widely discussed issue today in employment law relates to sexual harassment. Sexual harassment law is booming, and the U. S. Supreme Court currently has before it two cases that will likely shape the future of harassment law profoundly. In one case the issue is whether harassment can count as employment discrimination based on sex when the harasser and the victim are of the same sex; the second case involves a broader question of how strictly employers can be held liable for the harassment of subordinates by their supervisors.

Sexual harassment is a form of sex discrimination, violating Title VII of the Civil Rights Act of 1964. It consists of unwelcome sexual advances, requests for sexual favors and other verbal or physical conduct of a sexual nature, when submission to or rejection of this conduct explicitly or implicitly affects an individual's employment, unreasonably interferes with an individual's work performance or creates an intimidating, hostile or offensive work environment. Complaints of sexual harassment are filed with the Equal Employment Opportunity Commission (EEOC), which, when investigating allegations of sexual harassment, looks at the whole record: the nature of the sexual advances and the context in which the alleged incident occurred. A determination on the merits of the allegations is made from the facts on a case-by-case basis.

The number of cases of alleged sexual harassment being reported over the past several years has risen. The damages that are awarded by juries can be staggering. A major automobile manufacturer recently agreed to pay a record $34 million to 350 women to settle allegations that they were groped and insulted on the assembly line at its Illinois factory and that managers did nothing to stop it.

Prevention is the best tool to eliminate sexual harassment in the workplace. Employers and those employees in a supervisory capacity are encouraged to take steps necessary to prevent sexual harassment from occurring. There should be a clear communication to employees that sexual harassment will not be tolerated. The employer should have a written policy against sexual harassment; post federal and state bulletins describing applicable laws; establish an effective complaint or grievance process; and take immediate and appropriate action when an employee complains, including making a full investigation of the incident and documenting the findings. Complaints of sexual or any other form of harassment should be taken seriously. If someone brings an incident to the manager's attention, he/she should consult with the company's human resources department. The goal is to make sure that the complaining party is reassured that he or she is being taken seriously and that positive steps to prevent another occurrence are being taken. The negative consequences for not doing so can be enormous and can lead to significant monetary awards against the company and even against the individual offender; substantial amounts of downtime by managers and employees; substantial legal expenditures both for the company's defense of the action and on behalf of the individual bringing the claim; and the destruction of careers and even marriages. Employers and those having responsibility over employees should do all they can to prevent such conduct from occurring and to deal with such conduct promptly and effectively.

FAMILY AND MEDICAL LEAVE ACT

The Family and Medical Leave Act (FMLA) covers all employers with fifty or more employees. The FMLA provides that eligible employees can take up to twelve work weeks of leave during a twelve-month period for: (1) the birth or adoption of a child; (2) placement of a foster child with an employee; (3) time off to care for such child; (4) the serious health condition of a parent, spouse or child; or (5) the employee's own serious health condition. To be eligible for FMLA leave, an employee must: (1) have been employed for at least twelve months; (2) have worked at least 1,250 hours in the twelve-month period preceding the leave commencement date; and (3) work at a company facility that employs fifty or more employees at that facility or within seventy-five miles of it. Leave must be taken consecutively, with the exception of leaves for serious health conditions (of the employee or a covered family member) that may be taken on an intermittent or reduced work schedule basis. The FMLA requires that employees provide thirty days' advance notice of leave or as much advance notice as practicable in unforeseen circumstances, such as an accident necessitating the employee's time away from work. Employers may require employees to submit medical or other certification to support their leave, such as a note from the employee's physician or a note from a covered family member's physician. Employers may require employees requesting a leave for a serious health condition to submit to a second-opinion medical exam by a physician at the employer's own expense. During an FMLA leave, an employee's group health insurance benefits must be continued, with the employer contributing the same amount toward these benefits as it would for an employee not on leave. The employee must also submit any employee-required premiums to the employer during the leave. All other employee benefits for employees on leave must be handled in accordance with the terms of each respective benefit plan, policy or practice of the employer, but employees may be treated no less favorably than employees on non-FMLA leave.

After an employee returns from FMLA leave, he/she must be reinstated to the same or an equivalent position with equivalent pay, status and all of the terms and conditions of employment. Exceptions exist for certain highly compensated employees, and for change in business circumstances. If, for example, the employee's position is eliminated during a reduction in force while an employee is on leave, the FMLA states that in these situations an employee is to be treated no differently than if he/she were not on leave.

OCCUPATIONAL SAFETY AND HEALTH ACT

The Occupational Safety and Health Act of 1970 requires employers to provide a workplace free from recognized safety and health hazards. OSHA's hazard communications standard requires employers to notify and train employees about hazardous chemicals in the workplace. Under OSHA most employers are required to maintain certain logs detailing workers' job-related injuries and illnesses, the dates and nature of the incidents and other relevant information. Copies of an annual log and summary must be posted by most employers in conspicuous places during the month of February of each year. The act is enforced by the Occupational Safety and Health Commission. Violations of OSHA are punishable by fines. Employers are prohibited from discriminating against, discharging or retaliating against an employee who has instituted or participated in a proceeding under OSHA. Employees who are discriminated against or discharged may be entitled to back pay and any lost benefits. Criminal penalties may be assessed against employers for willful violations of the law.

AMERICANS WITH DISABILITIES ACT

The Americans with Disabilities Act of 1990 (the ADA) prohibits private employers, state and local governments, employment agencies and labor unions from discriminating against qualified individuals with disabilities in job application procedures, hiring, firing, advancement, compensation, job training and other terms and conditions of employment. An individual with a disability is a person who: (1) has a physical or mental impairment that substantially limits one or more major life activities; (2) has a record of such impairment; or (3) is regarded as having such an impairment.

A qualified individual with a disability is someone who, with reasonable accommodation, can perform the essential functions of the job in question. Reasonable accommodation includes: (1) making existing facilities used by employees readily accessible to and usable by persons with disabilities; (2) job restructuring, including modifying work schedules, and work reassignment to a vacant position; or (3) acquiring or modifying equipment or devices, adjusting or modifying examinations, training materials or policies, and providing qualified readers or interpreters.

Employers are required to make accommodation to a known disability of a qualified applicant or employee if it would not impose an undue hardship on the operation of the employer's business. Undue hardship is defined as an action requiring significant difficulty or expense to the employer when considering such factors as the employer's size, financial resources and the nature and structure of its operation.

Questioning the Applicant. Employers cannot ask job applicants about the existence, nature or severity of a disability. Employers may ask an applicant about his/her ability to perform job-specific functions. A job offer may be conditioned on the results of a medical examination or inquiry, but only if the examination or inquiry is required of all entering employees in the job. Medical examinations or inquiries must be job related and consistent with the employer's business needs.

Filing a Complaint. Charges of employment discrimination on the basis of disability can be filed at any field office of the U.S. Equal Employment Opportunity Commission.

Accessibility. The manager also should understand ADA requirements as they affect the shopping center. For example, the shopping center must be accessible by wheelchair, which will require appropriate curb cuts, ramps and sufficiently wide entrances. The latter may extend to requiring that tenants' storefronts accommodate wheelchairs. While the landlord's (and therefore the manager's) obligations generally extend only to the common areas and the areas of the shopping center reserved for shopping center employees, the manager may want to establish written rules and regulations that require tenants to comply with the ADA. The shopping center will ultimately suffer if customers are denied access, regardless of who is responsible for ADA compliance.

Execution of Contracts

The manager should seek clear direction from the property owner as to the scope of the manager's authority to enter into agreements on behalf of the property owner. Additionally, the manager should examine state law to determine if the contract has to be in writing and who can sign it. Before signing any contract on behalf of the owner, it is recommended that the manager review the management agreement to develop a clear understanding as to the scope of his/her authority. Many property owners have specific limitations that are set forth in the management leasing agreement that prohibit the manager from signing leases. There may also be limitations imposed based on the duration of the contract or dollar limitations. Some owners require, for example, that all service contracts contain a provision that they can be canceled without penalty on thirty days' notice. Most owners impose a cap on the manager's contracting for a property expenditure without obtaining the owner's prior written consent and may even require that the manager award contracts based on competitive bidding.

STATE LAW

State law governs the types of contracts that have to be signed, in writing, and who can sign those contracts. Some states, such as South Carolina, require in writing all management and leasing agreements identifying the property and containing all of the terms and conditions under which the property is to be managed and leased, including the commissions to be paid; a definite expiration date; and provisions for the payment of the management fees. Some states further require that if the management agreement requires the property manager to collect any sums on behalf of the owner, the qualifying real estate broker for the management company sign the management agreement.

INDEMNIFICATION

The management agreement will typically include an indemnification for the manager for claims, losses and damages resulting from actions taken by the manager which are within the scope of the manager's authority under the management agreement. The indemnification usually does not apply to criminal acts, gross negligence, fraud or willful misconduct. From a business perspective, the manager needs to be sure that he/she has followed the owner's direction on the types of contracts the manager can sign on the owner's behalf. Failure to follow the owner's direction can result in lost business with the owner and potential liability for the management company, particularly where the indemnifications provided within the management agreement are lost because the manager has acted beyond the scope of his/her authority.

Public Access to Shopping Centers

The issue of public access to shopping centers really revolves around the First Amendment's guarantee of freedom of speech. The First Amendment of the United States Constitution protects the exercise of free speech in public forums against interference by the state. Many people believe that a shopping center is a place of public accommodation and that they are entitled access to the center to exercise their

First Amendment rights. However, the First Amendment only protects against governmental interference with free speech; it does not protect free speech activities in privately owned shopping centers.

The Supreme Court of the United States has adamantly held that property does not lose its private character merely because the public is generally invited to use it for designated purposes. The essentially private character of a store does not change by virtue of its being large or clustered with other stores in a modern shopping center. Several Supreme Court decisions have reaffirmed that the First Amendment does not authorize the government to take away a property owner's right to exclude others from exercising their right to free speech. A private property owner (and hence, a shopping center owner) retains the right to use its property as it sees fit and may exclude others from entering upon the property. Important exceptions to this general concept follow.

LABOR ORGANIZATIONS

A shopping center manager can deny one group access to the shopping center while allowing another group to solicit. However, this right is subject to some very important exceptions. First, labor organizations (like unions) are governed by different requirements than average groups seeking to gain access to the property. Whether or not picketers and union organizers are allowed access to the property depends on the nature of their activity and the conditions in the shopping center. Labor organizations and related employment issues are subject to the requirements set forth in the National Labor Relations Act (NLRA). This act gives union members and organizers broad rights. If a shopping center manager is faced with an issue concerning access and a labor union, he/she should contact an attorney to determine if denying access violates the NLRA.

STATE LAW

The second exception to a shopping center manager's right to arbitrarily deny access is grounded in state constitutional policy. The Supreme Court determined that it is up to each state to individually address whether its constitution grants individuals freedom of speech at privately owned shopping centers. Most states that consider this issue are reluctant to expand the free speech guaranties of their constitutions beyond the scope of the First Amendment to private property, where there is generally no state action. However, the law is changing and varies from state to state. Some states, based on their individual constitutions, extend the rights granted by the First Amendment to places of public accommodation. For instance, California has upheld the right to engage in First Amendment–type activities in privately owned shopping centers. California's constitution effectively extends an individual's right to free speech to places of public accommodation.

In California, a shopping center owner cannot prohibit a particular group from exercising its right of expression. However, California shopping centers are allowed to place time and manner restrictions to prevent interference with commercial functions. In addition, some states that have considered this issue have decided to limit accessibility to political petitioning and allowed shopping centers to prohibit access for religious, social or other kinds of noncommercial activities.

If a shopping center manager is confronted with an accessibility issue and is inclined to deny a particular group access, he/she should contact an attorney to determine if doing so infringes on the individual's rights to free speech under the state constitution. Generally, the owner should establish specific rules and regulations concerning use of the shopping center for "community activities." The manager will then be obligated to consistently apply the rules and regulations in a nondiscriminatory manner. For example, the manager should not allow a local Boy Scout troop to camp overnight in the shopping center as part of a fund-raiser, yet deny the same access to a Girl Scout troop. Even if this denial does not violate public access laws, it has the potential to create a public relations nightmare.

Condemnation

STATUTORY GRANT

While it is not a common occurrence, the property owner may be faced with a situation in which a local governmental authority desires to take all or a portion of a shopping center for public purposes. The power of eminent domain, commonly referred to as condemnation, gives the state legislature the right through the officers of the state, through the medium of corporate bodies or by means of individual enterprise to take private property for public purposes. The power of eminent domain is typically delegated to transportation departments, counties, municipalities, housing authorities and public utilities. State law prescribes for what purposes the power of eminent domain may be utilized. Typical purposes include construction of rights-of-way for utilities; construction of power plants; construction and operation of waterworks; construction of petroleum and gas pipelines; construction of watershed projects; and construction of beacons and lighthouses. The United States also has the power of eminent domain.

METHOD OF TAKING

The process of taking varies state by state, but usually the process depends upon the condemning authority and the purpose of the condemnation. There are generally four methods of acquisition: summary proceedings; special master proceedings; in rem proceedings; and declaration of taking.

Summary Proceedings. Generally, a summary proceeding is a nonjudicial taking whereby the court does not become involved until after the issue of compensation for the taking has been decided by a board of assessors. Often the condemning authority will make an offer to the property owner to acquire the property to be taken, and if the offer is rejected the condemning authority files a notice of condemnation and the appropriate court will set a hearing date. Assessors for the hearing are selected, typically one by the condemning authority and one by the property owner; but if the property owner fails to select an assessor, the court will then appoint one. Once the two assessors have been selected, they select a third assessor. The assessors then conduct a hearing whereby the condemning authority and the property owner can produce evidence as to the value of the property. The assessors enter the findings as to the value of the property, and if a party is dissatisfied with the valuation it can file an appeal to the appropriate court.

Special Master Proceedings. The special master proceeding is a judicial method of acquiring property and is commenced by the condemning authority filing a petition of condemnation with the appropriate court. The court appoints a special master and requires the interested parties to appear before the special master at a hearing. At the time of the hearing, the special master serves in the same capacity as the board of assessors in the summary proceedings: The special master hears the evidence offered by the condemning authority and the property owner as to the value of the property. Any party dissatisfied with the award granted by the special master can file an appeal to the appropriate court.

In Rem Proceedings. The in rem proceeding is a hybrid of summary proceedings and special master proceedings in that it utilizes a board of assessors to determine the amount of just compensation for the property being taken, and that it is a judicial proceeding commenced by the condemning authority filing a petition with the appropriate court. Assessors are selected and a hearing is scheduled so that the parties can present their evidence to the assessors on the value of the property being taken. Any party dissatisfied with the assessors' determination of value may appeal to the appropriate court.

Declaration of Taking. The only method under which a condemning authority can take title to property without an evidentiary hearing to determine just compensation is under the declaration of taking method. This method of condemnation begins with the filing of a petition with the appropriate court. Along with the filing of the petition, a declaration of taking is filed with the court and is signed by the appropriate governmental officer of the authority seeking to condemn the property. At the time of filing the petition and declaration, the condemning authority is required to deposit with the court an amount which has been estimated in the declaration as just compensation for the property being taken. At this point, title to the property is vested in the condemning authority. The court has the authority to set aside the declaration of taking, but only for limited reasons, such as fraud or misuse of the power of eminent domain. The parties having an interest in the property have the right to file a petition with the court to have the money deposited by the condemning authority paid to them. The court has the right to fix the time period in which the property owner is to surrender possession of the property. Should the property owner or any other interested party be dissatisfied with the amount of compensation, that party has the right to file an appeal with the appropriate court.

THE ROLE OF THE SHOPPING CENTER MANAGER

In the event of a condemnation, the manager should review the tenant leases to determine what rights the tenants have to any portion of the award or if they have any right to terminate their leases. A simple road widening may result in the forced removal of a pylon sign, or the closing of an entrance to the shopping center or a reduction of parking spaces. The manager may find her/himself negotiating with a tenant over the value of its sign panel if a pylon is taken, or whether it has the right to terminate its lease or reduce its rent because an entrance to the shopping center has been closed or the parking has been reduced. The manager's assistance to the property owner may be invaluable as a liaison to the tenants to keep them apprised as to the status of the eminent domain proceedings. The manager may also be an important source for gathering together information on behalf of the property owner to present to appraisers hired to determine the value of the property. In determining just compensation, some states consider the market value of the portion of the property taken and the consequential damages to the remainder. The manager may be interviewed by the appraisers or asked to testify as a lay witness as to what impact the taking will have on the property.

Tax Appeals

In many states, property taxes are perhaps the largest expense for any commercial property. While most shopping center leases allocate a proportionate tax burden on the tenant, the landlord invariably makes up the shortfall between the assessed taxes and the amounts collected from tenants. Therefore, the landlord has an incentive to avoid increases in taxes.

In most states, property tax appeals can be categorized in two ways: first, an appeal can be initiated by the property owner or the manager during the first half of the tax year in question. Usually this kind of appeal is the result of being unhappy with the taxable value placed on the property for the prior year. Second, an appeal can be filed answering a "reassessment notice" indicating the taxable value has changed from the prior year. This type of appeal requires a response from the property owner or the manager within a time frame specified in the reassessment notice.

STAGES OF THE APPEAL PROCESS

In most states the first stage is an informal process during which a representative of the taxing jurisdiction meets the party appealing the tax in an open forum. Information is exchanged at this level and a resolution is sought using the data exchanged. The second stage is usually before a board of equalization/assessment. This stage is more formal and may involve a panel of citizens or real estate professionals deciding the outcome of the appeal. The third stage of the process occurs if the party appealing is still not satisfied with the taxable value arrived at after the second stage and files an appeal to the appropriate court.

THE MANAGER'S ROLE

Many property owners hire a third-party tax service to monitor the assessments on their properties and to pay the taxes. The manager will often be asked to work with the tax consultant by providing information to the consultant, such as the income generated from the property, which may be a factor in determining the property's assessed valuation, and to monitor the appeal process.

Recommended Readings

Current Topics in Shopping Center Law. New York: International Council of Shopping Centers, 1997.

Folger, Peter M., Esq., and Lisa McCabe van Krieken, Esq. *Union Access to Private Property: An Overview from Babcock and Wilcox to Lechmere.* New York: International Council of Shopping Centers, 1992.

ICSC Law Library: Construction Issues. New York: International Council of Shopping Centers, 1995.

ICSC Law Library: Environmental Issues. New York: International Council of Shopping Centers, 1996.

ICSC Law Library: Financing Issues. New York: International Council of Shopping Centers, 1996.

Key Shopping Center Legal Issues: Understanding Current Laws Impacting Leasing and Management. New York: International Council of Shopping Centers, 1995.

Keys, John R., Jr., Esq. *The Antitrust Aspects of Restrictive Covenants in Shopping Center Leases: 1994 Revision.* New York: International Council of Shopping Centers, 1994.

Kranzdorf, Norman M., Esq., ed. *Retailer Tenant Bankruptcy: A Retailer Bankruptcy Primer for Shopping Center Landlords.* New York: International Council of Shopping Centers, 1997.

This chapter was contributed by Colin M. Gromley, Esq., and Kevin M. Walsh, Esq., Attorneys-at-Law, Altman, Kritzer & Levick, P.C., Atlanta, Georgia.

13 ‖ Retailing

Shannon Alter, CPM

Property managers must contend with a variety of issues on a daily basis. Their days are always full and often frustrating, as they are tugged many ways by owners, tenants and vendors. To some shopping center managers, the very idea of learning about retailing seems a burdensome chore. After all, it's just one more thing to add to an already full plate. But learning more about retailers and their businesses can help the astute manager contribute to enhancing both the value of the center and the landlord-tenant relationship.

Any understanding of retailing must begin with understanding the unique nature of shopping centers and of retailers as tenants. Are shopping center tenants any different than tenants in other property types? Absolutely! Within reason, does it matter if an office tenant is an accountant or gives computer classes? Does it make a difference to the landlord whether office or industrial tenants' businesses increase? Not really, as long as the tenant continues to pay the rent and behaves well.

Therefore, it's reasonable to discuss why shopping centers and retailers are different. Retailers expect that landlords will provide the right tenant mix in a comfortable atmosphere that will encourage customers to shop. The primary reason a merchant is in a shopping center rather than in another property type is that he or she wants to derive the benefits that come from being near compatible merchants—in other words, merchants want to benefit from the synergy of a shopping center. In turn, landlords anticipate merchants will draw upon one another to achieve overall success for their stores and the shopping center. They also want to share in a merchant's success via percentage rent. Therefore, *sales matter!* Even if a merchant does not pay percentage rent it is important to collect sales reports, as sales are an important barometer of how individual tenants, as well as the entire center, are faring.

How can a property manager strike the delicate balance necessary to meet an owner's goals and desires and satisfy the merchants? To see increased revenue in the long run, managers must learn that while their goals are to enhance a center's value, a retailer's goals are to strengthen and enhance the value of its business through increased sales. In other words, landlord and tenant must essentially work as partners to achieve their goals. This chapter will look at how the property manager can be more successful by understanding these components of retailing:

- The relationship factor
- What to look for
- The retailer's business strategies
- Key retail business processes
- Signs of trouble

The Relationship Factor

Essentially, shopping center management is a relationship business. But what does that mean?

Say that John Smith, a property manager, has a large portfolio of shopping centers with several very demanding owners and intense reporting requirements. He is in a new job and anxious to prove himself, but he's also bogged down in paperwork. Consequently, he rarely gets out to visit his centers and depends on his assistant, Mary, to handle most calls because he just doesn't have the time. After all, he doesn't see any *need* to talk with the tenants as long as things are running without a hitch. Mary has never visited the centers. Around the fifth of each month, the receptionist makes calls regarding overdue rents. When John does call it's usually because there is a big problem.

Does this scenario sound familiar? All too often managers unwittingly set up what promises to be an adversarial relationship by overlooking the importance of friendly, personal, consistent contact with the merchants in their centers.

The fact is, the sheer volume of "stuff" a property manager must deal with can be overwhelming. So what's a busy property manager to do? Before John Smith can begin to learn anything about retailers and their businesses, he must first establish a relationship with them. After all, property managers have to "live" with their tenants. Most people enjoy talking about themselves and their interests. And what interests retailers most? Retailing, of course—the business they live and breathe. Establishing consistent communication can sometimes be difficult due to turnover in store managers, particularly those of chain tenants. However, you, as property manager, can learn more about your merchants' businesses and encourage them to talk if you pay them regular visits. At the same time, don't ignore the store managers of your major or chain tenants—they are often a wonderful source of information, both about their own stores and the center. If possible, try to get to know the district manager responsible for the area the center is in; such a relationship can be invaluable.

Ask how sales are going. Sometimes major tenants, for example, are not required to provide sales figures other than at specified times, and property managers are reluctant to ask for sales information in between. *Ask anyway.* Even if the store doesn't have to provide proprietary information, a good relationship with a store or district manager might net helpful information, such as how this store fares chainwide, whether sales as a whole were up or down and so on. Moreover, a good relationship with store management can be beneficial if you are having difficulty with another part of the chain's operations, accounting department or other areas.

What to Look For

What's a busy property manager to do? Let's say John has worked hard to develop a relationship with the retailers in his center. What does he need to understand first about the retailing business? Even uninitiated property managers can tell a lot about a store upon visiting it, so the first thing John should do is "shop" the store. He doesn't necessarily need to go shopping with an intent to purchase, but he should view the store from the customer's perspective. Here are some things to consider when *you* shop the retailers in your centers:

- What is the ambiance—the "feel"—of the store? Is it comfortable and pleasant to shop in?

- Are you greeted by a store employee and offered assistance, or is the clerk on the phone talking to a friend?
- Is merchandise displayed well, with prices clearly marked? Are price reductions clear and well marked?
- Is the store well stocked? Does its image come across clearly? Has the retailer taken every opportunity to display merchandise—on the wall or on endcaps, for example?
- Are the store's signage and advertising effective? Are signs professional and informative?
- Does the staff have good knowledge of the products and/or services offered?

You'll want to chat with your center's retailers about the things *you* noticed while you were shopping the store, but be sure to bone up before you go. This can take some finesse and knowledge on your part; you don't want to have merchants view the conversation as an inquisition.

One of the items mentioned above was that customers should be able to quickly discern the store's image, or focus, upon visiting it. The retailer, in turn, should clearly understand its target customers and the trade area from which it draws. In short, the retailer must have a demographic profile of its customers to be sure that the type of customer in the area is its type of customer. The retailer will also want to know about psychographics, which provide the lifestyle data of potential shoppers in its trade area. Psychographics tell retailers and property managers why customers shop in a certain store, when they shop, what type of quality or price they seek and other useful information. Here are some points you'll want to keep in mind as you chat with each merchant:

- Who are the store's core customers, those from whom the retailer generally gets 20 to 30 percent of its business? An example would be a store targeted toward surf- and beachwear for women under age twenty-five.
- What are the lifestyles and activities of those core customers? In this example, the customers would enjoy casual clothes and an outdoor lifestyle, mostly are single and have some discretionary income.
- What are their shopping habits? A surfwear customer may be going to school and available to shop during the day. She may take a bus or borrow a car to get to the center.

- Is the core customer value oriented or quality conscious? The customer may not require top-of-the-line clothing, but still wants fashion at a reasonable price.
- Last, but not least: which stores represent major competition? Does the retailer keep up with trends? Does the merchant regularly shop the competition?

The Retailer's Strategies

Have you ever had the unsettling experience of walking into a shop where you weren't quite sure what the retailer was selling, and whatever it was, there wasn't much of it on the shelves, and no one was available to help you anyway? You almost certainly ventured into a store where the retailer didn't have a strategy, a plan for how to get and keep its target customers.

Now that the property manager, John, has assured himself that his retailer understands its target customer, he'll want to take a look at the strategies retailers use to distinguish themselves from other retailers and draw that target customer into the store. A retailer's strategies should include areas such as merchandising, price points, growth, store ambiance, creativity, service and advertising. Listed below are a few of the items John (and you) may want to look at more closely as he comes to know his merchants' business better.

MERCHANDISING

As mentioned earlier, the store's direction and image should be very clear and immediately identifiable. There should be no mixed messages, so neither customers nor staff are confused. When property managers visit their retailers (either new or existing) they should consider several additional points concerning effective merchandising:

- Is the store a high-end, cutting-edge-of-fashion store or is it low-end, value-oriented?
- What assortment of items is offered? While it is important for a store to have depth and uniqueness, every retailer cannot offer everything. The range of merchandise must be narrow enough for a particular retailer to gain advantage over the competition in the area. Typically three to five classifications are offered.

- What is the store's lifestyle appeal? Does it have a special branded image?
- Does the store offer gift wrapping? Are customers reminded of gift-giving opportunities in the form of gift certificates, packaging, etc.?

AMBIANCE

The store's "look" or vision should be evident at a glance. The physical store itself should provide the shopper with a pleasant shopping experience and should support all of the information pertaining to it—for example, promotions, signage, displays. Has merchandise been categorized by color, product or use to draw attention to the items for sale? Some stores provide certain items on the floor for demonstration, so customers can try them out. Coffee stores or bakeries might provide samples of certain merchandise.

SERVICE

Nearly everyone has had the unfortunate experience of being the recipient of just plain poor service. The clerk was rude, a special order never arrived or you couldn't make a return because "it isn't store policy." Are you likely to return to stores with poor service? With the quality of service declining in many areas of today's time-pressured world, many customers refuse to shop at stores where they received inferior service. They simply don't have the time, particularly when they have errands that can just as easily be done elsewhere, in a more welcoming atmosphere.

If that isn't enough, many times customers don't bother to complain about inferior service—they just don't come back. But they *do* tell their friends. Service is truly an intangible but essential part of a retailer's "inventory," and substandard service can have a considerable negative impact. Outstanding service distinguishes a retailer from its competition and is clearly a way the retailer can add value. Retailers must do things differently today to gain advantage and market share over competitors. Focusing on service is an excellent way to do precisely that.

Just as the retailer must understand its target customer, so too it must comprehend *what that customer expects* once he or she arrives in the store. For example, today people seem to have more leisure time than ever, yet they are also busier than ever and have increasing demands on their time. Consequently, a grocery store customer might *expect* convenient services such as banking and dry cleaning to be available. He or she might *expect* delivery service, or the ability to order specific products. He or she definitely *expects* to save time. All of these things can add value to the shopper's experience.

What, then, does the category of service include? What do your retailers' customers expect? Here are some things to look for:

*   Friendly, empathic, responsive staff
*   High-quality merchandise
*   Convenient hours
*   Easy store layout
*   Guaranteed satisfaction
*   Availability of desired merchandise
*   Outstanding knowledge of products or services
*   Ability to place special orders
*   Creativity; special gift wrapping
*   Owner/store manager on-site (for independent stores)
*   Personal phone calls or notes regarding sales or promotions; newsletters
*   Training, training, training

Service, it is said, begins and ends with the employees. You know how frustrating it is to encounter an apathetic, inconsiderate or impolite attitude toward service.

Think of the stores you know of with excellent service. Are you likely to return to them? Probably, because they make things easier and more pleasant for you as a shopper. Customer-friendly employees can be an invaluable asset for a retailer.

Property managers can often be a valuable source of industry information for merchants, particularly smaller ones. There are many excellent trade magazines that print articles relating to retailing. Merchants often do not see these, so it is helpful to provide them with copies of pertinent articles.

ADVERTISING

As with merchandising, a retailer's chosen advertising must be very specific. Typically, a retailer will spend between 2 and 5 percent of annual sales on advertising. Retailers sometimes view advertising only as an added expense when it is really an investment in the future. Not just any ad will do; it must be focused and consistent, and appear at the right time and in the right place. For example, is the store part of a chain that has regular direct mailings? Does the center have a promotion fund or a merchants' association in which the merchant participates? Although this is a good starting point, most merchants cannot live by center advertising alone and must have their own program.

The objective, of course, is for a retailer to be able to further build its image and awareness and create sales. First, a retailer must understand why customers shop at its store. It must then tie in its advertising concepts to support the store's merchandise and appeal to its target customers. It must develop an ad plan and create a calendar. Only then will it be able to turn visits into sales and first-time customers into loyal clients.

Key Retail Business Processes

Now that the stage is set, a property manager will want to pay attention to some of the retailer's key business processes. Retailers engage in some activities similar to property managers: supervising and training staff, developing and managing budgets, planning advertising. In addition, they must know how to effectively buy, display and manage merchandise. Armed with knowledge about a retailer's key business processes, a property manager can better understand that a combination of factors points to a merchant's success or lack thereof.

When calculating many of these key business ratios, a merchant's net sales figures are used. *Net sales* are gross sales less refunds to the customer. It is a good idea, by the way, to periodically doublecheck your merchants' sales reports to be sure they are correctly calculated according to the lease.

OCCUPANCY COST

One of the first benchmarks a property manager can use to gauge how a merchant is performing is *occupancy cost,* which measures how well the store's sales volumes support its cost. Rent, common area maintenance (CAM) charges, taxes, insurance and percentage rent are typically all included in occupancy cost ratio even though the numerator is often labeled just "rent." The ratio looks like this:

$$\frac{\text{Annual rent}}{\text{Annual sales}} = \% \text{ Occupancy costs}$$

As an example, take a retailer in 1,500 square feet doing $225 per square foot (psf) in annual sales, with rent of $1.50 and CAM of $0.40

per square foot per month, including taxes and insurance. The retailer does not yet pay any percentage rent. This retailer's occupancy costs might be as follows:

Rent: $1.50 per month × 12 = $18.00 psf × 1,500 sf = $27,000 annual rent
CAM: $0.40 per month × 12 = $4.80 psf × 1,500 sf = $7,200 annual CAM
Total: $1.90 per month × 12 = $22.80 psf × 1,500 sf = $34,200 annual costs

Total annual sales: 1,500 sf × $225 psf per year = $337,500

$$\frac{\$34,200 \text{ (annual rent)}}{\$337,500 \text{ (annual sales)}} = 10\% \text{ occupancy cost}$$

(As a rule of thumb, your merchant's occupancy cost percentage should not be more than double its rate of percentage rent. Say you have a retailer who does not have a percentage rent requirement in its lease. What do you do then? You can still check what the percentage rate normally would be by investigating industry sources. One great way to estimate likely rates of percentage rent is to take a look at similar retailers in like locations within your own portfolio. Another way is to check with outside brokers you may use, or with other property managers. Professional associations may provide you with networking opportunities, giving you the chance to compare notes with other shopping center managers.)

What if the sample merchant's occupancy cost had turned out to be 18 percent rather than 10 percent? When a merchant's occupancy cost is higher than desired, it is a sign that the store's sales cannot support its costs and that it is likely headed for trouble. Just as property managers use this ratio as a measure of the viability of a store location, merchants too must be aware of and analyze their success. It's easy to see, then, why increasing store sales volumes must be the retailer's primary focus.

INVENTORY TURNOVER

Another ratio that is critical for a retailer is that of *inventory*, or *stock*, *turnover*. This ratio tells you how many times the retailer's average inventory has been turned over, or how many times it has been sold. In other words, inventory turnover is the rate at which inventory is sold. *Average inventory* is the sum of the retail inventories at the beginning of each month added to the total inventory at the end of the month, then divided by two. Average inventory is calculated on either the beginning of the month (BOM) stock or end of the month (EOM) stock, as shown below:

$$\frac{\text{Total inventory}}{\text{Number of inventories}} = \text{Average inventory}$$

A retailer's goal is to have a lot of what people want and very little of what they don't want. Merchandise that is not sold represents a financial investment which is tied up and occupies valuable shelf space that could be used for newer, quicker-moving items. Consequently, a higher turnover rate is desirable, since it generally is indicative of greater productivity and higher profit. Inventory control is important because it is a measure of how efficient a retailer is at buying, selling and managing its inventory. As well, the merchant likely has a better chance of gaining repeat business through greater merchandise exposure. Inventory turnover is calculated as follows:

$$\frac{\text{Net sales}}{\text{Average inventory}} = \text{Inventory turnover}$$

Compare the inventory turnover for two stores:

	Store #1	Store #2
Sales	$1,200,000	$900,000
Average inventory	300,000	300,000
Number of turns	4	3

Typically, stores such as supermarkets will have high turnover rates, while stores selling higher-end items, such as jewelry stores, will have lower turnover rates. Average turnover rates for different types of retailers can be found in a number of industry publications.

MARKUP

In order for a retailer to manage inventory well, it must know how to price the merchandise so that it will sell well once it gets into the store. Merchants know their prices must be in line with their competition, yet they must also manage to make a profit. When a retailer buys goods, it will then plan to *mark up* a planned profit over the initial cost of the goods and all related costs, such as transportation and preparation.

The terms *markup* and *markon* are synonymous and show the difference between the cost of an item and the selling price. Markup is always expressed in terms of the marking relative to the retail price, not the cost, either in dollars or as a percentage. The *retail sales price* results from a combination of the cost of goods and the initial markup. If you know the retail price and the cost of the merchandise item, it is possible to calculate the markup percentage, as follows:

$$\frac{\$\text{Retail price} - \$\text{cost}}{\$\text{Retail price}} = \text{Markup percentage}$$

As an example, if the cost of an item is $9.00 and the retail price is $16.00, the markup is 44 percent:

$$\frac{\$16.00 - \$9.00}{\$16.00} = 44\%$$

Retailers may also use a specific markup to establish the sales price. The ingredients of the formula remain the same, using the *cost complement* (reciprocal percentage):

$$\frac{\$\text{Cost}}{100\% - \text{Markup}\%} = \$\text{Retail price} \quad \text{or} \quad \frac{\$9.00}{100\% - 44\%} = \$16.00$$

Another method of markup is called *keystone markup*, which exactly doubles the cost of an item—the markup is 50 percent. For example, a dress that cost the retailer $75.00 will be priced at $150.00. The only potential problem with this method is that it does not focus on the demand for the item. If the item is in demand, or unique to a particular store, then the item should be marked up accordingly.

MARKDOWNS

Of course, a retailer hopes that all its merchandise will be sold at the original retail price, but it may also have to mark down merchandise in order to move it. *Markdowns* are reductions in the original price of an item with the express purpose of getting it to sell. The inability to sell merchandise at the previously determined sales price may occur due to poor timing (i.e., carrying peak stock too late in the season), incorrect pricing or simply a buying mistake. Markdowns reflect depreciation in the cost value of the merchandise; therefore, it is important for retailers to analyze which vendors' merchandise sells.

Markdowns are important to a retailer because they affect its ability to turn over goods and add new merchandise for the new season. For example, retailers may choose to carry lower stock levels in January when business is typically slower and when they want to make space available for new merchandise to spark customers' interest and bring in new sales. Usually a retailer will take repeated markdowns until the merchandise is finally sold.

Signs of Trouble

Go back to property manager John Smith. He's recently taken over management of a community shopping center and has visited the center's gift store for the first time. The owner is an independent, but is out at the time of John's visit. There is one employee in the store who is friendly and offers assistance. John notices that the store seems to have a little bit of this and a little of that. Things appear to be difficult to find; there does not appear to be much selection, and some shelves look rather empty. The display case at the front counter is cluttered. Is this retailer in trouble?

This retailer clearly has some challenges related to merchandising and *is* likely headed for trouble. John cannot be entirely sure at this point that the retailer is not salvageable, as he does not have enough information. Prior to visiting this merchant, there are several things he could have examined for a more complete picture:

- *Monthly sales figures:* Have there been any changes and why? Has store ownership changed? How does this merchant compare to others in a similar category in the center or in the landlord's other centers? Have the sales reports been correctly computed according to the lease?
- *Payment history:* Is the merchant making monthly rent and common area payments on time? Has he or she objected to a rent increase or requested a rent reduction?
- *Occupancy cost:* As discussed earlier, a retailer's occupancy cost includes all costs—rent, common area, promotions, etc. The store's sales must support its occupancy costs. Recall the rule of thumb which dictates that a store's occupancy cost should not be more than double its percentage rent rate. Therefore, a store with an occupancy cost of 20 percent and a percentage rent rate of 6 percent is likely treading in troubled waters.
- *Outside influences:* Are there other extenuating circumstances in the center which may have influenced this retailer? For example, did the grocery store right next to the gift shop move out six months ago?

Is the main city street bordering the center undergoing prolonged construction?

Generally, even less-experienced property managers who take the time to visit merchants regularly can discern when a store is headed for trouble. Here are some ways to tell when trouble looms ahead:

- The merchant is paying slowly or is always late.
- The merchandise is too scattered and lacks focus.
- The visual presentation of merchandise is poor and does not confirm the store's image.
- The stock is low or the shelves are empty. Just like a full buffet table, full shelves induce confidence.
- There's always a sale, complete with hand-lettered signs.
- The store and windows are dirty.
- The inventory is old and stale. No changes are made in the merchandise, even when seasonal changes should occur.
- The retailer has stopped advertising because it's too expensive.
- The employees are apathetic, unfriendly or unknowledgeable.

How the Manager Can Help

Offering help to a retailer can be a challenge for a variety of reasons. Most common are (1) the retailer might not recognize he or she needs help, (2) the property manager may not have the knowledge or the resources necessary to help or (3) the merchant may not be inclined to listen because he or she does not have a good relationship with the manager. Whatever the reason, evaluating and assisting a retailer with the right kind of help can take finesse on the manager's part. Some ways in which the manager can assist merchants are listed below:

- Continually monitor and stay on top of merchant sales reports. Talk with merchants about any material change in sales.
- Be a resource: provide information to merchants, such as the results of surveys or focus groups, pertinent articles, etc.
- Schedule a presentation for merchants by an in-house expert or an outside consultant on things such as better storefront displays or effective visual merchandising. Advertising or newspaper vendors may offer free assistance and advice. This type of presentation is usually effective, but it is often difficult

to get those merchants who particularly need help to attend. Once again, the manager-merchant relationship is crucial.

- Pay for an outside consultant to help a tenant merchandise, making sure that the most important issues are the ones addressed and that recommended solutions are in fact feasible.
- Keep a running list of troubled stores, or of those on the edge. Develop an action plan with the landlord for working with these merchants.

Taking the time to learn more about retailers' businesses can truly benefit the shopping center manager's relationship with merchants and enhance the long-term value of the center. An involved, interested manager can contribute to the success of his or her merchants by first understanding the key business strategies retailers use and then knowing how to monitor retailers and assist them when needed.

Recommended Readings

The Best of The Retail Challenge. New York: International Council of Shopping Centers, 1991.

Developing a Shopping Center Retail-Training Program. New York: International Council of Shopping Centers, 1995.

Dollars and Cents of Shopping Centers. Washington, D.C.: Urban Land Institute.

Eight Steps to Effective Retail Selling. Audiocassette. New York: International Council of Shopping Centers, 1992.

The Grocery Industry. Murray Hill, NJ: Dun & Bradstreet Information Services.

The ICSC Guide to Value Retailing the Smart Way. New York: International Council of Shopping Centers, 1997.

Increasing Retail Productivity: A Guide for Shopping Center Professionals. New York: International Council of Shopping Centers, 1998.

Industry Norms and Key Business Ratios. Murray Hill, NJ: Dun & Bradstreet Information Services.

International Foodservice Manufacturers Association (IFMA). Chicago, IL.

The Retail Challenge: Tips for Shopping Center Retailers. Quarterly. New York: International Council of Shopping Centers.

Retailing in the 1990s. Murray Hill, NJ: Dun & Bradstreet Information Services.

Shopping Centers Today. Monthly. New York: International Council of Shopping Centers.

Stores. Washington, D.C.: National Retail Federation (NRF).

The Tenant Retention Solution. Chicago, IL: Institute of Real Estate Management.

Value Retail News. Monthly. New York: International Council of Shopping Centers.

This chapter was contributed by Shannon Alter, CPM, Owner, Retail Management Services, Tustin, California.

Glossary

The following shopping center definitions have been compiled by the ICSC Research Department.

The term "shopping center" has been evolving since the early 1950s. Given the maturity of the industry, numerous types of centers currently exist that go beyond the standard definitions. Industry nomenclature originally offered four basic terms: neighborhood, community, regional and superregional centers. However, as the industry has grown and changed, more types of centers have evolved and these four classifications are no longer adequate. The International Council of Shopping Centers has defined eight principal shopping center types. See the table on page 286.

The definitions, and in particular the table that accompanies the text, are meant to be guidelines for understanding major differences between the basic types of shopping centers. Several of the categories shown in the table, such as size, number of anchors and trade area, should be interpreted as "typical" for each center type. They are not meant to encompass the operating characteristics of every center. As a general rule, the main determinants in classifying a center are its merchandise orientation (types of goods/services sold) and its size.

It is not always possible to precisely classify every center. A hybrid center may combine elements from two or more basic classifications, or a center's concept may be sufficiently unusual as to preclude it from fitting into one of the eight generalized definitions presented here.

There are other types of centers that are not separately defined here but nonetheless are a part of the industry. Some can be considered subsegments of one of the larger, defined groups, perhaps created to satisfy a particular niche market. One example would be the convenience center, among the smallest of centers, whose tenants provide a narrow mix of goods and personal services to a very limited trade area. A typical anchor would be a convenience store or other mini-mart. At the other end of the size spectrum are super off-price malls that consist of a large variety of value-oriented retailers, including factory outlet stores, department store close-out outlets and category killers in an enclosed megamall (up to 2 million sq. ft.) complex. Other smaller subsegments of the industry include vertical, downtown, off-price, home improvement and car care centers. The trend toward differentiation and segmentation will continue to add new terminology as the industry matures.

Simply stated, a shopping center is a group of retail and other commercial establishments that is planned, developed, owned and managed as a single property. On-site parking is provided. The center's size and orientation are generally determined by the market characteristics of the trade area served by the center. The two main configurations of shopping centers are malls and open-air strip centers.

Basic Configurations

There are two types of configurations: 1) Malls and 2) Strip Centers. Malls typically are enclosed, with a climate-controlled walkway between two facing rows of stores. The term represents the most common design mode for regional and superregional centers and has become an informal term for these types of centers.

A strip center is an attached row of stores or service outlets managed as a coherent retail entity, with on-site parking usually located in front of the stores. Open canopies may connect storefronts, but a strip center generally does not have enclosed walkways linking the stores. A strip center may be configured in a straight line, or have an "L" or "U" shape.

Shopping Center Types

Within the basic configurations, there are eight major types: Neighborhood Center, Community Center, Regional Center, Superregional Center, Fashion/Specialty Center, Power Center, Theme/Festival Center and Outlet Center.

Neighborhood Center: This center is designed to provide convenience shopping for the day-to-day needs of consumers in the immediate neighborhood. According to ICSC's *SCORE* publication, roughly half of these centers are anchored by a supermarket, while about a third have a drugstore anchor. These anchors are supported by smaller stores offering drugs, sundries, snacks and personal services. A neighborhood center is usually configured as a straight-line strip with no enclosed walkway or mall area, although a canopy may connect the storefronts.

Community Center: A community center typically offers a wider range of apparel and other soft goods than the neighborhood center. Among the more common anchors are supermarkets, super drugstores, and discount department stores. Community center tenants sometimes include off-price retailers selling such items as apparel, home improvement/furnishings, toys, electronics or sporting goods. The center is usually configured as a strip, in a straight line, an "L" or a "U" shape. Of the eight center types, community centers encompass the widest range of formats. For example, certain centers that are anchored by a large discount department store refer to themselves as discount centers. Others with a high percentage of square footage allocated to off-price retailers can be termed off-price centers.

Regional Center: This center type provides general merchandise (a large percentage of which is apparel) and services in full depth and variety. Its main attractions are its anchors: traditional, mass merchant or discount department stores of fashion specialty stores. A typical regional center is usually enclosed, with an inward orientation of stores connected by a common walkway, and parking surrounds the outside perimeter.

Superregional Center: Similar to a regional center, but because of its larger size, a superregional center has more anchors, a deeper selection of merchandise, and draws from a larger population base. As with regional centers, the typical configuration is an enclosed mall, frequently with multilevels.

Fashion/Specialty Center: A center composed mainly of upscale apparel shops, boutiques and craft shops carrying selected fashion or unique merchandise of high-quality and price. These centers need not be anchored, although sometimes restaurants or entertainment can provide the draw of anchors. The physical design of the center is very sophisticated, emphasizing a rich decor and high-quality landscaping. These centers usually are found in trade areas having high income levels.

ICSC Shopping Center Definitions

Type	Concept	Sq. Ft. Inc. Anchors	Acreage	Typical Anchor(s)		Anchor Ratio*	Primary Trade Area**
				Number	Type		
Neighborhood Center	Convenience	30,000–150,000	3–15	1 or more	Supermarket	30–50%	3 miles
Community Center	General merchandise; convenience	100,000–350,000	10–40	2 or more	Discount dept. store; supermarket; drug; home improvement; large specialty/discount apparel	40–60%	3–6 miles
Regional Center	General merchandise fashion (Mall, typically enclosed)	400,000–800,000	40–100	2 or more	Full-line dept. store; jr. dept. store; mass merchant; disc. dept. store; fashion apparel	50–70%	5–15 miles
Superregional Center	Similar to Regional Center but has more variety and assortment	800,000+	60–120	3 or more	Full-line dept. store; jr. dept. store; mass merchant; fashion apparel	50–70%	5–25 miles
Fashion/Specialty Center	Higher-end, fashion-oriented	80,000–250,000	5–25	N/A	Fashion	N/A	5–15 miles
Power Center	Category-dominant anchors; few small tenants	250,000–600,000	25–80	3 or more	Category killer; home improvement; discount dept. store; warehouse club; off-price	75–90%	5–10 miles
Theme/Festival Center	Leisure; tourist-oriented; retail and service	80,000–250,000	5–20	N/A	Restaurants, entertainment	N/A	N/A
Outlet Center	Manufacturers' outlet stores	50,000–400,000	10–50	N/A	Manufacturers' outlet stores	N/A	25–75 miles

*The share of a center's total square footage that is attributable to its anchors
**The area from which 60–80% of the center's sales originate

Power Center: A center dominated by several large anchors, including discount department stores, off-price stores, warehouse clubs, or "category killers," i.e., stores that offer tremendous selection in a particular merchandise category at low prices. Some of these anchors can be freestanding (unconnected). The center has only a minimum amount of small specialty tenants.

Theme/Festival Center: This center typically employs a unifying theme that is carried out by the individual shops in their architectural design and, to an extent, in their merchandise. The biggest appeal of this center is to tourists; it can be anchored by restaurants and entertainment facilities. The center is generally located in an urban area, tends to be adapted from an older, sometimes historic, building and can be part of a mixed-use project.

Outlet Center: Usually located in a rural or occasionally in a tourist location, an outlet center consists mostly of manufacturers' outlet stores selling their own brands at a discount. An outlet center typically is not anchored. A strip configuration is most common, although some are enclosed malls, and others can be arranged in a "village" cluster.

Following are additional key terms and definitions compiled from *ICSC's Guide to Shopping Center Terms* that relate to the shopping center management topics in this book.

A list of the ICSC publications from which the terms in this glossary were taken is given below. The number preceding each title corresponds to the footnote number shown in the definitions.

1. *ICSC Research Quarterly,* "Shopping Center Definitions."
2. *Marketing Your Shopping Center,* S. Albert Wenner.
3. *Fundamentals of Shopping Center Management.*
4. *ICSC Keys to Shopping Center Marketing Series.*
5. *Fundamentals of Shopping Center Marketing.*
6. *Market Research for Shopping Centers,* edited by Ruben A. Roca.
7. *ICSC Keys to Shopping Center Management Series.*
8. *Preparing a Budget for a Small Shopping Center,* Alan A. Alexander, CSM.
9. *Shopping Center Lease Administration,* Alan A. Alexander, CSM.
10. *The SCORE: ICSC's Handbook on Shopping Center Operations, Revenues & Expenses, 1993.*
11. *Construction Management Techniques,* Ray G. Simms.
12. *Carpenter's Shopping. Center Management,* edited by Robert J. Flynn, CSM.
13. *Advanced Shopping Center Management: Roofs.*
14. *Advanced Shopping Center Management: Parking Lots.*

accounts receivable   All income that has been billed and is still owed at any point in time.[4]

accrual basis of accounting
The method of accounting whereby revenues and expenses are identified with specific periods of time, such as a month or year, and are recorded as incurred, along with acquired assets, without regard to the date of receipt or payment of cash; distinguished from cash basis.[3]

An accounting method that tracks expenditures against the budget for a given time frame, indicating amounts already received and paid as well as anticipated receipts and planned expenditures.

addendum   Lease change or addition usually inserted at the end of the original lease form.[4]

add-on [rent charges]   Additional charges to the rent, which may include service charges for maintenance of common areas, merchants' association fees, contribution to the marketing fund, HVAC [heating, ventilation and air-conditioning] and electric charges, trash, insurance, or taxes.[4]

administrative marketing costs   The cost of payroll, benefits, rent, and bookkeeping and other administrative costs attributed to marketing.[4]

advertising   The nonpersonal communication of a sales message to actual or potential purchasers by a person or organization selling a product or service, delivered through a paid medium for the purpose of influencing the buying behavior of those purchasers.[3]

advertising campaign   Advertising and related efforts used on behalf of a shopping center in the attainment of predetermined goals.[2]

advertising fund   A fund set up by the [shopping center] developer for producing special ad campaigns or catalogs for the shopping center.[4]

advertising plan   A description of the message, themes, and creative elements of your advertising campaign. It includes a budget for creative and production services.[4]

anchor store
A major store (usually a chain store) in a shopping center having substantial economic strength and occupying a large square footage.[3]

A major department store branch in a shopping center.[2]

The stores and other uses that occupy the largest spaces in a center and serve as the primary traffic generators. Freestanding anchors are excluded.[10]

asset   Any owned physical object (tangible) or right (intangible) having a monetary value.[5]

assignee   New tenant that assumes the rights and responsibilities of the original tenant.

assignment   The transfer to another party of all a tenant's interests in a lease for the remainder of the lease term. It is distinguished from a sublease, in which some portion of the terms of the lease remains with the primary tenant.[3]

bad debt allowance [Also known as credit loss.]   The allowance for uncollectible tenant billing balances. [10]

balance sheet
A statement of financial position of any economic unit disclosing as of a given moment in time its assets, at cost, depreciated cost, or other indicated value; its liabilities; and its ownership equities.[3]

A report showing a business's financial position on a specific date.[7]

See cash flow statement.[4]

bill-backs   All expense items enumerated in the lease—such as common area, taxes, insurance, and maintenance—that are paid by the landlord and then billed to the tenant.[8]

boiler and machinery insurance   Coverage for damage caused by or to boilers and machinery, including business interruption caused by boiler explosion or machinery breakdown.[7]

bookkeeping   The process of analyzing, recording, and classifying transactions for the purpose of establishing a basis for recording and reporting the financial affairs of the enterprise and the results of its operations.[3]

box ads   A print media term meaning advertisements, generally uniform in size, grouped together under a banner heading and promoting a cooperative event.[2]

breakpoint In percentage rent, the point at which rent due from a specific percentage of sales equals the minimum rent.[7]

broker A licensed insurance professional who represents and acts on behalf of clients rather than an insurance company.[7]

budget
An itemized listing and/or allotment of all estimated revenues anticipated and a listing (and segregation) of all estimated costs and expenses that will be incurred in obtaining those revenues over a fixed period of time.[7]

Any financial plan serving as an estimate of and a control over future operations.[5]

A summary of probable income and expenses for a given period of time.[8]

business interruption insurance Covers loss of net income, other than loss of rents, that would have been earned, including expenses incurred to reduce that loss.[7]

CAM *See* common area maintenance.

CAM administration fee Receipts from tenants for administering CAM [common area maintenance] charges.[10]

capital budget
Includes income from sale of assets, broken down as to gain or loss against book value, payments on the principal of a mortgage or other debt, and the year's outlays for repairs or additions to be capitalized for depreciation over future years. All numbers used in the capital budget are as-estimated going in and as-actual in the year-end report.[12]

An outline of expenditures for physical improvements to the property.[7]

capital expense
A structural repair such as the replacement of a storm sewer system.[7]

The annual amount required to pay interest on and provide for the ultimate return (depreciation or amortization) of the investment.[7]

capitalization The process of converting into a present value (obtaining the present worth of) a series of anticipated future annual installments of income.[7]

capitalization rate
The rate used to convert income into value.[7]

The capitalization rate varies with the availability of money, the going interest rate in the center's geographical location, the relative amount of risk estimated by a lender, and the overall bargaining position of the developer. [12]

cash basis   A basis of keeping accounts (in contrast to the accrual basis) whereby revenue and expenses are recorded on the books of account when received and paid, respectively, without regard to the period to which they apply.[5]

cash disbursement journal   A monthly record of all payments.[4]

cash flow analysis   A projection of anticipated income and expenses according to the actual or anticipated times of receipt and disbursement. It indicates a positive or negative cash flow and allows for any necessary adjustments throughout the year.[4]

cash flow statement   A financial picture for a determined period of time. It provides an overview of assets and liabilities, and any variance between them. Also called a balance sheet.[4]

cash method   This report indicates exactly what was received and what was paid to date and relates specifically to the projected cash flow prepared with the budget.[4]

certificate of insurance
A document that is evidence that an insurance policy has been issued.[7]

A document that verifies the type and amounts of insurance carried by a policyholder.[7]

coinsurance clause   A clause penalizing the insured if the amount insured for is less than a pre-agreed specified percentage of the value of the property insured.[7]

commencement date   The day on which a tenant's lease term begins; not to be confused with occupancy date.[7]

commercial general liability policy   A broad form of third-party insurance that covers the policyholder in the event of bodily injury, personal injury, and property damage claims.[7]

common area
The walkways and areas onto which the stores in a center face and which conduct the flow of customer traffic.[2]

The portions of a shopping center that have been designated and improved for common use by or for the benefit of more than one occupant of the shopping center.[5]

common area HVAC energy   Heating, ventilation, and air-conditioning (HVAC) energy expenses for the common area only.[11]

common area maintenance (CAM)
The amount of money charged to tenants for their shares of maintaining a center's common area.[7]

The charge that a tenant pays for shared services and facilities such as electricity, security, and maintenance of parking lots.[7]

The area maintained in common by all tenants, such as parking lots and common passages. This area is often defined in the lease and may or may not include all physical areas or be paid for by all tenants.[7]

Items charged to common-area maintenance may include cleaning services, parking lot sweeping and maintenance, snow removal, security, and upkeep.[12]

concession   The privilege of maintaining a subsidiary business within certain premises.[3]

construction allowance   Money or financial incentives given to tenants for the cost of constructing their store space in a center.[7]

Consumer Price Index (CPI)
An indicator of rising prices or inflation used to measure the impact of inflation upon consumers; published by the Bureau of Labor Statistics at the end of every month.[6]

Various statistical indexes gathered and published by the federal government as economic indicators.[7]

A monthly government report of prices paid for a standard market basket of goods in various classifications.[4]

Consumer Price Index adjustment   An adjustment to the agreed-upon marketing contribution based on changes in the consumer price index.[4]

Consumer Price Index rents   Rents that are pegged to rises in the consumer price index.[7]

contract
An agreement by which two legally competent persons promise to obligate each other to do something.[3]

In media usage, a written agreement (usually one year's duration) to use a specified amount of space (print) or air time (radio and TV).[2]

cost approach
A method in which the value of a property is derived by estimating the replacement cost of the improvements, deducting the estimated depreciation, and adding the value of the land, as estimated by use of the market-data approach.[7]

The value of a property obtained by estimating the replacement cost of the improvements, deducting the estimated depreciation, and adding the value of the land, as estimated by the use of the market-data approach. A high percentage of appraisals include the cost approach in the analysis, and, in some states, it is obligatory for the assessor to include it in his considerations.[12]

co-tenancy   A term that refers to a clause inserted into a tenant's lease stipulating that a reduced rent or no rent be paid until an agreed-upon percentage of the center is occupied.[7]

covenant   Words used in a contract whereby the person who is getting or giving something binds himself to the other for the performance (or nonperformance) of a particular act.[3]

cross-shopping   Purchasing complementary items at different stores or in different departments of a single store.[4]

current asset
Unrestricted cash or other asset held for conversion within a relatively short period into cash or other similar asset, or useful goods or services. Usually the period is one year or less.[5]

Assets that can be converted into cash within 12 months.[7]

current liability
A short-term debt, regardless of its source, including any liability accrued and deferred and unearned revenue that is to be paid out of cur-

rent assets or is to be transferred to income within a relatively short period, usually one year or less.[5]

Those things owed and due within 12 months.[7]

debit A bookkeeping entry or posting recording the creation of or addition to an asset or expense, or the reduction or elimination of a liability.[5]

debt service The payments consisting of amortization of and interest on a loan.[7]

demographic characteristics Basic objective data about the shoppers of a center or residents of a market area. The statistics might include age, gender, income, education, and occupation.[4]

demographic market A demographic group or segment from which a shopping center draws its shoppers and sales.[4]

demographic study A study of socioeconomic facts concerning individuals or households—such as car ownership, income, age, marital status, and education—studied by advertisers and merchandisers in order to make their sales and advertising programs more effective.[5]

demographics
Vital statistics of the marketing area; that is, average income, age, number of children, cost of homes, education, and ethnic factors.[2]

Basic objective data about the shoppers in [a geographic] market area. Demographic statistics include age, sex, income, education, and occupation.[7]

The statistical characteristics of population groups, sorted out by such things as age and income, used to identify markets.[7]

department store type merchandise (DSTM)
DSTM includes the kind of goods sold in shopping centers, such as apparel, shoes, jewelry, gifts and other merchandise usually found in department stores and shopping centers. DSTM excludes personal services, entertainment, food service, drugs, groceries, and automotive, all of which may be found in shopping centers. DSTM sales potential is a component of a center's share of market calculation.[4]

DSTM includes merchandise normally found in variety, apparel, furniture, and appliance stores, and in other outlets such as jewelry, sporting goods, stationery, luggage, and camera stores, as well as department stores.[6]

General merchandise, apparel, furniture, and other merchandise (GAFO) as defined by the Department of Commerce, *Census of Retail Trade.*[6]

depreciation
The process of estimating and recording lost usefulness. Loosely, any wasting away of a physical asset and hence its cost, especially where not accompanied by a change in outward appearance, as in a slow-moving inventory of styled goods; functional loss of value.[5]

A loss from the upper limit of value caused by deterioration and/or obsolescence.[7]

The amount the value of a property deteriorates in a year; how much the total value is reduced by wear and tear.[7]

directors and officers liability [insurance]   Protects a company's directors and officers in the event of a suit brought by stockholders or the public for negligence in the performance of their responsibilities.[7]

discount rate   An interest rate commensurate with perceived risk; used to convert future payments or receipts to present value.[7]

effective rent   A combination of the minimum and percentage rent paid by a tenant.[7]

enclosed common area   A term applied to enclosed malls and measured in square feet of floor area. It includes the mall, public restrooms, receiving and distribution facilities for the common use of tenants, and other enclosed common areas.[10]

enclosed mall   An enclosed mall has a walkway or mall that is enclosed, heated and cooled, insulated, and lighted. The mall corridor is flanked on one or both sides by storefronts and entrances. The configuration of the center may vary, but on-site parking is usually provided around the perimeter of the center.[10]

equity   The net value of a property, obtained by subtracting from its total value all liens and other charges against it. The term is frequently applied to the value of the owner's (as opposed to the lender's) interest in the property in excess of all claims and liens.[7]

errors and omissions [insurance] coverage   Protects against liability arising out of errors and omissions in the performance of professional services.[7]

estoppel letter   The tenant or the landlord represents as to the current relationship of the tenant and landlord; that is, an estoppel letter will set forth whether there are any defaults or whether rent has been paid in advance. This document would have each party agree that the lease is in full force and effect and that no covenant [has been] breached.[7.]

exclusives
A term referring to a store's being given the exclusive right to sell a particular category of merchandise within a shopping center.[7]

An existing tenant may have negotiated the right to be the only one in the center to offer particular goods or services, and therefore space may not be leased to another tenant offering the same goods or services in competition with the first tenant.[7]

exhibits   Attachments, usually to the end of an original lease, specifying the location, legal description, and tenant's construction specifications.[7]

expense recovery   Total receipts from tenants to recover operating expenses for maintenance and repair, utilities, security, insurance, taxes, and other expenses.[10]

expenses   Charges involved in running the business. *See* fixed expenses.[7]

expiration date   The date on which a tenant's lease term is complete.[7]

financial reports   Monthly statements of how much an account had at the start and the end of the month; they provide both budgeted and actual information for the current month and year to date.[4]

fixed assets   Things used in a business that are not for sale.[4]

fixed contributions   [Insertion into] the original lease of a provision limiting the landlord's contribution in the total real estate burden to a fixed amount—usually expressed as so many cents per square foot of GLA [gross leasable area]—with all taxes over that figure to be spread among the tenants pro rata to their share of the total GLA. The sum to be paid by the landlord is [usually] pegged at approximately the total amount anticipated for the first year.[12]

fixed expenses   Also called indirect expenses, these are operating expenses that are not affected by increases or decreases in sales volume.[7]

fixed minimum rent   The amount of basic rent paid by the tenant, usually stated as an amount per square foot charged on an annual basis. This figure does not include any other fees or assessments typically charged in a shopping center. Also called base rent.[4]

flat rent   A specific rent on square footage paid by a tenant for a specified period of time.[7]

focus group
A group representing a cross-section of the center's customers, brought together to discuss their needs and preferences.[4]

A group of consumers who are assembled to candidly discuss their opinions on a particular subject.[4]

food court   In enclosed malls, an area devoted to permanent vendor stalls offering a range of prepared foods for on-premises consumption and served by a common seating area.[10]

food court expenses   All expenses specifically attributable to a food court operation. These include: 1. housekeeping labor—the payroll and employee benefits associated with the janitorial function of the food court, and 2. supplies/other—all costs of supplies and other miscellaneous expenses relating specifically to the food court.[10]

GAFO   An acronym for General merchandise, Apparel, home Furnishings, and Other merchandise (such as books, toys, and food sold away from home), which are normally sold in regional shopping centers.[6]

general and administrative expenses   All expenses related to the management of the shopping center, office staff, office supplies, office equipment rental expenses, management fees, leasing fees and commissions, and professional services. [Line items include bad debt allowances, leasing fees and commissions, legal and audit expenses, management fees, office equipment expenses, on-site payroll, and benefits.][10]

gross income   Revenues before deducting any expenses.[5]

gross leasable area (GLA)
Normally the total area on which a shopping center tenant pays rent. The GLA includes all selling [space] as well as storage and other miscellaneous space.[6]

The square footage of a shopping center that can generate income by being leased to tenants. This figure does not include the area occupied by department stores or anchor tenants.[4]

The measurement used to define how much space a tenant has leased in a center. GLA is determined by measuring the distance between the middle walls of a space and the distance between front outside wall to back outside wall.[7]

The total floor area designed for tenant occupancy and exclusive use, including basements, mezzanines, and upper floors. It is measured from the center line of joint partitions and from outside wall faces. In short, GLA is that area on which tenants pay rent; it is the area that produces income.[12]

gross lease   A lease in which the landlord pays 100% of all taxes, insurance, and maintenance associated with the operation of a shopping center.[7]

gross margin   The difference between the sales and the total cost of merchandise sold.[7]

gross profit
Net sales less cost of goods sold but before considering selling and general expenses, incidental income, and income deductions.[3]

Markup multiplied by sales price.[7]

gross sales   Total sales from all transactions.[7]

heating, ventilation and air-conditioning (HVAC) units   Fairly large machines that handle all the heating, cooling, and ventilation uses associated with a center.[7]

housekeeping expenses   The cost of janitorial services for the interior common area of the center, whether performed by mall personnel or an outside service. For mall personnel, it includes payroll, employee benefits, and materials and supplies. For outside service contracts, it includes time charges for labor and any charges for equipment use and maintenance supplies.[10]

income, net Difference between [the shopping center's] total effective income and total operating expenses.[6]

income, per capita Total personal income of residents divided by the resident population.[6]

income, real The amount of income one can spend on goods and services one may enjoy.[6]

income, total Money "cash" income, including wages, salaries, self-employment, Social Security, and retirement pension.[6]

income, total personal Money income plus noncash types of income, including food stamps and imputed income.[6]

income approach
An appraisal technique in which the anticipated net income is processed to indicate the capital amount of the investment that produces it. The capital amount, called the capitalized value, is, in effect, the sum of the anticipated annual rents less the loss of interest until the time of collection.[7]

A technique that takes the historical net income as a basis on which to calculate the capital value of the investment producing that net income. According to this method, the value of income-producing property, such as a shopping center, tends to be set by the amount of future income that can reasonably be expected, and the present value of the property is the present value of the future income.[12]

income statement A report showing a business's financial performance over a specific period of time.[7]

indemnification Protection against a [law-]suit or [unanticipated] expenses.[7]

insurance A contract between a risk-taker (the insurer) and another party (the insured) in which, for a fee (the premium), the insurer agrees to pay the insured for losses to something specific (the risk) due to named causes (hazards or perils). The insurer may also assume the obligation to pay a third party (the claimant) on behalf of the insured.[7]

insurance expense   This major category includes all premiums and costs incurred for insurance covering structures, public liability, rental value, equipment, and bonding of employees. It includes the cost of an insurance consultant. Line items include: Liability insurance: the net premium cost of public liability insurance; Property insurance: the net premium cost of property insurance; Special coverage: the net premium cost of special coverage, such as earthquake or flood insurance; and Other: the net premium costs of other types of insurance, such as auto, boiler and machinery, bonding of employees, and insurance consultants, if any.[10]

insurance revenue   Receipts from tenants to recover the cost of insurance for the center.[10]

insuring agreement   The section of an insurance policy that states what the policy covers.[7]

interest   Money paid for the use of capital. It is usually expressed as a rate or percentage of the capital, called the interest rate.[7]

key money   Money from the tenant to the landlord for the right to operate a business in the center.[7]

kick-out clause   An option that allows a landlord or tenant to terminate the lease before the end of the term. [In the tenant's case, generally tied to the presence of another retailer.][7]

kiosks   Booths located in the common areas of the center or mall and generally housing small-item merchandise or services; for example: hosiery, photo developing.[2]

landlord   The owner of real property (or of a leasehold interest in real property) who leases the property to a tenant for value consideration.[3]

landscaping expenses   The cost of landscaping contracts, services or groundskeepers, and normal replacement of trees, shrubs, and flowers on the exterior and in the interior common area of the mall. It covers the cost of mall personnel, if any, performing these services.[10]

lease
A contract transferring the right to the possession and enjoyment of [property] for a definite period of time.[3]

The signed agreement between landlord and tenant that establishes responsibility, sets standards and states what is recoverable from tenants for the maintenance process.[7]

lease summary report   An abstract of information about the status of the leasable space in a center as well as pertinent information from each tenant's lease.[4]

leasing fees and commissions   The expenses incurred for commissions paid to secure tenants for a center.[10]

lessee   The tenant; one who rents or leases property from another.[3]

lessor   The owner; one who rents or leases property to another.[3]

letter of intent   Generally a document submitted prior to a formal lease. It serves to delineate the intentions between the landlord and the tenant. Basic issues, including minimum rent, percentage rent, pass-through expenses and other major points of negotiation, are outlined. [Generally subject to execution of a complete contract.][7]

liability
An amount owed by one person (a debtor) to another (a creditor).[5]

A legal obligation or responsibility.[7]

liability insurance   *See* commercial general liability policy.

lien   A charge, security, or encumbrance upon property for the payment of a debt.[3]

liquidation   The sale of assets and the settlement of debts in the winding up of a business, estate, or other economic unit.[3]

long-term liabilities   Those things owed after 12 months.[7]

maintenance
The upkeep of the various physical assets and common area of a shopping center.[7]

Maintenance involves the preservation of what is already there. For example, patching the parking lot and relamping the lights; painting wall surfaces and replacing deteriorated caulking; rodding the sewer line and changing the oil in the Jeep; and in general doing these things that prolong the economic life of the property in its present form.[12]

maintenance and repair expenses   Expenses related to the maintenance and repair of the shopping center. They may include the costs of payroll, employee benefits (taxes, workers' compensation, pension contributions, etc.), service contracts, and maintenance materials and supplies purchased for the center. They usually do not include major capital improvements or maintenance and repair services that are for the benefit of individual tenants and billed directly to the tenants.[10]

mall [The typical mall is] enclosed, with a climate-controlled walkway between two facing rows of stores. The term represents the most common design mode for regional and superregional centers and has become an informal term for these types of centers.[1]

management fee
The fee charged by the fee manager or the owner to cover rental collection, administration, common area, maintenance, and tenant relations activities.[8]

A tenant and/or landlord charge. The management fee is calculated from a negotiated percentage of the gross collectible of a shopping center. The fee usually includes the CAM [common area maintenance] charge.[7]

The fee, whether a flat fee or a percentage of gross receipts, charged to the center for management services provided by the management company.[10]

markdown
A reduction in the retail price of merchandise, primarily for clearance, special sales events, or to meet competition.[2]

A decrease from the original price of an item. The markdown percentage is usually stated as a percentage of the reduced selling price.[5]

A retail price reduction caused by the inability to sell goods at the original or subsequently determined retail price.[7]

market analysis The process of determining the characteristics of the market and the measurements of its capacity to appeal to a community.[6]

market area The area surrounding a shopping center from which the center draws its customers.[7]

market benchmarks Comparisons of a center's market demographics with other markets in the U.S.[4]

market data   The demographic and economic characteristics of a center's market area (based on census data).[4]

market penetration   The percentage of the desired market reached by the proposed [advertising] schedule.[4]

market plan
Quite literally, a blueprint for the company's total marketing effort. It charts specific directions, objectives, strategies, and tactics for achieving optimum success in marketing efforts.[3]

A detailed document explaining all the steps and activities a shopping center will use to promote itself during a one-year period.[7]

market profile   A demographic description of the people and households of the primary and secondary markets.[2]

market research   The initial and ongoing studies needed to make marketing decisions. A survey conducted for the developer before commitment to build and on a recurring basis for the marketing director, who disseminates pertinent information to tenants. Reports define demographics and psychographics of the market area.[2]

market share   The portion of trade-area retail potential attributable to proposed facilities, after consideration of their known market strength and relative position vis-à-vis comparable competition.[6]

marketing fund
A pool of marketing dollars, to which all tenants contribute, that is administered by the marketing director and is an advisory board of tenants.[4]

An alternative to the merchants' association, a marketing fund requires contributions from each tenant; the recipient is not a merchants' association but the fund, which is controlled solely by the developer. Under this arrangement, some sort of advisory board is set up, composed of merchant representatives, and the developer consults with this board on the use of the promotional fund.[5]

The pooling and distribution of money paid by tenants for the overall marketing of the shopping center. The marketing fud is overseen by the center's marketing director and staff and is used for advertising and promotion activities. [7]

Established by a fee paid to the landlord, this is a pool of monies for which shopping center landlords are totally responsible. The fund has a tenant advisory board. A clause in the lease covers increases in the fee.[7]

[marketing fund] advisory board   A group of tenants representing all aspects of the tenant mix that administers a marketing fund along with the marketing director.[4]

markup
The difference between the retail selling price of the merchandise and the cost of the merchandise to the retailer.[7]

The difference between the cost price as billed (before deductions for cash discount) and the retail price at which the merchandise is originally offered.[5]

media
In advertising, the means or instruments of communication: radio, television, newspapers, magazines, direct mail, and billboards.[4]

The vehicles—including radio, television, newspapers, magazines and newsletters—through which public relations messages are transmitted.[4]

merchandise mix
The variety and categories of merchandise offered by the retail tenants assembled in a particular shopping center.[7]

A merchandise mix is a group of products that are closely related because they satisfy a class of needs, are used together, or are sold to the same basic market targets. It is made up of a series of demand-related merchandise items, which are specific versions of a product that has a separate designation.[5]

merchants' association
A merchants' association is a not-for-profit corporation organized to conduct merchandising programs, community events, shopping center decoration programs, advertising programs, and publicity programs, and to coordinate joint member cooperative advertising and marketing functions, events, and endeavors for the general benefit of the shopping center. The association acts as a clearinghouse for suggestions, ideas and programming of merchandising events, and it serves as a quasi-court for handling complaints and differences of opinion.[5]

The tenant group organized to promote the center through cooperative advertising, public relations activity, and community involvement.[2]

An organization of merchants that works to advertise and promote a shopping center. It is a nonprofit, independent corporation.[7]

A not-for-profit, independent corporation with a board of directors who vote and sign checks. The members pay dues. Monthly meetings and an annual report are required.[7]

[merchants' association] articles of incorporation   Papers filed with the secretary of the state in which the center is located that declare the [merchants'] association's status as a not-for-profit organization and state the association's purpose.[4]

merchants' association by-laws   The basic rules of governance of a merchants' association.[4]

merchants' association dues   The financial obligation of member tenants and landlord, fixed by a predetermined structure and used for center-wide promotion, special events, and community activities.[2]

minimum rent
The basic rent a tenant pays; usually expressed as a price per square foot.[7]

Rent that is not based on a tenant's sales.[7]

The specific dollar amount paid by a tenant for the amount of square footage leased.[7]

mixed-use centers   These centers typically combine at least three revenue-producing uses from among retail, office, parking, restaurant, hotel, residential, and entertainment facilities. They may be built in suburban or urban areas. In downtown areas, where land costs are high, a multilevel or high-rise, single-mass design is commonly used to minimize the land area needed.[12]

mortgage constant   The total annual payment of principal and interest (annual debt service) on a level-payment amortized mortgage, expressed as a percentage of the initial principal amount of the loan. It is used in mortgage-equity analysis as well as in estimating cash flows generated by income-producing real estate.[7]

mortgage, wraparound The owner takes a second mortgage that encompasses the first mortgage. It is a method of refinancing often used when property value has increased significantly and the owner wants to obtain extra funds based on the property's current market value. When a wraparound is used, the borrower avoids losing the benefit of a favorable (lower) interest rate on the original loan even though the new, second mortgage money is borrowed at a higher rate.[12]

national tenant A retailer who operates a chain of stores on a nationwide basis.

negligence The act of being extremely careless. The failure to use such care as a reasonably prudent and careful person would use under similar circumstances. If found negligent in a court of law, a center can be held liable for the actions of a guard or a criminal.[7]

net What remains after specified deductions from the gross amount.[7]

net income *See* income, net.

net operating income The income after deducting from gross income the operating expenses, including property taxes, insurance, utilities, management fees, heating and cooling expenses, repairs and maintenance, and replacement of equipment.[7]

net price Sometimes called retailer's cost price. The amount a retailer must pay for a particular item.[7]

net profit
The amount of money left after all expenses have been paid.[4]

The profit over a specified period of a corporation or other business after deducting operating costs and income deductions; equals net income.[5]

net sales Gross sales less returns and allowances, freight-out, and often cash discounts allowed. In recent years the trend has been to report as net sales the net amount finally received from the customer.[5]

net worth What the owner actually owns in the business.[7]

occupancy area The total square footage of a center, including all vacant spaces.[10]

occupancy cost   The sum of a tenant's fixed rent, percentage rent, and add-ons. Also called total rent.[4]

office equipment expenses   The cost of renting or servicing office equipment such as copiers, personal computers, and other office equipment ([sometimes] excluding telephones).[10]

offset
A reduction in the cost of percentage rent when a tenant meets a pre-arranged goal in another area, usually sales.[7]

A deduction of specified expenses or investments from all or a portion of percentage rent.[7]

operating budget
An outline of how much income a shopping center has and how that income will be spent.[7]

Includes all income other than sale of capital assets, offset by all items of expense other than depreciation and interest on debt and payments on debt principal or added investment.[12]

operating expenses
Generally speaking, all expenses, occurring periodically, that are necessary to produce net income before depreciation. Under some conditions these expenses are placed in two categories: operating expenses and fixed charges.[7]

Monies needed to operate a business, as distinct from outlays to finance the business.[7]

operating statement
A management statement that provides net sales, costs, and expenses and net operating profit or loss for a fixed period.[7]

A financial statement showing income and expenses by specific category and for a specific time frame.[8]

outparcels   Unused portions of a shopping center's site that constitute the perimeter areas, not including the center facility or parking lot, and that may be used or developed for similar or nonsimilar purposes.[7]

overages   Rent paid in addition to an agreed-upon minimum rent.[7]

overhead   A synonym for fixed expenses.[4]

pad   The exact parcel of land on which a department store's building stands.[12]

pad tenant   A tenant, usually freestanding, located on a separate parcel at the front of a shopping center. Also called an out-lot tenant.[8]

parking area   The space in a shopping center devoted to parking, including aisles, walks, islands, minor landscaping, and other features incidental to parking.[6]

parking lot cleaning/sweeping/repair expenses   All costs (payroll, benefits, materials, service contracts and supplies) incurred in the striping, repairing of potholes, cleaning, and sweeping of the parking lot, sidewalks and service courts. They also include all expenses incurred in the maintenance and repair of the parking lot sweeping equipment.[10]

parking ratio   The relationship of space used for parking and necessary vehicular and pedestrian movement to land area covered by buildings or space within the buildings. This relationship can be expressed in the number of car spaces per 1,000 square feet of rentable area.[6]

pass-through expenses   A tenant's portion of expense composed of common area maintenance, taxes and insurance, and any other expenses determined by the landlord to be paid by the tenant.[7]

percentage rent
A percentage of the tenant's total annual sales paid in addition to fixed rent. This additional rent is normally paid after a predetermined sales level has been achieved. The percentage factor is then applied to all sales over the present level (breakpoint).[4]

The payment by a tenant as rent of a specified percentage of the gross income from sales made upon the premises. Developers in shopping centers customarily charge a minimum rent plus a percentage rent when sales exceed a certain volume.[5]

Percentage rent is a function of sales activity. A tenant's sales during a lease year are multiplied by the percentage rent rate(s); any excess over the minimum rent is percentage rent.[7]

Extra rent paid to a landlord if a tenant's sales figures exceed a pre-arranged figure.[7]

primary market
The geographic market from which a center's predominant shoppers and/or sales come. *See* secondary market.[4]

A geographic term used to define the immediate trading area of a shopping center.[2]

primary research   The process of gathering original information because existing data on an issue are not available. *See* secondary research.[4]

primary trading area   The geographic area around a particular retail facility from which approximately 60% to 70% of the facility's customers come. The geographic radii and driving times to the primary zone vary among center types.[6]

pro forma   The developer's estimate of all costs of planning, developing, building, and operating the center. Then he develops estimates of income, primarily from rents to be paid by tenants. From these estimated expenses and income, the developer computes the anticipated net income for the shopping center. From that item, the projected value of the completed, operating shopping center may be calculated through application of a capitalization rate.[12]

profit   A general term for the excess of revenue, proceeds, or selling price over related costs.[5]

profit and loss statement   A financial statement showing revenues earned by a business, the expenses incurred in earning the revenues, and the resulting net income or net loss; also called operating statement, variance report, income statement, or statement of income and expenses.[5]

promotions or special events expenses   The cost of producing special events and promotional activities within the center, except at Christmastime. They include labor, decorations, signs, point-of-purchase materials, special entertainments, etc., attributable to such events.[10]

public relations   The establishment and maintenance of goodwill, promulgated by participation and concern for communitywide activities.[2]

publicity
Newsworthy information that, when released to the media, will be published or broadcast as news. It is used as free advertising.[7]

The use of selected media to carry messages and stories without cost.[4]

The dissemination of news and information concerning a person or organization through channels of communication such as newspapers, magazines, television, and radio, the use of which is not paid for by the publicity seeker.[5]

radius [restriction] clause
A clause inserted into a shopping center retail lease establishing the distance from the center that the retailer may operate another, similar store.[7]

A specific trade radius in which a tenant may not operate another business, usually of the same type or name.[7]

recapture A right, usually held by major tenants, to deduct such items as common area maintenance or insurance paid from percentage rents that may be owing.[8]

recapture rate The annual rate at which capital investment is returned to an investor over a specified period of time; the annual amount, apart from interest or return on interest (compound interest), that can be recaptured from an investment, divided by the original investment. Also called capital recovery rate.[7]

regional center This center type provides general merchandise (a large percentage of which is apparel) and services in full depth and variety. Its main attractions are its anchors: traditional, mass merchant or discount department stores or fashion specialty stores. A typical regional center is usually enclosed, with an inward orientation of the stores connected by a common walkway, and parking surrounds the outside perimeter.[1]

regional tenant A retailer who operates stores in a particular region of the country.[7]

relocation clause [A lease clause that] gives a landlord the ability to move the tenant to another location within the shopping center premises.[7]

renewal option   An agreement at the time of the original lease as to the terms of a tenant's extension of lease term.[7]

rental area
The square footage of a building that can actually be rented. (Halls, lobbies, elevator shafts, maintenance rooms, and lavatories are excluded.)[5]

That part of gross floor area used exclusively by individual tenants and on which rent can be obtained.[6]

replacement   In a strict sense, it implies removing some portion of the property and restoring the missing part on a like-for-like basis.[13]

replacement cost   Today's cost of construction, without considering depreciation.[7]

replacement value   The basis for loss payment can, by endorsement (specifying changes in or additions to the policy) and additional premium, be changed from actual cash value (replacement cost less depreciation) to replacement value, which is the full cost of replacement as of that date. This change adds to the annual expense of insurance.[12]

retailing   The business activities concerned with selling goods to ultimate consumers.[5]

return on investment (ROI) analysis   A formula used to determine the relative worth of an asset. There are many different kinds of analyses: they're usually used to determine if an asset should be repaired or replaced.[7]

risk management   The branch of management that is concerned with protecting a business against the risks of accidental loss.[7]

sales   The amounts received by or accrued to the store in exchange for merchandise sold to customers during an accounting period.[4]

sales analysis report   A report of actual sales and percentage of change over a given time. It also shows sales per square foot for each tenant or merchandise category.[4]

sales area   Rentable area minus storage space. The proportion of rentable store area devoted to sales varies among store types and among stores of the same type, so that calculations of sales or rent are more uniform if made on the basis of total store area.[6]

sales benchmarks   Allows comparisons of the center to other shopping centers in terms of sales, rent, and other statistics.[4]

sales contribution   An estimate of how much of a center's sales come from a geographic or a demographic group. Sales contribution is a component of a center's share of market calculation.[4]

sales efficiency ratio   A comparison, expressed as a ratio, of the percentage of a merchandise category's total square footage to its percentage of gross sales. The ratio is an indicator of category productivity.[4]

sales per square foot   Total annual sales divided by the total number of square feet of rentable area.[6]

sales potential
Estimates of how much money the people who live in a market will spend on consumer goods and services.[4]

Total retail spending by trade area residents, usually stated in terms of store type. This potential is the product of the multiplication of population and per capita expenditures. The sales potential provides the support base for the planned new facilities as well as for existing competitive facilities both within and beyond the trade area.[6]

sales/rent report   Information that helps evaluate the sales performance of a center and its stores. It is considered the center's "report card" and is an ongoing measure of productivity.[4]

secondary market
The geographic market located outside the primary market from which a center obtains shoppers or sales. *See also* primary market.[4]

A geographic term used to designate areas outside the primary market, the fringes of the market and beyond.[2]

secondary research   Information that has already been gathered by another party and is available. *See* primary research.[4]

security expenses   This major category includes costs associated with security at the center. These include payroll and employee benefits of center-employed security personnel, the costs of contracted security services, equipment, uniforms, and supplies attributable to the security function.[10]

shopping center A group of retail and other commercial establishments that is planned, developed, owned, and managed as a single property. On-site parking is provided. The center's size and orientation are generally determined by the market characteristics of the trade area served by the center. The two main configurations of shopping centers are malls and open-air strip centers.[1]

site A specific tract of land proposed for center development, exhibiting qualities of size, shape, location plus accessibility, and zoning, and suited for the development of a center.[6]

snow removal expenses The cost of snow removal from the building roof and parking lot and salting or sanding of the parking lot. It includes manpower, equipment, and material provided by an outside contractor or by the center.[10]

special event A centerwide, merchants' association-sponsored promotion aimed at generating increased customer traffic. [*See also* promotions or special events expenses][2]

step-down rents Rents that are structured so that percentages paid on total sales by a tenant decrease as sales grow.[7]

step-up rents Rents that are structured so that they increase at specific times during the life of a lease.[7]

stock turnover
The degree of balance between a retailer's inventory and sales and the speed with which its merchandise moves into and out of a department or store.[7]

The number of times inventory turns over in a given period of time. It is calculated by dividing average inventory at retail into the net sales for the year. Average yearly inventory is the sum of the retail inventories at the end of each month added to the initial opening inventory and divided by 13, the number of inventories used.[5]

strip center
A strip center consists of an attached row of at least three retail stores, managed as a coherent retail entity, with on-site parking in front of the stores. GLA [gross leasable area] for the center must be at least 10,000

sq. ft. Open canopies may connect the storefronts, but a strip center does not have enclosed walkways or malls linking the stores. A strip center may be configured in a straight line, or have an "L" or "U" shape.[10]

A straight line of stores with parking in front and a service lane in the rear. The anchor store, commonly a supermarket in small strip centers, is placed either at one end or in the center of the strip. A strip center is usually a small neighborhood center, and the terms have come to be used interchangeably, although a strip may also be a large center.[12]

subcontractors   [Sources of] skilled labor from specialized trades such as mechanical, electrical, fire protection, carpentry, painting, HVAC (heating, ventilation, and air-conditioning), and floor and ceiling fixtures.[11]

sublease
The renting or leasing of premises by a tenant to a third party, but with some portion or interest in them still being retained. Either all or part of the premises may be subleased, for either the whole term of the original lease or a portion of it. However, if the tenant relinquishes his or her entire interest, it is no longer considered a sublease but an assignment.[3]

The original tenant remains liable for the lease while a new tenant assumes occupancy.[7]

subrogation   The right of an insurance company to recover its loss from the responsible party after paying the policyholder's claim.[7]

superregional center   Similar to a regional center, but because of its larger size, a superregional center has more anchors, a deeper selection of merchandise, and draws from a larger population base. As with regional centers, the typical configuration is as an enclosed mall, frequently with multilevels.[1]

surety bonds
Payment and performance bonds usually used on significant construction jobs.[7]

Stand behind the general contractor's obligations to the owner under the terms and conditions of the contract. Generally such surety bonds cost ½% to 1% of the total contract amount.[11]

tenant improvements   Building improvements that enhance a tenant's space. May be paid for by either landlord or tenant.[8]

tenant mix
The distribution of store types within a retail complex.[4]

The types and price levels of retail and service businesses within a shopping center.[7]

tenant roster   The tenant roster is a master record. It lists such basic information as each tenant's name, the space number occupied, and the type of business being operated. It also lists key details in the tenant's leases, such as the square footage occupied, the rent per square foot and the total monthly rent, the lease date (which could be either the date it is prepared or the date it is signed), the commencement and expiration dates of the lease, and any special provisions.[9]

termination

1. Interruption of the lease before the term expires.[7]

2. The firing of an employee.[7]

total income   *See* income, total.

total personal income   *See* income, total personal.

total rent   The minimum and percentage rent paid by a tenant, coupled with any extra charges that the tenant must pay.[7]

trade area

The geographic area from which a center draws its shoppers. Limits that define a trade area may be distance, natural barriers such as rivers, or man-made obstructions such as a highway that is difficult to cross.[7]

The geographic area from which the sustaining patronage for steady support of a shopping center is obtained. The extent of the trade area is governed in each instance by a number of factors, including the matter of the center itself, its accessibility, the extent of physical barriers, the location of competing facilities, and limitations of driving time and distance.[6]

The territory from which 80% to 90% of retail trade will come on a continuing basis.[12]

trade fixture   An item specific to a tenant's business, usually not attached to the walls or floor; usually removed at lease expiration.[7]

trade name   The name under which a tenant operates a business.[7]

traffic   The number or volume of shoppers who visit a shopping center during a specified period of time.[7]

triple net lease   A lease in which 100% of all taxes, insurance, and maintenance associated with a shopping center is paid by the tenant.[7]

turn key   The landlord builds and finishes out a retail space; the tenant shows up with merchandise and is ready for business.[7]

use clause
A clause inserted into a shopping center retail lease that restricts the category of merchandise or items that a retailer is allowed to sell.[7]

An outline of the exact type of merchandise to be sold or business to be conducted in the premises.[7]

Tenants are restricted to providing the categories of merchandise or services specified in their leases and must obey any lease restrictions on how they operate.[9]

utilities expenses   This major category includes the cost of all utilities used in the common area of the center. It includes expenses for electricity, gas, and oil related to the common area, including exterior lighting. It does not include utilities purchased by the center and resold to individual tenants for consumption within their lease premises.[10]

utilities revenue   Any receipts from tenants for electrical or other utilities.[10]

vacancy rate   The square footage that is unoccupied, even if leases are signed and rents are being collected, expressed as a percentage of the total occupancy area of each store category.[10]

vanilla box   A space partially completed by the landlord based on negotiations between tenant and landlord. Although every landlord's definition is different, a vanilla box normally means HVAC [heating, ventilation and air-conditioning], walls, floors, stockroom wall, basic electrical work, basic plumbing work, rear door, and storefront.[7]

variance report   Usually part of the financial package provided to managers on a periodic basis. It shows the difference between budgeted expectations and actual results.[7]

workmen's compensation   *See* workers' compensation.[7]

workers' compensation   A social insurance that entitles an employee to medical care and replacement of at least part of his or her wages if he or she is injured on the job. In return for this, the employee gives up the right to sue his or her employer. Claims are generally paid by private insurers, but the rates are set by state boards.[7]

zero-based budgeting   A method of developing a current budget without basing it on any previous years' budgets; the starting point for each budget item is zero.[3]

Index